c

EN

KOREAN

DICTIONARY

romanized

THE AUTHOR:—Born and raised in Korea, where she has lived a total of almost twenty years. After schooling in England, married Horace Underwood, younger member of the well-known missionary family. Missionary to Korea from the Presbyterian Board of Foreign Missions, New York. Studied Korean from private tutors and at missionary language schools in Korea and Japan. Teacher at Chosun Christian University. Presently in the United States preparing for further missionary work in Korea.

concise

ENGLISH
KOREAN
DICTIONARY
romanized

by Joan V. Underwood

TUTTLE PUBLISHING
Tokyo • Rutland, Vermont • Singapore

Published by Tuttle Publishing, an imprint of Periplus Editions (HK) Ltd., with editorial offices at 364 Innovation Drive, North Clarendon, VT 05759 U.S.A. and 61 Tai Seng Avenue #02-12, Singapore 534167.

© 1954 by Charles E. Tuttle Co., Inc.
All rights reserved.

LCC Card No. 55005891
ISBN 978-0-8048-0118-8

First edition, 1954

Printed in Singapore

Distributed by:
North America, Latin America & Europe
Tuttle Publishing
364 Innovation Drive,
North Clarendon,
VT 05759-9436 USA
Tel: 1 (802) 773 8930 Fax: 1 (802) 773 6993
info@tuttlepublishing.com
www.tuttlepublishing.com

Japan
Tuttle Publishing
Yaekari Building 3F
5-4-12 Osaki, Shinagawa-ku
Tokyo 141-0032, Japan
Tel: (81) 3 5437 0171 Fax: (81) 3 5437 0755

Asia-Pacific
Berkeley Books Pte Ltd
61 Tai Seng Avenue #02-12,
Singapore 534167
Tel: (65) 6280 1330 Fax: (65) 6280 6290
inquiries@tuttlepublishing.com.sg
www.periplus.com

13 12 11 10   54 53 52 51

TUTTLE PUBLISHING® is a registered trademark of
Tuttle Publishing, a division of Periplus Editions (HK) Ltd.

*Dedicated to
my husband and my son
with deep appreciation
for their patience*

PREFACE

There has long been a great need for a small simple pocket dictionary of the Korean language, so when I was approached and asked to supply that need, I agreed to do so. This is the result. In this book I have attempted to collect together some 8000 or so words which will be useful for a foreigner in Korea. As near as was in me possible I have tried to take the most commonly used meanings in English and translate them into the most nearly equivalent words in Korean, taking into consideration to a certain extent the connotation of those words. I am by no means a Korean scholar and those who know more than I will perhaps feel that I have either simplified too much or have picked the wrong word, but in as limited a work as the present much has had to be left out.

The original basis of my choice of words was Thorndike's list of 5000 most commonly used English words. However, among those words are many which are of no use in a foreign language, and those were excluded. For the extra words included, two other dictionaries were used: Taiseido's *Pocket Romanized English-Japanese Dictionary* edited by Morio Takahashi, and Dr. H. H. Underwood's *English-Korean Dictionary*. Where the word was found in both dictionaries I tended to include it, though there were many exceptions. Because of present circumstances, I have also included many more military, medical and political terms than I would normally have considered necessary. Then too, I have taken special pains to include some of those words which in any language are used by those native to that language, but which a foreigner most frequently fails to utilize and a dictionary seldom specifically mentions. For instance, in a predominantly agricultural country like Korea, there are separate words for "rice" in its various stages of growth and use; because of the closeness of the family ties, as compared with the Anglo-Saxon world, there are different words for such relationships as younger or older brothers and sisters as used by men and women, and for the in-laws. In a civilization where politeness is actually indicated in speech rather than implied by tone of voice, there are different words used when talking about one's own possessions, or

viii

those of another, or when speaking to or of a superior. Though a good deal of this distinction is now disappearing, there are still differences, which I have tried to indicate where possible.

One of the biggest drawbacks to the compiling of a Korean dictionary at the present time is the fluidity of the spelling. Korean spelling can be compared with that in Elizabethan England at the time when Shakespeare was writing. The Republic of Korea Government has issued some specific spelling rules, which are being used in the schools, in classes and text books, but these have as yet not been widely disseminated, due to the shortage of time the government has had in which to accomplish this task, and the difficulties under which it is now working. I have tried to use this spelling, though with the lack of adequate Korean dictionaries it has not been entirely possible. The Korean spelling I have used has been, therefore, based on a comparison of Hyungki Lew's *New Life Korean-English Dictionary*, the Min Jung Publishing Company's *School English-Korean Dictionary* (compiled for the use of Koreans) and, as final arbiter, *Our Language Dictionary* in Korean.

The romanization of the Korean words has been based throughout on my interpretation of the McCune-Reischauer system of romanization, in my opinion the best so far devised. The reader will find an explanation of this on the following pages.

I wish here to express my great appreciation and indebtedness to Mr. Hugh Nam Pang, who gave freely of his spare time, for his unfailing assistance, and to my husband, Horace G. Underwood, without whose help I would have been unable to finish this work.

Yokohama, Japan
October 15, 1953

THE KOREAN LETTERS
AND THEIR SOUNDS

VOWELS

ㅏ   As the **a** of "father"
ㅑ   As the **ya** of "yacht"
ㅓ   Between the **u** of "put" and the **u** of "hut"
ㅕ   As the **you** of "young"
ㅗ   As the **aw** of "law"
ㅛ   As the word "**yaw**"
ㅜ   As the **ue** of "rue"
ㅠ   As the **u** of "useful"
ㅡ   As the **eu** of the French "deux"
ㅣ   Sometimes as the **i** of "sit", and sometimes as the **i** of "machine"

DIPHTHONGS

ㅐ   As the **a** of "sat"
ㅒ   As the **ya** of "yam"

세	A sound between the **e** of "set" and the **ai** of "air"
셰	Same basic vowel sound as above, except preceded by "**y**"
ㅚ	Close to the **eu** in the French "peur"
ㅟ	As the **wie** of "wield"
ㅢ	Approximately the sound of the **u** of the French "lune" followed by the **i** of "machine"
ㅘ	As the **wa** of "wand"
ㅝ	As the **wo** of "won"
ㅙ	As the **wa** of "wag"
ㅞ	As the **we** of "wet"

CONSONANTS

	Initially	Medi-ally	Finally	Changes
ㄱ	una. **k**	**k** or **g**	light **k**	finally **ng** before **m** & **n**
ㄴ	**n**	**n**	**n**	medially **l** before another **n** or **r**

	Initially	Medially	Finally	Changes
ㄷ	una. **t**	or between vowels, una.**t** or **d**	light **t**	
ㄹ	**r**	**r** or **l**	**l**	medially **l** before another **r**
ㅁ	**m**	**m**	**m**	
ㅂ	una. **p**	or between vowels, una. **p** or **b**	light **p**	**m** before **n**
ㅅ	**s** or **sh**		**d, t, n, s**	
ㅇ			nasal **ng**	
ㅈ	una. **ch** of **Charles**	between **ch** of **church** and **j** of **judge**	light **t**	
ㅊ	More aspirate than **ch** of **church**			
ㅋ	More aspirate than **c** of **cow**			

	Initially	Medi-ally	Finally	Changes
ㅌ	More aspirate than **t** in **t**ea			
ㅍ	More aspirate than **p** in **p**ea			
ㅎ	**h**	pronounced before a vowel; aspirates a following consonant		
ㄲ	**g**	long **k**	long **k**	
ㄸ	**d**	long **t** (as in A**tt**a)		
ㅃ	**b**	**b**		
ㅆ	long **s**	long **s** (as in Mu**ss**olini)		
ㅉ	between **ts** of pi**ts** and **tch** of pi**tch**			

(**una.** stands for **unaspirated**)

xiv

PRONUNCIATION
OF
ROMANIZATION

CONSONANTS

k	As k of "kite"
n	As n of "night"
t	As t of "tight"
r	As r of "radio"
l	As l of "live"
m	As m of "mine"
p	As p of "put"
s	As s of "sit"
sh	As sh of "shall"
ng	As ng of "sang"
ch	As ch of "Charles"
j	As j of "jar"
ch'	More aspirate than ch of "church"
k'	More aspirate than c of "cow"
t'	More aspirate than t of "tea"
p'	More aspirate than p of "pea"
h	As h of "hot"
g	As g of "go"

d	As **d** of "**d**og"
b	As **b** of "**b**ad"
ss	As **ss** of "Mu**ss**olini"
tch	As **tch** of "pi**tch**"

VOWELS

a	As **a** of "father"
ya	As **ya** of "**ya**cht"
o	Between **u** of "put" and **u** of "hut"
yo	As **you** of "**you**ng"
o	As **aw** of "law" lengthening to **o** of "go"
yo	As **yaw** of "**yaw**"
u	As **ue** of "rue"
yu	As **u** of "**u**seful"
u	As **eu** of French "**deu**x"
i	As **i** of "sit"
i	As **i** of "machine"

DIPHTHONGS

ae	As **a** of "sat"
yae	As **ya** of "**ya**m"
e	Between **e** of "set" and **ai** of "**ai**r"
ye	As **yea** of "oh **yea**h"
oe	Close to **eu** of French "**peu**r"
wi	As **wie** of "**wie**ld"

ui	As **u** of French "lune" follow- ed by **i** of "machine"
wa	As **wa** of "wand"
wo	As **wo** of "won"
wae	As **wa** of "wag"
we	As **we** of "wet"

The romanized words have been
written in syllables; therefore each
consonant and each vowel in each
syllable is pronounced. The only
exceptions are where two vowels
form a diphthong, and are in that
case pronounced as a single vowel,
and where **ch**, **sh**, **ng** and **tch** have
been used within a syllable.

〔 A 〕

a *art.* not normally used in Korean;
   (one) han 한;   (a certain) ŏt-tŏn
   어떤

abacus *n.* chu-p'an 주판

abandon *v.* pŏ-ri-da 버리다

abbess *n.* su-nyŏ-won-jang 수녀원
   장

abbot *n.* sŭng-won-jang 승원장

abbreviate *v.* chur-i-da 줄이다

abbreviation *n.* yak-ja 약자

abdicate *v.* t'oe-wi ha-da 되위하다

abdomen *n.* pae 배

abduct *v.* goe-yŏ-nae-da 꾀여내다

abhor *v.* sir-ŏ ha-da 싫어하다

ability *n.* nŭng-yŏk 능력

able, to be, *v.* hal-su it-da 할수있다

abnormal *adj.* pyŏn-t'ae-jŏk 변태적

abolish *v.* p'ye-ji ha-da 폐지하다

abolition *n.* p'ye-ji 폐지

abortion *n.* yu-san 유산

abound *v.* p'ung-sŏng ha-da 풍성하
   다

about *prep.* (concerning) …e kwan-
   ha-yŏ …에관하여;(approximately)
   yak 약

above *prep.* wi-e 위에

abridge *v.* chur-i-da 줄이다

abroad *adv.* hae-oe-e 해외에

abrogate *v.* p'ye-gi ha-da 폐기하다

abrupt *adj.* ch'ang-jol han 창졸한

abscess *n.* pu-sŭ-rŏm 부스럼

absent *adj.* kyŏl-sŏk-ĭn 결석인

absolute *adj.* chŏl-dae-jŏk 절대적

absolutely *adv.* chŏl-dae-ro 절대로

absolution *n.* sa-myŏn 사면

absolve *v.* sa-myŏn ha-da 사면하다

absorb *v.* hŭp-su ha-da 흡수하다

abstain *v.* chŏl-che ha-da 절제하다

abstract *adj.* ch'u-sang-jŏk 추상적

absurd *adj.* maeng-nang han 맹랑한

abundance *n.* p'ung-bu 풍부

abundant *adj.* p'ung-bu han 풍부한

abundantly *adv.* p'ung-bu ha-ge 풍부하게

abuse *n.* (verbal) yok-sŏl 욕설;
(of authority) nam-yong 남용; *v.*
(revile) yok-sŏl ha-da 욕설하다 ;
(misuse)nam-yong ha-da 남용하다

abusive *adj.* nam-yong ha-nŭn 남용하는

acacia *n.* a-k'a-si-a 아카시아

academy *n.* hak-wŏn 학원

accede *v.* tong-ŭi ha-da 동의하다

accelerate *v.* ba-rŭ-ge ha-da 빠르게 하다

accent *n.* aek-sen-t'ŭ 액센트; *v.* pa-da-tŭ-ri-da 받아들이다

acceptable *adj.* su-nak hal-man han 수낙할만한

access *n.* chŏp-kŭn 접근

accessible *adj.* kak-ka-i kal-su-i-nŭn 가까이갈수있는

accession *n.* ch'wi-chik 취직

accident *n.* sa-go 사고

accidental *adj.* u-yŏn-ŭi 우연의

accidentally *adv.* u-yŏn-hi 우연히

accommodate *v.* chŏk-ŭng si-k'i-da 적응시키다

accommodation *n.* suk-so 숙소

accompaniment *n.* pan-chu 반주

accompany *v.* kach-i-ka-da 같이가다

accomplice *n.* kong-bŏng-in 공범인

accomplish *v.* i-ru-da 이루다

accomplishment *n.* i-rum 이룸

accord *n.* il-ch'i 일치

according *adv.* da-rŏ-sŏ 따러서

accordingly *adv.* da-rŏ-sŏ 따러서

account *v.* kye-san ha-da 계산하다; *n.* kye-san 계산

accumulate *v.* ssa-d'a 쌓다

accuracy *n.* chŏng-hwak 정확

accurate *adj.* chŏng-hwak han 정확한

accusation *n.* ko-bal 고발

accuse *v.* ko-bal ha-da 고발하다

accustom *v.* pŏ-rŭt tŭ-ri-da 버릇들이다

acetylene *n.* a-se-ch'il-lin 아세칠린

ache *v.* a-p'ŭ-da 아프다; *n.* a-p'ŭm 아픔

achieve *v.* i-ru-da 이루다

achievement *n.* sŏng-ch'wi 성취

acid *adj.* sin 신

acknowledge *v.* in-chŏng ha-da 인정하다

acorn *n.* to-t'o-ri 도토리

acquaint *v.* chal al-ge ha-da 잘알게하다

acquaintance *n.* suk-ji 숙지

acquiesce *v.* muk-ĭn ha-da 묵인하다

acquire *v.* ŏt-da 얻다

acquit *v.* choe-ŏp-da ha-da 죄없다하다

acre *n.* e-i-k'a 에이카

acrobat *n.* kwang-dae 광대

across *prep.* & *adv.* kŏn-nŏ-sŏ 건너서

act *v.* haeng ha-da 행하다; *n.* haeng-wi 행위

acting *adj.* chak-yong ha-nŭn 작용하는; (substitute) tae-ri-ŭi 대리의

action *n.* tong-jak 동작

active *a.j.* hwal-bal-han 활발한

activity *n.* hwal-tong 활동

actor *n.* nam-ja pae-u 남자배우

actress *n.* yŏ-ja pae-u 여자배우

actual *adj.* sil-che-ŭi 실제의

acute *adj.* nal-k'a-ro-un 날카로운

adapt *v.* mat-ge ha-da 맞게하다

add *v.* tŏ ha-da 더하다   「지다

addicted, to be a. to, *v.* ba-ji-da 빠

addition *n.* chŭng-ga 증가

additional *adj.* ch'u-ka-ŭi 추가의

address *v.* (speak to) yŏn-sŏl ha-da 연설하다; (a letter) chu-so sŏng-myŏng-ŭl ssŭ-da 주소성명을쓰다; *n.* chu-so 주소

adequate *adj.* chŏk-dang han 적당한

adhere *v.* put'-da 붙다

adhesion *n.* ko-ch'ak 고착

adjacent *adj.* pu-kŭn-ŭi 부근의

adjective *n.* hyŏng-yong-sa 형용사

adjourn *v.* p'ye-hwoe ha-da 폐회하다

adjust *v.* chŏk-ŭng ha-ge ha-da 적응하게하다

adjutant *n.* pu-kwan 부관

adjutant-general *n.* pu-kwan 부관

administer *v.* ch'ŏ-ri ha-da 처리하다

administration *n.* haeng-chŏng 행정

admirable *adj.* kam-bok hal-man-han 감복할만한

admiral *n.* hae-gun tae-chang 해군대장

admiration *n.* kam-t'an 감탄

admire *v.* kam-t'an ha-da 감탄하다

admission *n.* (confession) hŏ-yong 허용

admit *v.* tŭ-ri-da 들이다

admittance *n.* ip-chang-hŏ-ga 입장허가

admonish *v.* sŏl-yu ha-da 설유하다

admonition *n.* sŏl-yu 설유

adolescence *n.* ch'ŏng-nyŏn-gi 청년기

adopt *v.* (a son) yang-ja-ro sam-ta 양자로 삼다; (a daughter) yang-nyŏ-ro sam-ta 양녀로 삼다

adopted-son *n.* yang-ja 양자

adore *v.* sung-bae ha-da 숭배하다

adorn *v.* gu-mi-da 꾸미다

adrift *adv.* p'yo-ryu ha-yŏ 표류하여

adulation *n.* a-ch'ŏm 아첨

adult *n.* ŏ-rŭn 어른

adulterate *v.* p'um-chil-ŭl ŏ-rŏ-tŭ-ri-da 품질을 떨어뜨리다

adultery *n.* kan-t'ong 간통

advance *v.* chŏn-jin ha-da 전진하다

advanced *adj.* chŏn-jin doen 전진된

advantage *n.* i-ik 이익

advantageous, to be, *v.* yu-ri han 유리한

advent *n.* ch'ul-hyŏn 출현

adventure *n.* mo-hŏm 모험

adventurer *n.* mo-hŏm-ga 모험가

adverb *n.* pu-sa 부사

adversary *n.* won-su 원수

adverse, to be, *v.* kŏ-ku-ro-ŭi 거꾸로의

adversity *n.* yŏk-kyŏng 역경

advertise *v.* kwang-go ha-da 광고하다

advertisement *n.* kwang-go 광고

advice *n.* ch'ung-go 충고

advisable *aj.* kwon-hal-man-han
권할만한

advise *v.* ch'ung-go ha-da 충고하다

adviser *n.* ko-mun 고문

advocate *v.* ch'ang-do ha-da 창도하
다; *n.* ch'ang-do-ja 창도자

adze *n.* ga-kwi 까뀌

aerodrome *n.* pi-haeng-jang 비행장

aeroplane *n.* pi-haeng-gi 비행기

affable *adj.* puch-ĭm-sŏng i-nŭn
붙임성있는

affair *n.* il 일

affect *v.* kam-dong si-k'i-da 감동
시키다

affectation *n.* gu-mi-nŭn t'ae-do
꾸미는태도

affection *n.* ae-jŏng 애정

affectionate *adj.* ta-jŏng han 다정한

affectionately *adv.* chŏng-dap-ge
정답게

affirm *v.* hwak-ŏn ha-da 확언하다

affix *v.* ch'ŏm-bu ha-da 첨부하다

afflict *v.* koe-rop hi-da 괴롭히다

afflicted *adj.* koe-rom-pat-nŭn 피
롬받는

affliction *n.* pul-haeng 불행

afford *v.* …hal yŏ-yu-ga it-da …할
여유가있다

affront *n.* mo-yok 모욕; *v.* mo-yok
ha-da 모욕하다

afire *adv.* pul-t'a-sŏ 불타서

afloat *adj.* dŏ-i-nŭn 떠있는

afraid *adj.* mu-sŏ-wo ha-da 무서워하다

A-frame *n.* chi-ge 지게

after *adv.* twi-e 뒤에; (time) hu-e 후에; *prep.* …ŭi-twi-e …의뒤에

afternoon *n.* o-hu 오후

afterward(s) *adv.* hu-e 후에

again *adv.* ta-si 다시

against *prep.* …e pan (dae) ha-yŏ …에반 (대) 하여

age *n.* na-i 나이

aged *adj.* nŭlg-ŭn 늙은

agency *n.* tae-ri 대리

agent *n.* tae-ri-ĭn 대리인; **secret a.** *n.* mĭl-jŏng 밀정

aggravate *v.* ak-hwa sĭ-k'i-da 악화시키다

aghast *adj.* nol-lan 놀란

agile *adj.* mĭn-ch'ŏp han 민첩한

agitate *v.* kyŏk-dong ha-da 격동하다

ago *adv.* ye-jŏn-e 예전에

agony *n.* ko-mĭn 고민

agree *v.* tong-ŭi ha-da 동의하다

agreeable *adj.* ma-ŭm-e tŭ-nŭn 마음에드는

agreement *n.* hyŏp-yak 협약

agricultural *adj.* nong-ŏp-jŏk 농업적

agriculture *n.* nong-ŏp 농업

aground *adv.* chi-sang-e 지상에

ahead *adv.* ap'-e 앞에

aid *v.* top-da 돕다; *n.* cho-ryŏk 조력

ail *v.* kwi-ch'yan'-ke ha-da 귀찮게 하다

ailment *n.* pyŏng 병

aim *v.* kyŏ-nu-da 겨누다; *n.* mok-jŏk 목적

air *n.* kong-gi 공기

airman *n.* pi-haeng-sa 비행사

airplane *n.* pi-haeng-gi 비행기

air-pressure *n.* ki-ap 기압

aisle *n.* chwa-sŏk sa-i-ŭi kil 좌석 사이의길

alacrity *n.* mĭn-hwal 민활

alarm *n.* kyŏng-bo 경보

alarm-clock *n.* cha-myŏng-jong 자 명종

alarming *adj.* nol-la-un 놀나운

alas *interj.* a-i-go 아이고

album *n.* al-bŏm 알범

alcohol *n.* al-k'ol 알콜

alcoholism *n.* al-k'ol chung-dok 알 콜 중독

alder *n.* chŏk-yang 적양

ale *n.* maek-ju 맥주

ale-house *n.* maek-ju p'a-nŭn chĭp 맥주파는집

alert *adj.* chŏng-sĭn-ch'ae-rĭn 정신 채린

algebra *n.* tae-su 대수
alibi *n.* hyŏn-jang pu-jae-jŭng-myŏng 현장부재증명
alien *n.* oe-guk-ĭn 외국인 「하다
alienate *v.* so-won-hi ha-da 소원히
alight *v.* nae-ri-da 내리다
alike, to be, *v.* kat'-da 같다
alive, to be, *v.* sar-a it-da 살아있다
all *adj.* mo-dŭn 모든; *n.* chŏn-bu 전부; *adv.* a-ju 아주
allegiance *n.* ch'ung-ŭi 충의
alley *n.* kol-mok 골목
alliance *n.* yŏn-hap 연합
alligator *n.* ak-ŏ 악어
all-important *adj.* ka-jang chung-yo han 가장중요한
allot *v.* hwal-tang ha-da 활당하다
allow *v.* hŏ-rak ha-da 허락하다
alloy *n.* hap-gŭm 합금
ally *n.* tong-maeng-ja 동맹자
almanac *n.* ch'aek-yŏk 책력
almighty *adj.* chŏn-nŭng 전능; *n.* (God) chŏn-nŭng-ŭi sĭn 전능의신
almond *n.* sal-gu-ssi 살구씨
almost *adv.* kŏ-ŭi 거의
alms *n.* ŭi-yŏn-gŭm 의연금
aloft *adv.* wi-e 위에
alone *adj.* hon-ja 혼자
along *prep.* & *adv.* da-ra-sŏ 따라서
aloud *adv.* nop'-ŭn so-ri-ro 높은소리로

alphabet *n.* ael-p'a-bet' 앨파벨

alphabetically *adv.* ka-na-da sun-sŏ-ro 가나다 순서로

already *adv.* i-mi 이미

also *adv.* yŏk-si 역시

altar *n.* che-dan 제단

alter *v.* pyŏn-gyŏng ha-da 변경하다

alteration *n.* pyŏn-gyŏng 변경

alternate *v.* kyo-dae ha-da 교대하다

alternative *n.* tal-li chwi-hal su-dan 달리 취할 수단

although *conj.* pi-rok…il-chi-ra-do 비록…일지라도

altitude *n.* nop'-i 높이

alto *n.* ael-t'o 앨토

altogether *adv.* ta-kach-i 다같이

aluminum *n.* ael-mi-ni-um 앨미니움

alumnus *n.* chor-ŏp saeng 졸업생

always *adv.* hang-sang 항상

amateur *n.* a-ma-ch'u-ŏ 아마추어

amaze *v.* nol-la-ge ha-da 놀라게하다

amazement *n.* nol-la-um 놀라움

amazing *adj.* nol-la-un 놀라운

ambassador *n.* tae-sa 대사

amber *n.* ho-bak (tol) 호박 (돌)

ambiguous *adj.* mo-ho han 모호한

ambition *n.* kong-myŏng sïm 공명심

ambitious *adj.* p'ae-gi i-nun 패기 있는

ambulance *n.* pyŏng-won ch'a 병원
차

ambush *n.* pok-byong 복병; *v.* pok-
byong ha-da 복병하다

amend *v.* ko-ch'i-da 고치다

amendment *n.* ko-ch'ĭm 고침

amends *n.* po-sang 보상

America *n.* mi-guk 미국

American *adj.* mi-guk 미국; *n.*
mi-guk sa-ram 미국사람

amethyst *n.* cha-saek-su-jŏng 자색
수정

amiable *adj.* sa-rang-sŭ-rŏ-un 사
랑스러운

amid, amidst *prep.* …ŭi ka-un-de
…의가운데

ammonia *n.* am-mo-ni-a 암모니아

ammunition *n.* t'an-yak 탄약

amnesty *n.* tae-sa 대사

among, amongst *prep.* …ŭi ka-un-
de …의 가운데

amount *n.* ch'ong-ge 총계

ample *adj.* p'ong-bu han 풍부한

amplify *v.* nŏlb-hi-da 넓히다

amputate *v.* chŏl-dan ha-da 절단하
다

amputation *n.* chol-dan 절단

amulet *n.* pu-jak 부작

amuse *v.* chae-mi-sŭ-rŏp-ge ha-da
재미스럽게하다

amusement *n.* nak 낙

amusing *adj.* cha-mi i-nun 자미있
는

an *art.* not normally used in Korean;
(one) han 한; (a certain) ŏt-
tŏn 어떤

anaemia *n.* pin-hyŏl-jŭng 빈혈증

analysis *n.* pun-hae 분해

analyze *v.* pun-hae ha-da 분해하다

anarchism *n.* mu-jŏng-bu-ju-ŭi
무정부주의

anarchist *n.* mu-jŏng-bu-ju-ŭi-ja
무정부주의자

anarchy *n.* mu-jŏng-bu 무정부

anatomy *n.* hae-bu 해부

ancestor *n.* sŏn-jo 선조

ancestral *adj.* sŏn-jo-ŭi 선조의

ancestry *n.* ka-mun 가문

anchor *n.* tat' 닻; *v.* tach-ŭl tŏn-
ji-da 닻을 던지다

anchorage *n.* chŏng-bak-ji 정박지

ancient *adj.* yen-nal-ŭi 옛날의

and *conj.* (between noun and noun)
wa 와; (everywhere else) do 또

anecdote *n.* ĭl-hwa 일화

anesthetic *n.* ma-ch'wi-je 마취제

angel *n.* ch'ŏn-sa 천사

anger *n.* no-yŏ-um 노여움; *v.* no-
ha-ge ha-da 노하게하다

angle *n.* mo 모; *v.* (fish) nak-si-jĭl
ha-da 낚시질하다

angler *n.* nak-si-gun 낚시군

angrily *adv.* sŏng-nae-sŏ 성내서

angry *adj.* sŏng-nan 성난

anguish *n.* kyŏk-sim han ko-t'ong 격심한 고통

animal *n.* tong-mul 동물

animism *n.* man-yu-jŏng sil-lon 만유정신론

animosity *n.* mi-wo ham 미워함

ankle *n.* pok-song-a byŏ 복송아뼈

annals *n.* yŏn-bo 연보

annex *v.* tŏ-ha-da 더하다

annexation *n.* pyŏng-hap 병합

annihilate *v.* chŏl-myŏl 절멸

anniversary *n.* ki-nyŏm-il 기념일

announce *v.* pal-p'yo ha-da 발표하다

announcer *n.* a-na-un-sŏ 아나운서

annoy *v.* koe-rop-ge ha-da 피롭게 하다

annoying *adj.* kwi-ch'yan'-ŭn 귀찮은

annual *adj.* yŏn-nyŏn-ŭi 년년의

another *adj.* ta-rŭn 다른; *pron.* ta-rŭn-gŏt 다른것

answer *v.* tae-dap ha-da 대답하다; *n.* tae-dap 대답

ant *n.* kae-mi 개미

antagonism *n.* chŏk-dae 적대

antagonist *n.* pan-dae-ja 반대자

anthem *n.* sŏng-ga 성가; **national a.** *n.* kuk-ga 국가

anthracite *n.* mu-yŏn-t'an 무연탄
anticipate *v.* ye-gi ha-da 예기하다
anticipation *n.* ye-gi 예기
antiseptic *n.* pang-bu-je 방부제
antler *n.* nog-yong 녹용
anus *n.* hǔng-mun 홍문
anvil *n.* mo-ru 모루
anxiety *n.* kŏk-jŏng 걱정
anxious *adj.* kŏk-jŏng ha-nun 걱
  정하는
anxiously *adv.*   kŏk-jŏng-sǔ-rŏ-i
  걱정스러이
any *adj.* ŏ-nǔ 어느   「든지
anybody *pron.* nu-gu-dǔn-ji 누구
anyhow *adv.* ŏ-tŏ-ke ha-yŏ-sŏ-ra-
  do 어떻게하여서라도
anyone *pron.* nu-gu-dǔn-ji 누구든지
anything *pron.* mu-ŏs-i-dǔn-ji 무
  엇이든지
anyway *adv.* yŏ-ha-gan 여하간
anywhere *adv.* ŏ-de-dǔn-ji 어데든지
apart *adv.* dŏr-ŏ-jyŏ-sŏ 떨어져서
apartment *n.* a-p'a-a-t'ǔ 아파아트
ape *n.* won-sung-i 원승이
apologize *v.* pyŏn-myŏng ha-da 변
  명하다
apology *n.* sa-jwa 사좌
apoplexy *n.* chol-do 졸도
apostle *n.* sa-do 사도
apothecary *n.* yak-che-sa 약제사
apparatus *n.* chang-ch'i 장치

apparent *adj*. myŏng-paek han 명백한

apparently *adv*. myŏng-paek-hi 명백히

appear *v*. na-t'a-na-da 나타나다

appearance *n*. ch'ul-hyŏn 출현

appendicitis *n*. maeng-jang-yŏm 맹장염

appendix *n*. pu-rok 부록

appetite *n*. sĭk-yok 식욕

applause *n*. pak-su 박수; *v*. pak-su ha-da 박수하다

apple *n*. sa-gwa 사과

applicant *n*. chi-won-ja 지원자

application *n*. sĭn-ch'ŏng 신청

applied *adj*. chŏg-yong doe-nŭn 적용되는

apply *v*. pal-lŭ-da 바르다; (make application) sĭn-ch'ŏng ha-da 신청하다

appoint *v*. ĭm-myŏng ha-da 임명하다

appointed *adj*. ĭm-myŏng doen 임명된

appointment *n*. yak-sok 약속

appreciable *adj*. p'yŏng-ga hal-su ĭ-nŭn 평가할수있는

appreciate *v*. p'yŏng-ga ha-da 평가하다

appreciation *n*. kam-sang 감상

apprehend *v*. put-chap-da 붓잡다

apprehensive *adj.* tu-rŏ-wo ha-nŭn 두려워하는

apprentice *n.* yŏn-gi-si-hwan 연기시환

approach *v.* ka-ka-i ka-da 가까이 가다; *n.* chŏp-gŭn 접근

appropriate *adj.* chŏk-dang han 적당한; *v.* sa-yong ha-da 사용하다

approval *n.* si-ĭn 시인

approve *v.* si-ĭn ha-da 시인하다

approximately *adv.* tae-gang 대강

apricot *n.* sal-gu 살구

April *n.* sa-wol 사월

apron *n.* ap'-ch'i-ma 앞치마

apt *adj.* …ha-gi swi-un …하기쉬운

arable *adj.* kyŏng-jak-e chŏk-dang han 경작에 적당한; **a. land** *n.* kyŏng-jak-ji 경작지

arc *n.* kung-hyŏng 궁형

arch *n.* a-a-ch'wĭ 아아취

archaeology *n.* ko-go hak 고고학

archbishop *n.* tae-sŭng-jŏng 대승정

archer *n.* sa-su 사수

architect *n.* kŏn-ch'uk-ga 건축가

arduous *adj.* hĭm tŭ-nŭn 힘드는

area *n.* (space) myŏn-jŏk 면적; (district) chi-gu 지구

argue *v.* chaeng-non ha-da 쟁논하다

argument *n.* non-jaeng 논쟁; (reason) non-jŭng 논증

arise *v.* na-t'a-na-da 나타나다

arithmetic *n.* san-su 산수

arm *n.* p'al 팔; *v.* mu-jang ha-da 무장하다

armament *n.* kun-bi 군비

arm-chair *n.* al-lak ŭi-ja 안락의 자

armed *adj.* mu-jang han 무장한

armistice *n.* hyu-jŏn 휴전

armored vehicle *n.* chang-gap ch'a-ryang 장갑차량

armour *n.* kap-ju 갑주

army *n.* yuk-gun 육군

around *adv. & prep.* tul-le-e 둘레에

arouse *v.* gae-u-da 깨우다

arrange *v.* (put in order) ka-jŭ-rŏn-hi ha-da 가즈런히하가; (make ready for) chun-bi ha-da 준비하다

arrangement *n.* chŏng-don 정돈; (preparation) chun-bi 준비

arrest *v.* chap-da 잡다; *n.* ch'e-p'o 체포

arrival *n.* to-ch'ak 도착

arrive *v.* to-ch'ak ha-da 도착하다

arrogance *n.* o-man 오만

arrow *n.* hwa-sal 화살

art *n.* ye-sul 예술

artery *n.* tong-maek 동맥

article *n.* (newspaper) ki-sa 기사; (things) mul-p'um 물품

artificial *adj.* ĭn-gong-jok 인공적

artillery *n.* tae-p'o 대포; (branch of service) p'o-byŏng 포병

artist *n.* ye-sul-ga 예술가

artistic *adj.* ye-sul-jŏk 예술적

as *conj.* …wa kach-i …와같이; *adv.* ch'o-rŏm 처럼

as far as (and including) *adv.* ga-ji 까지

as much as kŭ-man-kom 그많곰

ascend *v.* o-rŭ-da 오르다

ascent *n.* ol-la kam 올라감

ascertain *v.* cho-sa ha-da 조사하다

ash tray *n.* chae-tŏr-i 재떨이

ashamed *adj.* pu-kŭ-rŏ-wo ha-da 부끄러워하다

ashes *n.* chae 재

ashore *adj.* hae-byŏn-e 해변에

Asia *n.* a-se-a 아세아

aside *adv.* kyŏt-ŭ-ro 곁으로

ask *v.* kan-jŏng ha-da 간정하다; (questions) mut-da 묻다

asleep, to be, *v.* cha-go it-da 자고 있다

asparagus *n.* a-sŭ-p'a-ra-ga-ssŭ 아스파라가쓰

aspect *n.* hyŏng-se 형세

asphalt *n.* a-sŭ-p'al-t'ŭ 아스팔트

aspire *v.* yŏl-mang ha-da 열망하다

ass *n.* na-gwi 나귀

assailant *n.* kong-gyŏk-ja 공격자

assassin *n.* am-sal-ja 암살자

assassinate v. am-sal ha-da 암살
하다

assassination n. am-sal 암살

assault v. kong-gyŏk ha-da 공격하
다

assemble v. mo-i-da 모이다

assembly n. chĭp-hoe 집회

assent n. tong-ŭi 동의; v. tong-ŭi
ha-da 동의하다

assert v. chu-jang ha-da 주장하다

assets n. cha-san 자산

assign v. hwal-tang ha-da 활당하다

assist v. top-da 돕다

assistance n. cho-ryŏk 조력

assistant n. cho-su 조수

associate v. yŏn-hap ha-da 연합하
다; n. tong-nyo 동료

association n. yŏn-hap 연합

assume v. dŏ-mat-da 떠맡다

assumption n. ŏk-ch'ŭk 억측

assurance n. po-jŭng 보증

assure v. po-jŭng ha-da 보증하다

aster n. ssuk-bu-jang-i 쑥부장이

asthma n. ch'ŏn-sĭk 천식

astonish v. gam-jak nol-la-ge ha-da
깜짝놀라게하자

astonishment n. nol-la-um 놀라움

astrology n. chŏm-sŏng-hak 점성학

astronomer n. ch'ŏn-mun hak-ja
천문학자

astronomy n. ch'ŏn-mun hak 천문학

asylum *n.* p'i-nan-ch'ŏ 피난처

at *prep.* e 에

athlete *n.* sŏn-su 선수

athletic *adj.* un-dong kyŏng-gi-ŭi
운동경기의

athletics *n.* un-dong kyŏng-gi 운동
경기

Atlantic *adj.* tae-sŏ-yang 대서양

atlas *n.* chi-do-sŏ 지도서

atmosphere *n.* tae-gi 대기

atom *n.* won-ja 원자

atrocity *n.* p'ok-haeng 폭행

attach *v.* puch-i-da 붙이다

attachment *n.* pu-ch'ak 부착

attack *v.* kong-gyŏk ha-da 공격하다;
n. kong-gyŏk 공격

attain *v.* to-dal ha-da 도달하다

attainment *n.* to-dal 도달

attempt *v.* goe ha-da 꾀하다;
n. ki-do 기도

attend *v.* (wait upon) mo-si-da 모
시다; (go to) ta-ni-da 다니다

attendance *n.* ch'ul-sŏk 출석

attendant *n.* su-haeng-won 수행원

attention *n.* chu-ŭi 주의

attentive *adj.* cho-sĭm-sŏng i-nŭn
조심성있는

attic *n.* ta-rak-pang 다락방

attitude *n.* t'ae-do 태도

attorney *n.* pyŏn-ho-sa 변호사

attract *v.* gŭl-da 끌다

attraction *n.* mae-ryŏk 매력

audible *adj.* tŭr-ŭl-su i-nŭn 들을수
있는

audience *n.* ch'ŏng-jung 청중

audit *v.* kŏm-sa ha-da 검사하다;
n. hoe-gye kŏm-sa 회계검사

auditor *n.* hoe-gye kŏm-sa-gwan
회계검사관

augment *v.* put-da 붇다

August *n.* p'al wol 팔월

aunt *n.* a-ju-mŏ-ni 아주머니

author *n.* chŏ-ja 저자

authorities *n.* tang-guk-ja 당국자

authority *n.* kwon-wi 권위

authorize *v.* kwon-han-ŭl chu-da
권한을주다

autobiography *n.* cha-sŏ-jŏn 자서
전

automatically *adv.* cha-dong-jŏk-
ŭ-ro 자동적으로

automobile *n.* cha-dong-ch'a 자동
차

autumn *n.* ka-ŭl 가을

available *adj.* i-yong hal-su i-nun
이용할수있다

avalanche *n.* nun-sa-t'ae 눈사태

avarice *n.* yok-sĭm 육심

avenge *v.* won-su-kap'-da 원수갚다

avenue *n.* ka-ro 가로

average *n.* p'yŏng-gyun 평균

avert *v.* p'i-ha-da 피하다

aviator *n.* pi-haeng-ga 비행가
avoid *v.* p'i-ha-da 피하다
await *v.* ···ŭl ki-da-ri-da ···을 기
다리다
awake *v.* cham-ŭl gae-da 잠을 깨
다; *adj.* gae-wo i-nŭn 깨워있는
award *v.* chu-da 주다
aware *adj.* al-da 알다; **to become
a.** *v.* gae-dat-da 깨닫다
away *adv.* mŏl-li 멀리
awe *n.* tu-ryŏ-um 두려움
awful *adj.* mu-sŏ-un 무서운
awhile *adv.* cham-gan 잠간
awkward *aj.* (situation) kŏ-buk
han 거북한; (green) sŏ-t'u-rŭn
서루른
awl *n.* song-got pa-nul 송곳바눌
ax, axe *n.* to-ki 도끼
axle *n.* cha-ch'uk 자축
azalea *n.* chin-dal-lae 진달래;
(waxy kind) ch'ŏl-chuk 철쭉

〔 B 〕

baboon *n.* sŏng-sŏng-i 성성이
baby *n.* a-gi 아기
bachelor *n.* ch'ong-gak 총각
back *n.* (of body) hŏ-ri 허리;
adj. & adv. twi 뒤
back-bone *n.* ch'ŏk-ju 척주
background *n.* pae-kyŏng 배경

backward(s) *adv.* twi-ro 뒤로;
adj. (wrong way.) kŏ-ku-ro 거꾸
로

bacon *n.* pe-i-k'on 베이콘

bacteria *n.* se-kyun 세균

bad *adj.* na-pŭn 나쁜

badge *n.* bae-chi 뺏지

badger *n.* nŏ-ku-ri 너구리

badly *adv.* na-pŭ-ge 나쁘게

baffle *v.* chwa-jŏl si-k'i-da 좌절
시키다

bag *n.* chu-mŏ-ni 주머니

baggage *n.* so-ha-mul 소하물

baggage-room *n.* so-ha-mul ch'wi-
gŭp-sïl 소하물취급실

bail *n.* po-sŏk-gŭm 보석금; *v.* p'ŏ-
nae-da 퍼내다

bait *n.* mi-gi 미기; *v.* mi-gi-ro
goe-i-da 미기로꾀이다

bake *v.* kup-da 굽다 「굽는사람

baker *n.* bang kup-nŭn sa-ram 빵

bakery *n.* bang-chip 빵집

balance *n.* (equality) kyun-hyŏng
균형; *v.* kyun-hyŏng-ŭl yu-ji ha-
da 균형을유지하다

balcony *n.* no-dae 노대

bald *adj.* tae mŏ-ri doen 대머리된

bale *n.* mung-t'ŏng-i 뭉텅이

ball *n.* kong 공

ballast *n.* pae-mit'-chïm 배밑짐;
(road) cha-gal 자갈

balloon *n.* kyŏng-gŭi-gu 경긔구

ballot *n.* t'u-p'yo 투표

balmy *adj.* hyang-gi-ro-un 향기로운

bamboo *n.* tae 대

ban *v.* kŭm-ji ha-da 금지하다; *n.* kŭm-ji 금지

banana *n.* pa-na-na 바나나

band *n.* (sash) di 띠; (group) de 떼

band *v.* (together) tan-gyŏl ha-da 단결하다; (a box) gŭn-ŭ-ro muk-da 끈으로묵다; *n.* (music) ak-dae 악대

bandage *n.* pung-dae 붕대; *v.* pung-dae-ro kam-da 붕대로감다

bandit *n.* san-jŏk 산적

bang *n.* t'ang-so-ri 탕소리

banish *v.* kwi-yang po-nae-da 귀양보내다

banishment *n.* kwi-yang 귀양

bank *n.* ŭn-haeng 은행; (of river) ka 가

banker *n.* ŭn-haeng-ga 은행가

bank-note *n.* ŭn-haeng-gwon 은행권

bankruptcy *n.* p'a-san 파산

banner *n.* kun-gi 군기

baptism *n.* se-rye 세례

Baptist *n.* ch'im-ye kyo 침례교

baptize *v.* se-rye-rul chu-da 세례를주다

bar *n.* ba-a 빠아; (stick) mong-dung-i 몽둥이; *v.* ka-ru mak-da 가루막다; *n.* (law) pŭp cho-gye 법조계

barbarian *n.* ya-man-ĭn 야만인

barbarous *adj.* ya-man-ŭi 야만의

barber *n.* i-bal-sa 이발사

barb–wire *n.* ka-si-ch'ŏl-sa chul 가시철사줄

bare *adj.* maen …맨…

bare foot *n.* maen pal 맨발; *adj.* maen pai pŏs-ŭn 맨발벗은

barely *adv.* kan-sĭn-i 잔신이

bargain *n.* ssan-mul-gŏn 싼물건; *v.* oe-nu-ri ha-da 외누리하다

barge *n.* kŏ-ru 거루

bark *n.* (wood) na-mu gŭp-jĭl 나무껍질; *v.* chĭt-da 짖다

barley *n.* po-ri 보리

barn *n.* kwang 광

barnacle *n.* so-ra chong-yu 소라종류

barometer *n.* ch'ong-u-gye 청우계

barracks *n.* pa-rak-k'ŭ 바라크

barrel *n.* t'ong 통; (of gun) ch'ong-dae 총대

barren *adj.* pul-ĭm-ŭi 불임의

barrier *n.* chang-ae 장애

barrister *n.* pyŏn-ho-sa 변호사

barter *v.* kyo-yŏk ha-da 교역하다

base *n.* (foot) mit' 밑; (foundation)
ki-ch'o 기초; (of operations) kŭn-
gŏ-ji 근거지; *adj.* chŏn han 전한
baseball *n.* ya-gu 야구
baseless *adj.* kŭn-gŏ ŏp-nŭn 근거
없는
basement *n.* chi-ha-sĭl 지하실
bashful *adj.* pu-kŭ-rŏ-un 부끄러운
bashfully *adj.* pu-kŭ-rŏp-ge 부끄럽
게
basic *adj.* ki-bon-jŏk 기본적
basin *n.* (for washing) se-su tae-ya
세수대야
bask *v.* jo-i-da 쪼이다
basket *n.* large) kwang-ju-ri 광
주리; (small) pa-gu-ni 바구니
basket-ball *n.* nong-gu 농구
bass *n.* (fish) nong-ŏ 농어; (sound)
chŏ-ŭm-bu 저음부
bastard *n.* sŏ-ch'ul 서출
baste *v.* (clothes) si-ch'ĭm-jĭl ha-
da 시침질하다; (meat) ki-rŭm
ch'i-da 기름치다
bat *n.* baet' 뺄; (animal) pak-chwi
박쥐
bath *n.* mok-yok 목역
bathe *v.* myŏk-kam-da 멱감다
bathing *n.* mok-yok 목욕
bathroom *n.* mok-yok sĭl 목욕실
battalion *n.* tae-dae 대대
batter *v.* tu-dŭl-gi-da 두들기다

battery *n.* (electric) pat-de-ri 밧
데리; (artillery) p'o-byŏng chung-
dae 포병중대

battle *n.* ssa-um 싸움

battle line *n.* chŏn-sŏn 전선

battle-field *n.* ssa-um-t'ŏ 싸움터

battlement *n.* hyung pyŏk 흉벽

battleship *n.* chŏn-t'u-ham 전투함

bawl *v.* we-ch'i-da 웨치다

bay *n.* man 만

bayonet *n.* ch'ong-gŭm 총검

bazaar *n.* sang-p'um-jin yŏl-jang
상품진열장

be *v.* (existence) it-da 있다; (pred-
icative) i-da 이다; (honorific)
kye-si-da 계시다

beach *n.* hae pyŏn 해변

beacon *n.* pong-hwa 봉화

bead *n.* ku-mŏng-i i-nŭn ku-sŭl
구멍이있는구슬

beak *n.* chu-dung-i 주둥이

beam *n.* (wood) tae-dŭl-bo 대들보;
(of light) kwang-sŏn 광선

beaming *adj.* pit-na-nŭn 빛나는

bean *n.* k'ong 콩

bear *n.* kom 곰; *v.* (endure) kyŏn-
di-da 견디다; (yield) maet-da 맺
다; (a child) na-ta 낳다; (on
the back) chi-da 지다; (on the
head) i-da 이다; (on the shoulder)
mi-da 미다

beard *n.* su-yŏm 수염

bearer *n.* chi-ge kun 지게꾼

bearing *n.* t'ae-do 태도; (direction) pang-wi 방위

breast *n.* chim-sŭng 짐승

beat *v.* (hit) dae-ri-da 때리다; (defeat) chi-u-da 지우다

beater *n.* (hunting) mor-i-kun 모리꾼

beautiful *adj.* a-rŭm-da-un 아름다운

beautify *v.* a-rŭm-dap-ge ha-da 아름답게하다

beauty *n.* a-rŭm-da-um 아름다움

beauty parlor *n.* mi-jang-won 미장원

beaver *n.* su-dal-p'i 수달피

because *conj.* …gi-dae-mun-e …기 때문에

beckon *v.* son-jis-ŭ-ro pu-rŭ-da 손짓으로 부르다

become *v.* doe-da 되다

becoming *adj.* al-mat-nŭn 알맞는

bed *n.* ch'ĭm-sang 침상

bed-bug *n.* pĭn-dae 빈대

bedclothes *n.* i-bul 이불

bedding *n.* ch'ĭm-gu 침구

bedroom *n.* ch'im-sĭl 침실

bedstead *n.* ch'ĭm-dae 침대

bee *n.* gul-pŏl 꿀벌　　　　「나무

beech *n.* nŏ-do-pam na-mu 너도밤

beef *n.* so-ko-gi 소고기

beefsteak *n.* pi-p'ŭ-sŭ-t'e-ik' 비프
스테익

beehive *n.* gul-pŏl chǐp 꿀벌집

beer *n.* maek-ju 매주

beet *n.* sa-t'ang-mu 사탕무

beetle *n.* kap-ch'ung 갑충

before *adv.* ap'-e 앞에; *prep.* (time)
chŏn-e 전에; *prep.* (place) ap'-e
앞에; *conj.* …ha-gi-do-chŏn-e…하
기도전에

beforehand *adv.* mi-ri 미리

befriend *v.* to-wa chu-da 도와주다

beg *v.* ch'ŏng ha-da 청하다

beget *v.* na-ta 낳다

beggar *n.* kŏ-ji 거지

begin *v.* si-jak ha-da 시작하다

beginner *n.* ch'o hak-ja 초학자

beginning *n.* si-jak 시작

behalf *n.* i-ŭi 이의

behave *v.* ch'ŏ-sǐn ha-da 처신하다

behavior *n.* ch'ŏ-sǐn 처신

behead *v.* mok-ŭl pe-da 목을베다

behind *adv.* twi-e 뒤에; *prep.* …ŭi
twi-e …의뒤에

behold *v.* po-da 보다

being *n.* ǐn-gan 인간

belch *v.* t'ŭ-rǐm ha-da 트림하다

belief *n.* (trust) sin-yong 신용;
(faith) mid-ŭm 믿음

believe *v.* mit-da 믿다
bell *n.* chong 종
bellow *v.* k'un so-ri-ro ul-da 큰소
리로울다
bellows *n.* p'ul-mu 풀무
belong *v.* sok ha-da 속하다
beloved *adj.* sa-rang ha-nŭn 사랑하
는
below *adv.* a-rae 아래
belt *n.* hyŏk-dae 혁대
bench *n.* kŏl-sang 걸상
bend *v.* kup-hi-da 굽히다; (twist)
hwi-da 휘다
beneath *adv. & prep.* …ŭi pa-ro
a-rae-e …의바로아래에
benediction *n.* ch'uk-bok 축복
benefactor *n.* ŭn-in 은인
beneficial *adj.* yu-ĭk-han 유익한
benefit *n.* i-ĭk 이익
benevolence *n.* cha-sŏn 자선
bent *adj.* kup-hĭn 굽힌
bequeath *v.* nam-gi-da 남기다
bequest *n.* yu-mul 유물
bereaved of, to be *v.* sang-sĭl ha-da
상실하다
berry *n.* dal-gi 딸기
berth *n.* ch'ĭm-dae 침대
beseech *v.* kan-ch'ŏng ha-da 간청
하다
beside *prep.* …yop'-e …옆에
besides *prep.* oe-e 외에

besiege v. p'o-wi ha-da 포위하다
best adj. ka-jang choh-ŭn 가장좋은
bestow v. chu-da 주다
bet v. nae-gi 내기
betray v. pae-ban ha-da 배반하다
betroth v. hon-yak ha-da 혼약하다
better adj. tŏ-uk choh-ŭn 더욱좋은;
　adv. tŏ-uk choh-ge 더욱좋게
between prep. …sa-i-e …사이에
beverage n. ŭm-myo 음료
bewail v. t'an-sik ha-da 탄식하다
beware v. chu-ŭi ha-da 주의하다
bewilderment n. tang-hwang 당황
beyond prep. …ŭi chŏ-chok-e 의저
　쪽에; adv. chŏ-chok-e 저쪽에
bias n. p'yŏn-jung 편중
bib n. t'ŏk-pat-ki 턱받기
Bible n. sŏng-gyŏng 성경
biceps n. i-du-gŭn 이두근
bicycle n. cha-jŏn-gŏ 자전거
bid v. kap-sŭl no-ta 값을놓다
bier n. sang-yŏ 상여
big adj. k'ŭn 큰
bile n. tam-jŭp 담즙
bill n. kye-san 계산; (animal's)
　pu-ri 부리; **b. of lading** sŏn-ha
　chŭng-kwon 선하증권
billiards n. al-ch'i-gi 알지기
billow n. k'un-mul-gyŏl 큰물결
bind v. muk-da 묶다　　　「안경
binoculars n. ssang-an-gyŏng 쌍

biography *n.* chŏn-gi 전기
biology *n.* saeng-mul-hak 생물학
birch *n.* pŏt na-mu 벗나무
bird *n.* sae 새
birth *n.* ch'ul-san 출산
birthday *n.* saeng-il 생일
birthplace *n.* ch'ul-saeng-ji 출생지
biscuit *n.* pi-sŭ-k'et' 비스켙
bishop *n.* kam-dok 감독
bit *n.* (portion) so-pu-bun 소부분; (horse) cha-gal 자갈
bite *v.* mul-da 물다; *n.* mul-gi 물기
bitter *adj.* ssŭn 쓴
bitterly *adv.* mop-si 몹시
black *adj.* kŏm-ŭn 검은; *v.* ga-mah-ke ha-da 까맣게하다
blackboard *n.* ch'il-p'an 칠판
blacken *v.* ga-mah-ke ha-da 까맣게하다
blacksmith *n.* tae-jang-jaeng-i 대장쟁이
bladder *n.* pang-gwang 방광
blade *n.* nal 날
blame *v.* pi-nan ha-da 비난하다
blameless *adj.* hŏ-mul ŏp-nŭn 허물없는
blank *n.* paek chi 백지; *adj.* pin 빈
blanket *n.* tam-yo 담요

blaspheme *v.* mo-dok ha-da 모독
하다

blast *v.* (blow up) p'ok-p'a ha-da
폭파하다

blaze *n.* hwa-yŏm 화염; *v.* hwa-
yŏm-ŭl ol-li-da 화염을올리다

bleach *v.* hŭi-ge ha-da 회게하다

bleak *adj.* ssŭl-ssŭl han 쓸쓸한

bleat *v.* ul-da 울다

bleed *v.* p'i-na-da 피나다

blend *v.* twi-sŏk-da 뒤섞다

bless *v.* ŭn-hye-rŭl pe-p'ul-da 은혜
를베풀다

blessing *n.* ch'uk-pok 축복

blind *adj.* nun ŏ-du-un 눈어두운

blindman *n.* so-gyŏng 소경

blindness *n.* maeng-mok 맹목

blink *v.* nun-ŭl gam-bak kŏ-ri-da
눈을깜박거리다

bliss *n.* hui-yŏl 회열

blister *n.* pu-p'ur-ŭm 부풀음; *v.*
pu-p'ul-da 부풀다

block *n.* cho-gak 조각; *v.* mak-da
막다

blockade *n.* pong-swae 봉쇄

blood *n.* p'i 피

blood-vessel *n.* hyŏl-gwan 혈관

bloody *adj.* yu-hyŏl han 유혈한

bloom *v.* p'i-da 피다

blossom *n.* got 꽃 「tŏ-rŏm 더렵

blot *v.* tŏ-rŏp-hi-da 더럽하다; *n.*

blotter *n.* ap-ji 압지

blouse *n.* pu-ra-u-sŭ 부라우스

blow *v.* pul-da 불다; *n.* t'a-gyŏk 타격

blue *adj.* p'u-rŭn 푸른

bluebell *n.* to-ra-ji 도라지

blueprint *n.* ch'ŏng-sa-jin 청사진

bluff *n.* chŏl-byŏk 절벽; *v.* sok-i-da 속이다

blunder *n.* k'ŭn-sĭl-su 큰실수; *v.* pi-t'ŭl kŏ-rĭ-da 비틀거리다

blunt *adj.* tun-han 둔한; (frank) sol-jĭk han 솔직한

bluntly *adv.* sol-jĭk ha-ge 솔직하게

blur *v.* pul myŏng-yo ha-ge ha-da 불명료하게하다

blusn *v.* bal-gae-jĭ-da 빨개지다; *n.* pu-kŭ-rŏm 부끄럼

blushing, to be, *v.* pu-kŭ-rŏ-wo ha-da 부끄러워하다

boar, wild, *n.* san-to-ya-ji 산도야지

board *n.* p'an-ja 판자; (committee) wi-won 위원; *v.* (feed) sĭk-sa sĭ-k'i-da 식사시키다

Board of Directors i-sa-hoe 이사회

boarding-school *n.* ki-suk hak-kyo 기숙학교

boast *v.* cha-rang ha-da 자랑하다; *n.* cha-rang 자랑

boastful *adj.* cha-rang ha-nun 자
랑하는

boat *n.* pae 배

boatman *n.* sŏn-bu 선부

bobbin *n.* (sewing machine) puk 북;
(weaving) sĭl-ku-rĭt-dae 실꾸릿대

bodily *adj.* sĭn-ch'e 신체; *adv.* (as
a whole) t'ong-ch'ae 롱채

body *n.* mom 몸

bodyguard *n.* ho-wi-byŏng 호위병

bog *n.* chin-gu-rŏng 진구렁

boil *v.* (liquid) gŭl-ta 끓다; (solids)
salm-da 삶다; *n.* pu-sŭ-rŏm 부
스럼

boiler *n.* chŭng-gi ki-gwan 승기기
관

boisterous *adj.* ssi-kŭ-rŏ-un 씨끄
러운

bold *adj.* tam-dae han 담대한

bolt *n.* na-sa 나사

bomb *n.* p'ok-t'an 폭탄

bond *n.* ch'ae-gwon 채권

bondage *n.* no-ye 노예

bonds *n.* chĭl-gok 질곡

bone *n.* byŏ 뼈

bonnet *n.* pon-ne-t'ŭ 본네트

bonus *n.* sang-yŏ-kŭm 상여금

book *n.* ch'aek 책; *v.* ki-ip ha-da
기입하다

bookcase *n.* ch'aek chang 책장

bookkeeping *n.* pu-gi 부기

bookstore *n.* ch'aek-sa 책사

boot *n.* chang-hwa 장화

bootblack *n.* ku–du tak-nŭn sa-ram 구두닥는사람

booth *n.* ka-gae 가개

booty *n.* p'o-hoek-mul 포획물

boracic acid *n.* pung-san 붕산

border *n.* kyŏng-gye 경계; (on a dress) kat 갓; *v.* chŏp ha–da 접하다

bore *v.* sĭl–jŭng na-ge ha-da 실증 나게하다; (drill) dul–li-da 뚫리다

borrow *v.* pĭl–li-da 빌리다

bosom *n.* ka-sŭm 가슴

boss *n.* kam–dok-ja 감독자; *v.* t'ong-sol ha-da 롱졸하다

botany *n.* sing-mul hak 식물학

both *adj.* yang-chok-ŭi 양쪽의; *tron.* tul-ta 둘다; *adv.* …do …do …도…도

bother *v.* kwi-ch'yan'-ke ha-da 귀 찮게하다

bottle *n.* pyŏng 병

bottom *n.* mit' 밑

bottomless, to be, *v.* mit' ŏp-da 밑 업다

bough *n.* ka-ji 가지

boulder *n.* k'ŭn pa-wi 큰바위

bound *v.* (leap) d'wi-da 뛰다; *n.* cho-yak 조약; *suffix.* (New York-bound) …haeng …행

boundary *n.* kyŏng-gye 경계

boundless *adj.* han-jŏng ŏp-nŭn 한정없는

bounds *n.* pŏm-wi 범위

bouquet *n.* got ta-bal 꽃다발

bouy *n.* pu-p'yo 부표

bouyant *adj.* chal dŭ-nŭn 잘뜨는

bow *n.* chŏl 절; *v.t. & v.i.* chŏl ha-da 절하다

bow *n.* (archery) hwal 활

bowels *n.* nae-jang 내장

bowl *n.* sa-bal 사발

box *n.* sang-ja 상자

boxer *n.* kwon-t'u sŏn-su 권투선수

boxing *n.* kwon-t'u 권투

box-office *n.* p'yo-p'a-nŭn got 표파는곳

boy *n.* sa-nae a-i 사내아이

Boy Scouts *n.* sŭ-ka-ut' 스카웃

boyhood *n.* so-nyŏn si-jŏl 소년시절

boycott *n.* po-i-k'ŏt' 보이컷

brace *v.* (support) pŏ-t'i-da 버티다; *n.* pŏ-t'im 버팀

bracelet *n.* son-mok-kŏl-i 손목걸이

brackish *adj.* jan 짠

brag *v.* cha-rang ha-da 자랑하다

brain *n.* noe 뇌

brake *n.* pu-re-k'i 부레키

bramble *n.* ka-si-tŏm-bul 가시덤불

bran *n.* kyŏ 겨

branch *n.* ka-ji 가지 ; *v.* kal-la-ji-da 갈라지다

brand *n.* sang-p'yo 상표

brandy *n.* pu-raen-di-i 부랜디이

bracket *n.* pŏ-t'ĭm-mok 버림목

brass *n.* not-soe 놋쇠; **b.-dishes** not-kŭ-rŭt 놋그릇

brave *adj.* yong-gam han 용감한; *v.* yong-gam ha-ge ha-da 용감하게하다

bravely *adv.* yong-gam ha-ge 용감하게

bravery *n.* yong-gam 용감

bray *v.* na-gwi-ga ul-da 나귀가울다

brazier *n.* hwa-ro 화로

breach *n.* (violation) wi-ban 위반

bread *n.* bang 빵

breadth *n.* p'ok 폭

break *v.* pu-sŏ-ji-da 부서지다 ; *n.* p'a-goe 파괴

breakfast *n.* cho-ban 조반

breast *n.* ka-sŭm 가슴; (woman) chŏt 젖

breast-work *n.* hung-pyŏk 흉벽

breath *n.* sum 숨

breathe *v.* sum-swi-da 숨쉬다

breathless *adj.* sum-mak-hi-nŭn 숨막히는

breed *v.* pŏn-sĭk ha-da 번식하다 ; *n.* chong-jok 종족　「운바람

breeze *n.* ka-byŏ-un pa-ram 가벼

brethren *n.* tong-p'o 동포
brew *v.* man-dŭl-da 만들다
bribe *n.* noe-mul 뇌물; *v.* noe-mul-ŭl mŏk-i-da 뇌물을먹이다
bribery *n.* chŭng-hoe 승회
brick *n.* pyŏk-tol 벽돌
bride *n.* sĭn-bu 신부
bridegroom *n.* sĭl-lang 신랑
bridesmaid *n.* sĭn-bu tŭl-lŏ-ri 신부들러러
bridge *n.* ta-ri 다리
bridle *n.* kul-le 굴레
brief *adj.* jalb-ŭn 짧은
brier *n.* jil-le 찔레
brigade *n.* yŏ-dan 여단
brigadier-general *n.* yuk-kun chun-jang 육군준장
bright *adj.* pit-na-nŭn 빛나는
brighten *v.* pit-na-ge ha-da 빛나게 하다
brilliance *n.* kwang-ch'e 광체
brilliant *adj.* kwang-ch'e han 광체한
brim *n.* ka-jang 가장
brine *n.* jan-mul 짠물
bring *v.* ka-jyŏ o-da 가져오다
brink *n.* ka-jang-cha-ri 가장자리
brisk *adj.* hwal-bal han 활발한
briskly *adv.* hwal-bal ha-ge 활발하게
bristle *n.* kut-sen-t'ŏl 굳센털

Britain *n.* tae yŏng-guk 대영국

brittle *adj.* gae-jĭ-gi swi-un 깨지
기쉬운

broad *adj.* nŏlb-ŭn 넓은

broadcast *v.* pang-song ha-da 방
송하다; *n.* pang-song 방송

broadcasting station *n.* pang-
song-guk 방송국

brocade *n.* mu-nŭi i-nŭn pi-dan 무
늬있는비단

broil *v.* kup-da 굽다

broken *adj.* gae-jĭn 깨진

broker *n.* chung-mae-in 중매인;
house-b. *n.* chĭp chu-rim 집주
림

bronchia *n.* ki-gwan-ji 기관지

bronchitis *n.* ki-gwan-ji yŏm 기
관지염

bronze *n.* ch'ŏng-dong 청동

brood *n.* han-bae sae-ki 한배새끼;
v. cham-jam-hi saeng-gak ha-da
잠잠히생각하다

brook *n.* si-nae-mul 시냇물

broom *n.* pi 비

broth *n.* ko-gi-kuk 고기국

brothel *n.* kal-bo chĭp 갈보집

brother, elder, *n.* hyŏng-nĭm 형님;
brother, elder, (for women) op-ba
읍바; **brother, younger** *n.* tong-
saeng 동생; **brothers** *n.* hyŏng-
je 형제

brother-in-law *n.* (husband's older brother) a-ju-bŏ-ni 아주버니; (husband's younger brother) si-tong-saeng 시동생; (wife's brother) ch'ŏ-nam 처남; (sister's husband) mae-bu 매부

brow *n.* i-ma 이마

brown *adj.* kal-saek 갈색

bruise *v.* sang-ch'ŏ nae-da 상처내다

brush *n.* sol 솔; *v.* sol-jil ha-da 솔질하다

brushwood *n.* su-p'ul 수풀

brutal *adj.* chan-ĭn-han 잔인한

brute *n.* chan-ĭn han nom 잔인한놈

bubble *n.* kŏ-p'um 거품

bubonic-plague *n.* hŭk-sa pyŏng 흑사병

buck *n.* sut-sa-sŭm 숫사슴

bucket *n.* pa-ke-ssŭ 바게쓰

buck-wheat *n.* mo-mil 모밀

buckle *n.* hyŏk-dae kŏ-ri 혁대거리

bud *n.* pong-o-ri 봉오리

Buddha *n.* pu-ch'ŏ 부처

Buddhism *n.* pul-kyo 불교

Buddhist *n.* pul-kyo-ĭn 불교인; **Buddhist Scripture** *n.* pul-kyŏng 불경

budget *n.* ye-san 예산

bug *n.* pŏl-lŏ-ji 벌러지

bugle *n.* na-p'al 나팔

build *v.* se-u-da 세우다
building *n.* pil-ding 빌딩
bulb *n.* ku-gyŏng 구경; (electric)
chŏn-gu 전구
bulk *n.* tŏng-i 덩이
bulky *adj.* k'ŭn 큰
bull *n.* hwang-so 황소
bullet *n.* ch'ong al 총알
bulletin *n.* kong-bo 공보
bullfrog *n.* su-gae-gu-ri 수개구리
bump *v.* dak ma-ju ch'i-da 딱마주
치다; *n.* ch'ung-dol 충돌; (swelling) hŭk 흑
bunch *n.* ta-bal 다발
bundle *n.* ta-bal 다발
bunk *n.* ch'ĭm-sang 침상
burden *n.* chĭm 짐
burdensome *adj.* koe-ro-un 피로운
bureau *n.* chang-nong 장롱; (government) kuk 국
burglar *n.* kang-do 강도
burial *n.* mae-jang 매장
burn *v.* t'ae-u-da 태우다; (fire)
pul-put'-da 불붙다; *n.* hwa-sang
화상
burrow *n.* kul 굴; *v.* kul-ŭl p'a-da
굴을파다
burst *v.* t'ŏ-ji-da 터지다 *n.* p'ok-
bal 폭발
bury *n.* mut-da 묻다
bus *n.* ba-sŭ 빠스

bush *n.* tŏm-bul 덤불

busily *adv.* ρa-pŭ-ge 바쁘게

business *n.* sang-ŏp 상업

bust *n.* pan-sĭn-sang 반신상

bustle *v.* ya-dan-pŏp sŏk-dae-da
야단법석대다; *n.* ya-dan 야단

busy *adj.* pa-pŭn 바쁜

but *conj.* kŭ-rŏ-na 그러나; *prep.*
ŭi-oe-nŭn 의외는

butcher *n.* paek-jŏng 백정

butter *n.* pa-t'a 바타

butterfly *n.* na-bi 나비

button *n.* tan-ch'u 단추; *v.* tan-
ch'u-rŭl goe-da 단추를끼다

button-hole *n.* tan-ch'u ku-mŏng
단추구멍

buttress *n.* po-t'ĭm 버팀

buy *v.* sa-da 사다

by *adv.* kyŏt'-e 곁에; *trep.* …yŏp'-
e 옆에; (by means of) ŭi-ha-yŏ
위하여; (before) ga-ji 까지

bystander *n.* kyŏt'-e sŭn-sa-ram
곁에슨사람

〔C〕

cab *n.* t'aek-ssi 택씨

cabbage *n.* yang-pae-ch'u 양배추;
(Chinese) pae-ch'u 배추

cabin *n.* o-mak chĭp 오막집;(shĭp)
sŏn sĭl 선실

cabinet *n.* chang 장; (governmental) nae-gak 내각; **C. Minister** nae-gak tae-sĭn 내각대신

cable *n.* (rope) pat chul 밧줄; (underwater) hae-jŏ chŏn-sŏn 해저전선

caboose *n.* sŭng-mu-won-yŏl-ch'a 승무원렬차

cadet *n.* chang-kyo hak-kyo saeng-do 장교학교생도

cage *n.* (bird) sae-jang 새장

cake *n.* kwa-ja 과자

calamity *n.* chae-nan 재난

calculate *v.* kye-san ha-da 계산하다

calculation *n.* kye-san 계산

calendar *n.* tal-yŏk 달력; (lunar) ŭm-yŏk 음역; (solar) yang-yŏk 양역

calf *n.* song-a-ji 송아지; (leg) chong-a-ri 종아리

calico *n.* ok-yang-mok 옥양목

call *v.* pu-rŭ-da 부르다; (visit) pang-mun ha-da 방문하다; *n.* (visit) pang-mun 방문; *v.* (telephone) chŏn-hwa-rŭl kŏl-da 전화를걸다

calling *n.* ch'ŏn-jik 천직

calm *adj.* ko-yo han 고요한

calmly *adv.* ko-yo ha-ge 고요하게

camel *n.* nak-t'a 낙타

camera *n.* sa-jĭn-gi 사진기

camp *n.* ya-yŏng-so 야영소; *v.* ya-yŏng ha-da 야영하다

campaign *n.* kong-sŏng ya-jŭn 공성야전

camping ch'on-mak saeng-hwal 천막생활

can *n.* ham-sŏk-t'ong 함석통; *aux. v.* …hal su it-da …할수있다

canal *n.* un-ha 운하

canary *n.* k'a-na-ri-ya 카나리야

cancel *v.* ch'wi-so ha-da 취소하다

cancellation *n.* ch'wi-so 취소

candidate *n.* hu-bo-ja 후보자

candle *n.* yang ch'o 양초

candle-light *n.* ch'o pul 촛불

candlestick *n.* ch'o tae 촛대

candy *n.* sa-t'ang 사탕

cane *n.* chǐ-p'ang-i 지팡이; **sugar c.** *n.* sa-t'ang su-su 사탕수수

canned goods *n.* t'ong cho-rim 통조림

cannibal *n.* ǐn-yuk mŏk-nŭn-ja 인육먹는자

Canada *n.* ka-na-da 가나다

Canadian *n.* ka-na-da sa-ram 가나다사람; *adj.* ka-na-da-ǔi 가나다의

cannon *n.* tae-p'o 대포

cannon-ball *n.* p'o-t'an 포탄

cannot *v.* hal-su ŏp-ta 할수없다

canoe *n.* t'o-mak-pae 토막배

canopy *n.* ch'a-il 차일

canvas *n.* hwa-p'o 화포

canvass *v.* yu-se ha-da 유세하다

cap *n.* mo-ja 모자

capable *adj.* …hal su i-nŭn …할수
있는

capacity *n.* yong-jŏk 용적

cape *n.* ŏ-kae-man-to 어깨만또;
(headland) got 곶

capital *adj.* su-wi-ŭi 수위의; *n.*
(city) su-do 수도; (money) cha-
bon 자본

capitalism *n.* cha-bon-ju-ŭi 자본
주의

capitol *n.* ŭi-sa-dang 의사당

captain *n.* (army) tae-wi 대위;
(navy) tae-ryŏng 대령; (of warship) ham-jang 함장; (of merchant
ship) sŏn-jang 선장

captive *n.* pu-ro 부로

capture *n.* ch'e-p'o 체포; *v.* put-
chap-da 붓잡다

car *n.* ch'a 차; (auto) cha-dong-
ch'a 자동차

caravan *n.* tae-sang 대상

carbolic acid *n.* sok-t'an-san 석
탄산

carbon *n.* t'an-so 탄소

carburettor *n.* ki-hwa-gi 기화기

carcass *n.* si-ch'e 시체

card *n.* (playing) t'ŭ-rŏm-p'ŭ 트럼
프; (calling) myŏng-ham 명함

cardboard *n.* ma-bun-ji 마분지

care *v.* kŭn-sĭm ha-da 근심하다;
n. (worry) kŏk-jŏng 격정; **take
c.** chu-ŭi ha-da 주의하다

career *n.* il-saeng-ŭi haeng-no 일
생의행로

careful *adj.* chu-ŭi ha-nŭn 주의하
는

carefully *adv.* cho-sim-sŭ-rŏp-ge
조심스럽게

careless *adj.* mu-gwan-sim han 무
관심함

carelessly *adv.* cho-sĭm-sŏng ŏps-i
조심성없이

carelessness *n.* pul cho-sĭm-sŏng
불조심성 「다

caress *v.* ŏ-ru-man-ji-da 어루만지

cargo *n.* pae-chim 뱃짐

carol *n.* ch'uk-ha-ŭi no-rae 축하의
노래

carp *n.* ing-ŏ 잉어

carpenter *n.* mok-su 목수

carpet *n.* yang t'an-ja 양탄자

carrier *n.* (A-frame) chi-ge kun 지
게군; **aircraft-c.** *n.* hang-gong
mo-ham 항공모함

carrot *n.* ĭn-jĭn 인진

carry *v.* (take) ka-ji-da 가지다;
(on the head) i-da 이다; (on the

back) chi-da 지다; (in the arms) an-da 안다; (on the shoulder) mi-da 미다; (in the hand) tŭl-da 들다; (in the belt) ch'a-da 차다

cart *n.* ch'a 차; (hand) ku-ru-ma 구루마; (ox) ma-ch'a 마차

cartoon *n.* man-hwa 만화

carve *v.* cho-gak ha-da 조각하다

carver *n.* cho-gak-sa 조각사

carving *n.* cho-gak 조각

case *n.* (box) sang-ja 상자; (condition) kyŏng-u 경우; (affair) sa-gŏn 사건

casement *n.* ch'ang-ŭi mun-chak 창의문짝

cash *n.* hyŏn-gŭm 현금; *v.* chŏng-gŭm-ŭ-ro pa-ku-da 정금으로 바꾸다 「현금출납계

cashier *n.* hyŏn-gŭm ch'ul-nap-gye

cask *n.* t'ong 통

casket *n.* (coffin) kwan 관

cast *v.* tŏn-ji-da 던지다

castle *n.* sŏng 성

castor-oil *n.* p'i-ma-ju ki-rŭm 피마주기름

cat *n.* ko-yang-i 고양이

catalogue *n.* mok-nok 목록

catastrophe *n.* chae-pyon 재변

catch *v.* put-chap-da 붓잡다; **c. cold** kam-gi tŭl-da 감기들다; **c. fire** pul na-da 불나다

category *n.* pŏm-ju 범주

caterpillar *n.* pŏ-lŏ-ji 버러지

cathedral *n.* k'ŭn hoe-dang 큰회당

Catholic *adj.* (Roman) ch'ŏn-ju kyo 천주교

cattle *n.* ka-juk 가축

cause *v.* si-k'i-da 시키다; *n.* (origin) won-in 원인; *n.* (purpose) mok-jŏk 목적

caution *n.* cho-sĭm 조심

cautious *adj.* cho-sĭm-sŏng i-nŭn 조심성있는

cavalry *n.* ki-byŏng 기병

cave *n.* kul 굴

cavity *n.* ku-mŏng 구멍

cease *v.* kŭ-ch'i-da 그치다

ceaseless *adv.* gŭ-nĭm ŏp-nŭn 끄님없는

ceaselessly *adv.* gŭn'-ĭm-ŏps-i 끊임없이

cedar *n.* hi-mal-la-ya ŭ-ru-na-mu 히말라야으루나무

ceiling *n.* ch'ŏn-jŏng 천정

celebrate *v.* ch'uk-ha ha-da 축하하다

celebration *n.* ch'uk-ha 축하; (as suffix) …sĭk 식

celebrity *n.* myŏng-sa 명사

celery *n.* mi-na-ri 미나리

cell *n.* (hermit) am-ja 암자; (prison) kam-pang 감방

cellar *n.* chi-ha-sĭl 지하실

cemetery *n.* kong-dong myo-ji 공동묘지

census *n.* kuk-se cho-sa 국세조사

cent *n.* ch'ŏn 천

center *n.* chung-sĭm 중심

centigrade *adj.* pae-bun-do 배분도

centipede *n.* chi-ne 지네

central *adj.* chung-ang-ŭi 중앙의

century *n.* se-gi 세기

ceremony *n.* ye-sĭk 예식

certain *adj.* hwak-sĭl han 확실한;
  a certain ŏt-tŏn 어떤

certainly *adv.* hwak-sĭl-hi 확실히;
  (exclamation) mul-lon 물론

certificate *n.* chŭng-myŏng-sŏ 증명서

certify *v.* chŭng-myŏng ha-da 증명하다

chaff *n.* kyŏ 겨

chain *n.* soe-sa-sul 쇠사슬

chair *n.* ŭi-ja 의자

chairman *n.* hoe-jang 회장

chalk *n.* paek-muk 백묵

challenge *n.* cho-jŏn 조전; *v.* cho-jŏn ha-da 조전하다

champion *n.* sŏn-su 선수

chance *n.* (opportunity) ki-hoe 기회; (luck) un-su 운수

change *n.* pyŏn-dong 변동; *v.* pyŏn ha-da 변하다

changeable *adj.* pyŏn-ha-gi swi-un
변하기 쉬운

channel *n.* mul-kil 물길

chaos *n.* hon-don 혼돈

chapel *n.* ye-bae-dang 예배당

chapter *n.* chang 장

character *n.* sŏng-jil 성질; (written)
kŭl-ja 글자; (Chinese) han-mun-
ja 한문자

charcoal *n.* sut 숯

charge *v.* (attack) chin-gyŏk ha-da
진격하다

charitable *adj.* cha-bi kip'-ŭn 자비
깊은

charity *n.* cha-bi-sim 자비심

charm *v.* ki-pŭ-ge ha-da 기쁘게하
다; *n.* mae-ryŏk 매력; (amulet)
pu-jak 부작

chart *n.* hae-do 해도

charter *n.* t'ŭk-hŏ-jang 특허장

chase *v.* twi-rŭl jŭt-da 뒤를좇다;
n. ch'u-gyŏk 추격

chat *v.* han-dam ha-da 한담하다;
n. han-dam 한담

chauffeur *n.* un-jŏn-su 운전수

cheap *adj.* ssan 싼

cheaply *adv.* ssa-ge 싸게

cheat *v.* sok-i-da 속이다

check *v.* (entrust) mak-ki-da 막기
다; (hold back) ŏk-ge ha-da 억
게하다

check *n.* (bank) so-jŏl-su 소절수;
   v. p'yo ha-da 표하다
checkmark *n.* p'yo 표
checkerboard *n.* pa-dok-p'an 바둑
   판
cheek *n.* byam 뺨
cheer *n.* hwan-ho 환호; *v.* wi-an
   ha-da 위안하다
cheerful *adj.* ki-pŭn 기쁜
cheerfulness *n.* ki-pŭn-sŏng 기쁨성
cheese *n.* ch'i-ssŭ 치쓰
chemical *n.* hwa-hak che-p'um 화
   학제품; *adj.* hwa-hak-ui 화학의
chemist *n.* hwa-hak-ja 화학자
chemistry *n.* hwa-hak 화학
cherry *n.* pŏt 벗; (blossom) pŏt
   got' 벗꽃; (tree) pŏt na-mu 벗나
   무
chess *n.* chang-gi 장기
chest *n.* ka-sŭm 가슴; (box) kwe
   궤
chestnut *n.* pam 밤
chew *v.* ssĭp-da 씹다
chick *n.* pyŏng-a-ri 병아리
chicken *n.* t'ak 닭
chief *n.* su-ryŏng 수령
child *n.* a-i 아이
childhood *n.* yu-nyŏn-gi 유년기
chill *n.* han-gi 한기
chime *v.* chong-ŭl ul-li-da 종을을
   리다; *n.* (bell) chong 종

chimney *n.* kul-tuk 굴뚝

chimney-sweep *n.* kul-tuk-ssu-si-nŭn sa-ram 굴뚝쑤시는사람

chin *n.* t'ŏk 턱

china *n.* cha-gi 자기

China *n.* chung-guk 중국

Chinese *adj.* chung-guk-ŭi 중국의; (Nationalist) chung-hwa-ŭi 중화의; (Communist) chung-gong-ŭi 중공의

chip *n.* gak-a-naen cho-gak 까아낸 조각; *v.* gak-da 까다

chisel *n.* gŭl 끌

chlorine *n.* yŏm-so 염소

chloroform *n.* k'ŭl-lo-ro-p'om 클로로폼

chocolate *n.* ch'o-k'ol-le-t'ŭ 초콜레트

choice *n.* sŏn-t'aek 선택

choir *n.* hap-ch'ang-dan 합창단

choke *v.* sum mak-hi-da 숨막히다

cholera *n.* ho-yŏl-ja 호열자

choose *v.* sŏn-t'aek ha-da 선택하다

chop *v.* cha-rŭ-da 자르다

chopsticks *n.* chŏ 저

chorus *n.* hap-ch'ang 합창

Christ *n.* kŭ-rĭ-sŭ-to 그리스도

Christian *n.* ye-su kyo-ĭn 예수교인

Christianity *n.* ye-su-kyo 예수교

Christmas *n.* sŏng-t'an 성탄

chrysanthemum *n.* kuk hwa 국화

chuckle *n.* sok-us-ŭm 속웃음; *v.*
gĭl-gĭl ut-da 낄낄웃다

church *n.* ye-bae-dang 예배당

cicada *n.* mae-mi 매미

cider *n.* sa-gwa-mul 사과물

cigar *n.* ssi-ga-a tam-bae 씨가아
담배

cigarette *n.* ssi-ga-ret' tam-bae 씨
가레 담배

cinder *n.* chae 재

cinema *n.* hwal-dong sa-jin 활동
사진

circle *n.* won hyŏng 원형; *v.* hoe-
jŏn ha-da 회전하다

circuit *n.* (electric) hoe-ro 회로

circular *adj.* hwan-sang-ŭi 환상의

circulate *v.* sun-hwan ha-da 순환
하다

circulation *n.* sun-hwan 순환

circumference *n.* won-ju 원주

circumstance *n.* sa-jŏng 사정

circus *n.* kong-ma-jang 곡마장

cistern *n.* chŏ-su-t'ong 저수통

cite *v.* ĭn-yong ha-da 인용하다

citation *n.* hun-jang-jang 훈장장

citizen *n.* si-mĭn 시민

citizenship *n.* si-mĭn-gwon 시민권

city *n.* to-si 도시

civil *adj.* mĭn-gan-ŭi 민간의; (polite) chŏng-jung han 정중한

civilian *n.* ĭl-ban-ĭn 일반인

civilization *n·* mun-myŏng 문명

civilize *v·* mun-myŏng ha-ge ha-da
문명하게하다

claim *n·* yo-gu 요구; *v·* (insist)
chu-jang ha-da 주장하다;(demand)
yo-gu ha-da 요구하다

clam *n·* cho-gae 조개

clan *n·* ssi-jok 씨족

clap *n·* pak-su 박수; *v·* pak-su ha-
da 박수하다

clapper *n·* chong-ŭi hyŏ 종의혀

clash *v·* ch'ung-dol ha-da 충돌하다

clasp *v·* p'a-ak ha-da 파악하다

class *n·* kye-gŭp 계급; (school)
pan 반

classification *n·* pun-yu 분류

classify *v·* pun-yu ha-da 분류하다

classmate *n·* tong-ch'ang saeng 동
창생

classroom *n·* kyo-sil 교실

clause *n·* (in an agreement) cho-
hang 조항

claw *n·* pal-t'op 발톱

clay *n·* chin-hŭk 진흙

clean *adj·* gae-kŭt han 깨끗한; *v·*
so-je ha-da 소제하다

cleaning *n·* (clothes) k'ŭ-rin-ing
크린잉

cleanse *v·* so-je ha-da 소제하다

clear *adj·* myŏng-paek han 명백한;
v· che-gŏ ha-da 제거하다

clearly *adv.* myŏng-paek-hi 명백히

clench *v.* gwak chwi-da 꽉쥐다

clergyman *n.* mok-sa 목사

clerk *n.* sŏ-gi 서기

clever, to be, *v.* chae-ju it-da 재주 있다

cleverness *n.* chae-ju 재주

client *n.* ŭi-roe-in 의뢰인

cliff *n.* chŏl pyŏk 절벽

climate *n.* ki-hu 기후

climax *n.* chŏng-jŏm 정점

climb *v.* o-rŭ-da 오르다

cling *v.* tal-la put'-da 달라붙다

clip *n.* (gun) k'ŭl-li-p'ŭ 클리프

cloak *n.* man-t'o 만토

clock *n.* si-gye 시계

close *v.* tat-da 닫다; *adj.* ka-ka-i 가까이; *adj.* (near) ka-ka-un 가까운; (intimate) ch'in han 친한

closely *adv.* ka-kap-ge 가깝게

closet *n.* kol-pang 골방

clot *v.* ŏng-gin tŏng-ŏ-ri 엉긴덩어리

cloth *n.* ot kam 옷감

clothe *v.* ip-hi-da 입히다

clothes *n.* ot 옷

clothing *n.* ot 옷

cloud *n.* ku-rŭm 구름

cloudless *adj.* ku-rŭm ŏp-nŭn 구름 없는

cloudy *adj.* ku-rŭm gin 구름낀

clover *n.* k'ŭ-ro-o-ba 크로오바

clown *n.* ĭk-sal-gun 익살군

club *n.* kon-bong 곤봉

clue *n.* sil-mŏ-ri 실머리

clumsy *adj.* sŭ-t'u-rŭn 스투른

cluster *n.* song-i 송이; *v.* de-rŭl chit-da 떼를짓다

coach *n.* ka-rŭ-ch'ŏ chu-da 가르쳐 주다; *n.* (railway) kaek ch'a 객 차; (athletic) k'o-ch'wi 코-취

coal *n.* sŏk-t'an 석탄

coalition *n.* yŏn-hap 연합

coal mine *n.* t'an-gwang 탄광

coarse *adj.* kŏ-ch'in 거친

coast *n.* hae-an 해안

coat *n.* oe-t'u 외투

cobbler *n.* ku-du ko-ch'i-nŭn sa-ram 구두고치는사람

cobweb *n.* kŏ-mi-chul 거미줄

cock *n.* su-t'ak 수닭

cocoa *n.* k'o-k'o-a 코코아

coconut *n.* ya-ja yŏl-mae 야자열 매

cocoon *n.* ko-ch'i 고치

cod *n.* tae-gu 대구

cod-liver oil *n.* kan-yu 잔유

code *n.* (standard) ye-pŏp 예법; (secret) am-ho 암호

co-education *n.* kong-hak 공학

coffee *n.* k'a-p'i 카피

coffin *n.* kwan 관

coil *v.t.* hwi-kam-da 휘감다; *n.*
  k'o-il 코일

coin *n.* ton 돈

coincide *v.* il-ch'i doe-da 일치되
  다

coincidence *n.* am-hap 암합

cold *adj.* ch'an 찬; *n.* (in the head)
  kam-gi 감기; **be cold** ch'up-da
  춥다; (of hands and feet) si-ri-da
  시리다; **to catch cold** kam-gi
  tŭl-da 감기들다

collar *n.* k'al-la 칼라

colleague *n.* tong-ŏp-ja 동업자

collect *v.* mo-i-da 모이다

collection *n.* su-jip 수집;(offering)
  hŏn-gŭm 헌금

collective security *n.* chip-dan
  an-jŏn-po-jang 집단안전보장

college *n.* pun-gwa tae-hak 분과대
  학

collide *v.t.* ch'ung-dol ha-da 충돌
  하다

collision *n.* ch'ung-dol 충돌

colloquial *adj.* sok-ŏ-ŭi 속어의

colonel *n.* tae-ryŏng 대령

colonist *n.* sĭk-min 식민

colony *n.* sĭk-min-ji 식민지

color *n.* pit-kal 빛갈; *v.t.* & *i.*
  saek-ch'il ha-da 색칠하다

colt *n.* mang-a-ji 망아지

column *n.* won-ju 원주

comb *n.* pit 빗

combat *n.* chŏn-t'u 전투

combination *n.* kyŏl-hap 결합

combine *v.i.* kyŏl-hap ha-da 결할 하다

come *v.i.* o-da 오다

comedian *n.* hŭi-gŭk pae-u 회극배 우

comedy *n.* hŭi-gŭk 회극

comfort *n.* wi-an 위안; (ease) al-lak 안락; *v.t.* wi-ro ha-da 위 로하다

comfortable *adj.* p'yŏn-an han 편 안한

comic *adj.* hŭi-gŭk-jŏk 회극적

comma *n.* k'om-ma 콤마

command *n.* myŏng-yŏng 명령; *v.t.* myŏng-yŏng ha-da 명령하다

commander *n.* chi-hwi-gwan 지휘 관; (navy) chung-yŏng 중령; **c.-in-chief** ch'ong chi-hwi-gwan 총 지휘관

commemorate *v.t.* ki-nyŏm ha-da 기념하다

commence *v.t. & i.* si-jak ha-da 시작하다

commencement *n.* cho-rŏp sik 졸 업식

commend *v.* ch'ing-ch'an ha-da 칭 찬하다

comment *v.* chu-sŏk ha-da 주석하다

commerce *n.* sang-ŏp 상업
commercial *adj.* sang-ŏp-ŭi 상업의
commission *n.* wi-im 위임
commissioner *n.* wi-won 위원
commit *v.t.* haeng ha-da 행하다
committee *n.* wi-won-hwoe 위원회
commodity *n.* sang-p'um 상품
common *adj.* (mutual) kong-t'ong-ŭi 공통의; (ordinary) po-t'ong 보통
commonplace *adj.* p'yŏng-bŏm han 평범한
commonwealth *n.* yŏn-bang 연방
common sense *n.* sang-sĭk 상식
communicate *v.i.* & *t.* t'ong-sin ha-da 통신하다
communication *n.* t'ong-sin 통신
communications *n.* yŏl-lak 연락
communion *n.* (church) sŏng-ch'an sik 성찬식
communism *n.* kong-san chu-ŭi 공산주의
communist *n.* kong-san chu-ŭi-ja 공산주의자
community *n.* pu-rak 부락
compact *adj.* ch'i-mil han 치밀한
companion *n.* tong-mu 동무
company *n.* hoe-sa 회사; (army) chung-dae 중대
comparatively *adv.* pi-gyo-jŏk 비교적

compare *v.t.* pi-gyo ha-da 비교하다

comparison *n.* pi-gyo 비교

compartment *n.* ku-hoek 구획

compass *n.* na-ch'im-p'an 나침판

compassion *n.* tong-jŏng 동정

compel *v.t.* kang-yo ha-da 강요하다

compensate *n.* po-sang ha-da 보상
하다

compete *v.i.* kyŏng-jaeng ha-da 경
쟁하다

competent *adj.* cha-gyŏk i-nŭn 자
격있는

competition *n.* kyŏng-jaeng 경쟁

compile *v.* p'yŏn-ch'an ha-da 편찬
하다

complain *v.i.* pul-p'yŏng-ŭl mal
ha-da 불평을 말하다

complete *v.* wan-sŏng ha-da 완성
하다; *adj.* wan-jŏn-han 완전한

complex *adj.* pok-chap-han 복잡한

complicate *v.* hon-jap ha-ge ha-da
혼잡하게하다

complication *n.* hon-jap 혼잡

compliment *n.* ch'an-sa 찬사; *v.*
ch'ing-ch'an ha-da 칭찬하다

complimentary *adj.* ch'ing-ch'an
han 칭찬한

comply *v.i.* sŭng-nak ha-da 승낙하다

compose *v.t.* ku-sŏng ha-da 구성하
다

composer *n.* chak-kok-ga 작곡가

composition *n.* cho-sŏng 조성;
(written) chak-mun 작문

compound *v.t.* cho-hap ha-da 조합
하다

compress *v.* ap-ch'uk ha-da 압축하
다

compromise *n.* t'a-hyŏp 타협

compulsion *n.* kang-je 강제

compulsory *a j.* kang-je-jŏk 강제
적

comrade *n.* tong-mu 동무

conceal *v.t.* kam-ch'u-da 감추다

concede *v.* yang-bo ha-da 양보하다

conceit *n.* cha-bu-sĭm 자부심

conceive *v.* (imagine) an-ch'ul ha-
da 안출하다; (child) ae-gi pae-da
애기배다

concentrate *v.* chip-jung ha-da 집
…중하다

concern *n.* (worry) kŭn-sĭm 근심;
c. with kwan-gye 관계

concerning *prep.* …e kwan ha-yŏ
…에 관하여

concert *n.* ŭm-ak hwoe 음악회

concise *adj.* kan-dan han 간단한

conclude *v.* gŭt nae-da 끝내다

conclusion *n.* chong-gyŏl 종결

concrete *adj.* ku-ch'e-jŏk 구체적;
n. k'ong-k'ŭ-ri-i-t'ŭ 콩크리이트

concubine *n.* ch'ŏp 첩

concussion *n.* chĭn-t'ang 진탕

condemn *v.t.* pi-nan ha-da 비난하다

condense *v.* ŏng-gi-da 엉기다

condition *n.* (state) sang-t'ae 상태;
(in contracts) cho-gŏn 조건

condole *v.i.* cho-mun ha-da 조문하
다

conduct *n.* haeng-wi 행위; *v.*
(direct) chi-hwi ha-da 지휘하다;
(lead) in-do ha-da 인도하다

conductor *n.* (music) chi-hwi-ja
지휘자

cone *n.* won-ch'u 원추

confer *v.t.* chu-da 주다; **c. with**
v.i. sang-ŭi ha-da 상의하다

confess *v.t.* cha-baek ha-da 자백하
다

confession *n.* cha-baek 자백

confide *v. t. & i.* sin-im ha-da 신
임하다

confidence *n.* sin-im 신임

confine *v.t.* ka-du-da 가두다

confirm *v.* hwak-in ha-da 확인하다

confuse *v.t.* tang-hwang ha-ge ha-
da 당황하게하다

confusion *n.* tang-hwang 당황

congratulate *v.t.* ch'uk-ha ha-da
축하하다

congratulation *n.* ch'uk-ha 축하

congress *n.* kuk-hoe 국회

conjunction *n.* chŏp-sok-sa 접속사

connect *v.t.* yŏn-gyŏl ha-da 연결하다

connection *n.* yŏn-gyŏl 연결

connotation *n.* ŏ-gam 어감

conquer *v.t.* chŏng-bok ha-da 정복 하다

conqueror *n.* chŏng-bok-ja 정복자

conquest *n.* chŏng-bok 정복

conscience *n.* yang-sĭm 양심

conscientious *adj.* yang-sĭm-jŏk 양심적

conscious *adj.* ŭi-sik ha-go i-nŭn 의식하고있는

consciousness *n.* ŭi-sik 의식

consent *v.i.* sŭng-nak ha-da 승낙하 다; *n.* sŭng-nak 승낙

consequence *n.* kyŏl-gwa 결과

consider *v.t. & i.* saeng-gak ha-da 생각하다

considerable *adj.* sang-dang han 상당한

consist *v.i.* i-ru-ŏ-ji-da 이루어지다

consonant *n.* cha-ŭm 자음

constable *n.* kyŏng-gwan 경관

constabulary *n.* kyŏng-gwan-dae 경관대; (as quasi miliatry force, usually) kyŏng-bi-dae 경비대

constant *adj.* (same) han-kyŏl kat'-ŭn 한결같은; (continuous) pu-dan-ŭi 부단의

constellation *n.* sŏng-chwa 성좌

constituent *n.* (political) sŏn-gŭ-in 선거인

constitution *n.* hŏn-pŏp 헌법

construct *v.t.* kŏn-sŏl ha-da 건설
하다

construction *n.* (making) kŏn-sŏl
건설

constructive *adj.* kŏn-sŏl-jŏk 건설적

consul *n.* yŏng-sa 영사

consulate *n.* yŏng-sa-gwan 영사관

consult *v.* ŭi-non ha-da 의논하다

consume *v.t.* so-bi ha-da 소비하다

consumption *n.* so-bi 소비

contact *n.* chŏp-ch'ok 접촉

contagious *adj.* chŏn-yŏm-sŏng-ŭi
전염성의

contain *v.t.* p'o-ham ha-da 포함하
다

contaminate *v.* tŏ-rŏp-ch'i-da 더렵
치다

contempt *n.* kyŏng-myŏl 경멸

contend *v.i.* ta-t'u-da 다투다

content *adj.* man-jok han 만족한;
n. man-jok 만족

contentment *n.* man-jok 만족

contents *n.* nae-yong 내용

contest *n.* kyŏng-jaeng 경쟁

context *n.* mun-maek 문맥

continent *n.* tae-ryuk 대륙

continual *adj.* gŭn-nim ŏp-nŭn 끊
임없는

continue *v.t. & i.* kye-sok ha-da
계속하다

continuous *adj.* yŏn-sok ha-nŭn 연속하는

contraband *n.* kŭm-je-p'um 금제품; *adj.* kŭm-je-ŭi 금제의

contradict *v.* pan-bak ha-da 반박하다

contrary *adj.* pan-dae-ŭi 반대의

contrast *n.* tae-jo 대조

contribute *v.* ki-bu ha-da 기부하다

contribution *n.* ki-bu 기부

control *v.t.* chi-bae ha-da 지배하다; *n.* chi-bae 지배

convenience *n.* p'yŏn-ŭi 편의

convenient *adj.* p'yŏl-li han 편리한

convent *n.* su-nyŏ-won 수녀원

conversation *n.* hoe-hwa 회화

convert *v.t.* chŏn-hwan ha-da 전환하다

convoy *n.* ho-song-dae 호송대

cook *v.t. & i.* yo-ri ha-da 요리하다; *n.* yo-ri-in 요리인

cooking *n.* yo-ri 요리

cool *adj.* sŏ-nŭl han 서늘한; *v.t.* sik-hi-da 식히다

coop *n.* tak-jang 닭장

copper *n.* ku-ri 구리

copy *v.* pe-ki-da 베끼다

coral *n.* san-ho 산호

cord *n.* chul 줄

cordial *adj.* ma-ŭm-ŭ-ro pu-t'ŏ-ŭi 마음으로부터의

core *n.* sok 속

cork *n.* k'o-rŭ-k'ŭ 코르크

corn *n.* ok-su-su 옥수수

corner *n.* ku-sŏk 구석

cornfield *n.* ok-su-su-pat' 옥수수
밭

corporal *n.* chung-sa 중사

corps *n.* (army) kun-dan 군단

corpse *n.* si-ch'e 시체

correct *adj.* pa-rŭn 바른

correct *v.* ko-ch'i-da 고치다

correspond to *v.i.* il-ch'i ha-da 일
치하다; **c. with** *v.* t'ong-sĭn ha-
da 통신하다

correspondence *n.* p'yŏn-ji 편지

corridor *n.* pok-do 복도

cost *v.t.* kap na-ka-da 값나가다;
n. kaps 값

costly *adj.* pi-ssan 비싼

costume *n.* pok-jang 복장

cosy *adj.* al-lak han 안락한

cot *n.* chak-ŭn ch'im-dae 작은침대

cottage *n.* cho-kŭ-man chĭp 조그
만집

cotton *n.* som 솜; (cloth) mu-
myŏng 무명

couch *n.* nup-nŭn ŭi-ja 눕는의자

cough *n.* ki-ch'im 기침; *v.i.* ki-
ch'im ha-da 기침하다

council *n.* p'yŏng-ŭi hoe 평의회

counsel *n.* hun-su 훈수; *v.* hun-su
ha-da 훈수하다

count *v.* se-da 세다
counter *n.* kye-san-dae 계산대
counteract *v.t.* pan-dae ha-da 반대
하다
counterfeit *adj.* ka-cha-ŭi 가짜의
countersign *v.t.* pu-sŏ ha-da 부서
하다
country *n.* si-gol 시골; (nation)
na-ra 나라
county *n.* kun 군
couple *n.* han ssang 한쌍
courage *n.* yong-gi 용기
course *n.* (route) chin-haeng 진행;
(school) kwa-mok 과목
court *n.* (law) chae-p'an-so 재판소
courtesy *n.* chŏng-chung 정중
courtyard *n.* an dŭl 안뜰
cousin *n.* sa-ch'on 사촌
cover *v.* tŏp'-da 덮다; *n.* tŏp'-gae
덮개
covet *v.t.* pu-rŏ-wo ha-da 부러워
하다
cow *n.* am-so 암소
coward *n.* kŏp-jaeng-i 겁쟁이
cowardice *n.* kŏp 겁
cower *v.i.* gu-bŭ-ri-da 꾸부리다
crab *n.* ke 게
crack *n.* t'ŭm 틈; *v.t.* jo-gae-da
쪼개다; *v.i.* jo-gae-ji-da 쪼개지다
cracker *n.* pi-sŭ-k'et' 비스켈
cradle *n.* yo-ram 요람

craft *n.* (trade) chi-gŏp 직업; (skill) ki-sul 기술

craftsman *n.* ki-sul-ga 기술가

crafty *adj.* kan-sa-han 간사한

crane *n.* (bird) hak 학; (machine) ki-jung-gi 기중기

crash *n.* (collision) ch'ung-dol 충돌; *v.* ch'ung-dol ha-da 충돌하다

crate *n.* kwe-chak 궤짝

crater *n.* pun-hwa-gu 분화구

crave *v.t.* & *i.* kan-ch'ŏng ha-da 간청하다

crawl *v.i.* ki-da 기다

crayon *n.* k'ŭ-re-i-on 크레이온

crazy *adj.* mi-ch'in 미친

creak *v.i.* pi-gŏk-kŏ-ri-da 비걱거리다

cream *n.* k'ŭ-rim 크림

create *v.t.* ch'ang-jo ha-da 창조하다

creator *n.* ch'ang-jo-ja 창조자

creature *n.* saeng-mul 생물

credentials *n.* sĭn-im-jang 신임장

credit *n.* (money) ch'ae-gwon 채권; (belief) sin-yong 신용

creditable *adj.* ch'ing-ch'an hal-man han 칭찬할만한

creek *n.* nae 내

creep *v.i.* ki-da 기다

cremate *v.* hwa-jang ha-da 화장하다

crescent *n.* ch'o-saeng-dal 초생달

crevice *n.* t'ŏ-jĭn-t'ŭm 터진틈

crew *n.* (of ship) sŏn-won 선원

cricket *n.* kwi-tŭ-ra-mi 귀뜨라미

crime *n.* choe 죄

criminal *adj.* pŭm-choe-ŭi 범죄의;
n. choe-in 죄인

crimson *n.* chĭn-hong-saek 진홍색;
adj. sae-bal-gan 새빨간

cripple *n.* chŏl-lŭm pa-ri 절름바리

crisis *n.* wi-gi 위기

crisp *adj.* a-sak-a-sak ha-nŭn 아
삭아삭하는

critical *adj.* pi-p'yŏng-jŏk 비평적;
(crisis) wi-gŭp han 위급한

crocodile *n.* ak-ŏ 악어

crop *n.* su-hwak 수확

cross *n.* sip-ja-ga 십자가; *adj.*
am-sang-sŭ-ro-un 암상스로운;
v. kŏn-nŭ-da 건느다

crossing *n.* hoeng-dan 횡단

crossroads *n.* ne-gŏ-ri 네거리

crouch *v.i.* um-k'ŭ-ri-da 움크리다

crow *n.* ga-ma-gwi 까마귀; *v.i.*
(cock) ul-da 울다

crowd *n.* mu-ri 무리; *v.t.* mo-i-
da 모이다

crown *n.* wang-gwan 왕관; *v.t.*
kwan-ŭl ssi-u-da 관을씨우다

crucify *v.* sip-ja-ga-e mot-pak-da
십자가에못박다

cruel *adj.* chan-ĭn-han 잔인한

cruelty *n.* chan-ĭn 잔인

cruise *v.i.* sun-hang ha-da 순항하
다

cruiser *n.* sun-yang-ham 순양함

crumb *n.* bang pu-sŭ-rŏ-gi 빵부스
러기

crush *v.t.* nŭl-lŏ pu-sŭ-rŏ tŭ-ri-da
늘러부스러뜨리다

crust *n.* bang gŏp-jĭl 빵껍질

crutch *n.* chi-p'ang-i 지팡이

cry *v.i.* ul-da 울다; *v.t.* so-ri chi-
rŭ-da 소리지르다

crying *n.* ur-ŭm 울음

crystal *n.* su-jŏng 수정

cub *n.* sae-ki (짐승의) 새끼

cuckoo *n.* bŏ-kuk-sae 뻐꾹새

cucumber *n.* o-i 오이

cuff *n.* (of sleeve) so-mae 소매

culprit *n.* choe-in 죄인

cultivate *v.t.* kal-da 갈다

cultivation *n.* kyŏng-jak 경작

culture *n.* mun-hwa 문화

cup *n.* k'ŏp' 컵

cupboard *n.* ch'an-chang 찬장

cure *n.* ch'i-ryo 치료; *v.t.* ko-ch'i-
da 고치다

curiosity *n.* ho-gi-sim 호기심

curious *adj.* ho-gi-sim-i man-ŭn
호기심이많은

curl *n.* ko-sŭ-mŏ-ri 고스머리;

v. go-bŭ-rŏ-ji-ge ha-da 꼬브러
지게하다; **c. up** ko-bŭ-ri-da 꼬
브리다

curly *adj.* kop-sil-kop-sil han 곱
실곱실한

currant *n.* kŏn-p'o-do 건포도

current *n.* cho-ryu 조류; *adj.* i-jŭ-
ŭm-ŭi 이즈음의

curtain *n.* k'ŏ-ŏ-t'en 커어텐

curve *n.* kok-sŏn 곡선

cushion *n.* pang-sŏk 방석

custom *n.* p'ung-sok 풍속

customer *n.* ko-gaek 고객

customs *n.* kwan-se 관세; **c.-house**
se-gwan 세관

cut *n.* pe-gi 베기; **c. off** *v.* cha-
rŭ-da 자르다; **c. into** *v.* pe-da
베다

cutlery *n.* k'al-lyu 칼류

cycle *n.* chu-gi 주기

〔 **D** 〕

daffodil *n.* su-sŏn 수선

dagger *n.* tan-do 단도

dahlia *n.* ta-ri-a 다리아

daily *adv.* nal-ma-da 날마다; *n.*
il-gan sïn-mun 일간신문; *adj.*
mae-il-ŭi 매일의

dainty *adj.* mŏt-i-nŭn 멋있는

dairy *n.* u-yu ja-nŭn-de 우유짜는
데

daisy *n.* tŭl-guk-hwa 들국화

dam *n.* daem 땜; *v.t.* mak-da 막다

damage *n.* son-hae 손해; *v.t.* hae ha-da 해하다

damp *adj.* ch'uk-ch'uk han 축축한

dampen *v.* chŏk-si-da 적시다

dance *n.* ch'um 춤; *v.* ch'um ch'u-da 춤추다

dancer *n.* mu-yong-ga 무용가

dandelion *n.* mim-dul-le 밈들레

danger *n.* wi-hŏm 위험

dangerous *adj.* wi-hŏm han 위험한

dare *v.t.* kam-hi……ha-da 감히……하다

daring *adj.* yong-gam han 용감한

dark *adj.* ŏ-du-un 어두운; *n.* ŏ-dum 어둠

darken *v.* ŏ-du-wo-ji-da 어두워지다

darkness *n.* ŏ-dum 어둠

darn *v.t.* kip-da 집다; *n.* kip-nŭn-gŏt 집는것

dart *n.* hwa-sal 화살

dash *v.* (fling away, off, out) p'aeng-gae-ch'i-da 팽개치다; (rush against, upon) tol-jĭn ha-da 돌진하다

date *n.* (fruit) tae-ch'o 대초; (time) nal ja 날짜

daughter *n.* dal 딸; **d.-in-law** myŏ-nŭ-ri 며느리

dawn *n.* sae-byŏk 새벽

day *n.* nal 날

daybreak *n.* sae-byŏk 새벽

daylight *n.* hae-pit 햇빛

dazzle *v.t. & i.* nun-i pu-si-da 눈이부시다

dead *adj.* chuk-ŭn 죽은

deadly *adj.* ch'i-myŏng-jŏk 치명적

deaf *adj.* kwi-mŏk-ŭn 귀먹은

deafen *v.t.* kwi-mŏk-ge ha-da 귀먹게하다

deal *n.* kŏ-rae 거래; *v.t.* kŏ-rae ha-da 거래하다

dealer *n.* chang-sa-gun 장사꾼

dean *n.* pu kam-dok 부감독

dear *adj.* ch'in-ae ha-nŭn 친애하는; (expensive) pi-ssan 비싼

death *n.* sa-mang 사망

debate *v.t.* t'o-ron ha-da 토론하다; *n.* t'o-ron 토론

debt *n.* pit 빚

decay *n.* ssŏk-ŭm 썩음; *v.* ssŏk-da 썩다

decease *v.i.* chuk-da 죽다

deceit *n.* ki-man 기만

deceive *v.t.* sok-i-da 속이다

December *n.* sŏt dal 섣달; sip i wol 십이월

decent *adj.* chŏm-jan-ŭn 점잖은

decide *v.t. & i.* kyŏl-jŏng ha-da
결정하다

decision *n.* kyŏl-jŏng 결정

deck *n.* kap-p'an 갑판

declaration *n.* sŏn-ŏn 선언

declare *v.t. & i.* sŏn-ŏn ha-da 선언
하다

decline *v.i.* ki-ul-i-da 기울이다;
v.t. (refuse) kŏ-jŏl ha-da 거절하
다

decorate *v.t.* gu-mi-da 꾸미다

decoration *n.* gu-mi-gae 꾸미개;
(medal) hun-jang 훈장

decrease *v.t. & i.* chul-da 줄다;
n. kam-so 감소

decree *n.* pŏp-ryŏng 법령

dedicate *v.t.* pa-ch'i-da 바치다

deed *n.* haeng-wi 행위; (property)
chŭng-sŏ 증서

deem *v.t.* saeng-gak ha-da 생각하
다

deep *adj.* kip'-ŭn 깊은

deer *n.* no-ru 노루; **red d.** sa-sŭm
사슴

defeat *n.* p'ae-bae 패배; *v.t.* chi-
ge ha-da 지게하다

defect *n.* pu-jok 부족

defence *n.* pang-bi 방비

defenceless *adj.* pang-bi ŏp-nŭn
방비없는

defend *v.* pang-ŏ ha-da 방어하다

defendant *n.* p'i-go 피고

defer *v.t.* mul-li-da 물리다

defiance *n.* cho-jŏn 조전

deficit *n.* mo-ja-ra-nŭn ton 모자라는돈

definite *adj.* (sure) hwak-jŏng-jŏk 확정적; (limited) il-jŏng han 일정한

deformity *n.* ki-hyŏng 기형

defy *v.t.* ssa-um-ŭl kŏl-da 싸움을걸다

degree *n.* to 도; (school) hak-wi 학위; (rank) tŭng-gŭp 등급

deity *n.* sĭn-sŏng 신성

delay *v.t. & i.* nŭt-ch'u-da 늦추다; *n.* chi-ch'e 지체

delegate *n.* tae-p'yo-ja 대표자

delegation *n.* tae-p'yo-dan 대표단

deliberate *v.* sin-chung-hi saeng-gak ha-da 신중히생각하다; *adj.* il-bu-rŏ-ŭi 일부러의

deliberately *adv.* (on purpose) il-bu-rŏ 일부러

delicate *adj.* ko-un 고운

delicious *adj.* mat i-nŭn 맛있는

delight *v.* chŭl-gŏp-ge ha-da 즐겁게하다

delinquent *n.* t'ae-man han ja 태만한자

deliver *v.* ku-hae nae-da 구해내다

deliverance *n.* ku-je 구제

delivery *n.* pae-dal 배달

delude *v.t.* sok-i-da 속이다

demand *n.* yo-gu 요구; *v.t.* yo-gu ha-da 요구하다

democracy *n.* min-ju-ju-ŭi 민주주의

democratic *adj.* min-ju-ju-ŭi-jŏk 민주주의적

demonstrate *v.* po-i-da 보이다

demonstration *n.* de-mo 뎨도

den *n.* kul 굴

Denmark *n.* chŏng-mal 정말

denote *v.t.* p'yo-si ha-da 표시하다

denounce *v.* (blame) pi-nan ha-da 비난하다; (renounce) p'o-gi ha-da 포기하다

dense *adj.* baek-baek han 빽빽한

dentist *n.* ch'i-gwa-ŭi-sa 치과의사

deny *v.t.* pu-in ha-da 부인하다

depart *v.i.* dŏ-na-da 떠나다

department *n.* pu-mun 부문; (suffix) …bu …부; **d. store** *n.* paek-hwa-jŏm 백화점

departure *n.* ch'ul-bal 출발

depend *v.i.* ŭi-ji ha-da 의지하다

dependent *n.* sik-ku 식구

deposit *n.* ye-gŭm 예금; **d. with** *v.* mat'-ki-da 맡기다

depress *v.i.* na-ri-da 나리다; *v.* (mental) nak-sim sik-hi-da 낙심시키다

depression *n.* (commercial) pul-gyŏng-gi 불경기; (mental) nak-sim 낙심

deprive *v.* bae-at-da 빼앗다

depth *n.* kip'-i 깊이

deputy *n.* tae-ri 대리

derail *v.t.* t'al-sŏn si-k'i-da 탈선 시키다

derive *v.* yu-rae ha-da 유래하다

descend *v.* na-ri-da 나리다

descendant *n.* cha-son 자손

descent *n.* na-rim 나림

describe *v.t.* sŏ-sul ha-da 서술하 다

description *n.* sŏ-sul 서술

desert *n.* sa-mak 사막; *v.t.* (for-sake) pŏ-ri-da 버리다; *v.* (army) t'al-ch'ul ha-da 탈출하자

deserter *n.* t'al-ju-ja 탈주자

deserve *v.* kam-dang ha-da 감당하 다

design *n.* sŏl-gye 설계; *v.t.* sŏl-gye ha-da 설계하다

desire *n.* so-won 소원; *v.* won ha-da 원하다

desk *n.* ch'aek-sang 책상

despair *n.* chŏl-mang 절망; *v.i.* chŏl-mang ha-da 절망하다

desperate *adj.* kyŏl-sa-jŏk 결사적

despise *v.t.* myŏl-si ha-da 멸시하 다

dessert *n.* hu-sik 후식

destination *n.* mok-jŏk-ji 목적지

destitute *adj.* ka-nan han 가난한

destroy *v.t.* p'a-gwi ha-da 파괴하다

destroyer *n.* ku-ch'uk-ham 구축함

destruction *n.* p'a-gwi 파괴

detail *v.* (army) t'ŭk-p'a ha-da 특파하다; **details** *n.* sang-se 상세

detain *v.t.* ku-ryu ha-da 구류하다

detect *v.t.* a-ra-nae-da 알아내다

detective *n.* chŏng-t'am 정탐

determination *n.* kyŏl-sim 결심

determine *v.* kyŏl-jŏng ha-da 결정하다

develop *v.* pal-dal ha-da 발달하다

development *n.* pal-dal 발달

device *n.* ko-an 고안

devil *n.* ak-ma 악마

devise *v.t.* ko-an ha-da 고안하다

devote *v.t.* pa-ch'i-da 바치다

devotion *n.* hŏn-sĭn 헌신

devour *v.t.* t'am-sĭk ha-da 탐닉하다

dew *n.* i-sŭm 이슴

dial *n.* kŭl-ja-p'an 글자판

dialect *n.* sa-t'u-ri 사루리

dialogue *n.* tae-hwa 대화

diameter *n.* chik-kyŏng 직경

diamond *n.* kŭm-gang-sŏk 금강석

diarrhoea *n.* sŏl-sa 설사

diary *n.* il-gi 일기

dictate *v.t.* pat-a-ssŭ-da 받아쓰다; *v.* (order) myŏng-yŏng ha-da 명령하다

dictation *n.* pat-a-ssŭ-gi 받아쓰기

dictator *n.* tok-jae-ja 독재자

dictatorship *n.* tok-jae-jik 독재직

dictionary *n.* sa-chon 사전

die *v.i.* chuk-da 죽다

diet *n.* kuk-hoe 국회; (food) il-jŏng-han ŭm-sĭk mul 일정한음식물

differ *v.i.* ta-rŭ-da 다르다

difference *n.* ch'a-i 차이

different *adj.* ta-rŭn 다른

difficult *adj.* ŏ-ryŏ-un 어려운

difficulty *n.* kon-nan 곤난

dig *v.t.* p'a-da 파다

digest *v.* so-hwa ha-da 소화하다

digestion *n.* so-hwa 소화

dignified *adj.* tang-dang han 당당한

dignity *n.* wi-ŏm 위엄

dike *n.* duk 둑

diligence *n.* pu-ji-rŏn ham 부지런함

diligent *adj.* pu-ji-rŏn han 부지런한

diligently *adv.* pu-ji-rŏn-hi 부지런히

dim *adj.* ŏ-duk-ch'ĭm-ch'ĭm han
어둑침침한

dimension *n.* ch'i-su 치수

diminish *v.* chul-su 줄수

dimple *n.* (byam-ŭi) u-mul (뺨의)
우물

din *n.* si-kŭ-rŏ-un so-ri 시끄러운
소리

dine *v.* sik-sa ha-da 식사하다

dining-car *n.* sik-dang ch'a 식당차

dining-room *n.* sik-dang 식당

dining-table *n.* sik-t'ak 식탁

dinner *n.* chŏng-ch'an 정찬

dip *v.t. & i.* chŏk-si-da 적시다

diphtheria *n.* ti-p'ŭ-te-ri-a pyŏng
디프테리아병

diploma *n.* chor-ŏp-jang 졸업장

diplomacy *n.* oe-kyo 외교

diplomat *n.* oe-kyo-ka 외교가

dipper *n.* kuk-ja 국자

direct *adv.* kot-ŭn 곧은; *v.t.* chi-
do ha-da 지도하다

direction *n.* pang-hyang 방향

directly *adv.* chĭk-jŏp-ŭ-ro 직접으
로

director *n.* chi-do-ja 지도자

directory *n.* chu-so-sŏng-myŏng-
nok 주소성명록; (telephone) chŏn-
hwa pŏn-ho ch'aek 전화번호책

dirt *n.* chin-hŭk 진흙

dirty *adj.* tŏ-rŏ-un 더러운

disadvantage *n.* pul-li 불리

disagree *v.* pul-tong-ŭi ha-da 불동의하다

disagreeable *adj.* pul-k'wae han 불쾌한

disappear *v.i.* sa-ra-ji-da 사라지다

disappearance *n.* sa-ra-ji-nŭn-gŏt 사라지는것

disappoint *v.t.* sil-mang ha-ge ha-da 실망하게하다

disappointment *n.* sil-mang 실망

disapprove *v.* pan-dae ha-da 반대하다

disarm *v.* (reduce arms) kun-bi-ch'uk-so ha-da 군비축소하다; (completely disarm) mu-jang-hae-jang ha-da 무장해장하다

disaster *n.* chae-nan 재난

disastrous *adj.* pi-ch'am han 비참한

discharge *v.* (electricity) pang-jŏn ha-da 방전하다; (from army) che-dae ha-da 제대하다; (dismiss) joch'-a-nae-da 쫓아내다; **to be discharged** *v.* (from army) che-dae doe-da 제대되다

disciple *n.* che-ja 제자

discipline *v.* ching-gye ha-da 징계하다

disclose *v.* p'ok-no ha-da 폭로하다

discontent *n.* pul-man 불만

discount v. hal-in ha-da 할인하다;
n. hal-in 할인

discourage v. nak-sim si-k'i-da 낙
심시키다

discouragement n. nak-sĭm 낙심

discover v.t. pal-gyŏn ha-da 발견
하다

discovery n. pal-gyŏn 발견

discretion n. cho-sim-sŏng 조심성

discriminate v. ch'a-byŏl ha-da 차
별하다

discrimination n. ch'a-byŏl 차별

discuss v.t. ŭi-non ha-da 의논하
다

discussion n. ŭi-non 의논

disdain v. myŏl-si ha-da 멸시하다;
n. myŏl-si 멸시

disease n. pyŏng 병

disgrace v. yok po-i-da 욕보이다;
n. pul-myŏng-ye 불명예

disgraceful adj. su-ch'i-sŭ-rŏ-un
수치스러운

disguise v.t. pyŏn-jang ha-da 변장
하다; n. pyŏn-jang 변장

disgust n. yŏm-jŭng 염증

dish n. chŏp-si 접시

dishonest adj. pu-jŏng-jĭk han 부
정직한

dishonesty n. pu-jŏng-jĭk 부정직

dishonor n. pul-myŏng-ye 불명예;
v. yok-po-i-da 욕보이다

disinclination *n.* sir-hŏ-ham 싫어함

disinterested *adj.* kong-jŏng han 공정한

disk *n.* won-ban 원반

dislike *n.* sir-hŭm 싫음; *v.t.* sir-hŏ ha-da 싫어하다

disloyal *adj.* pul-ch'ung han 불충한

dismal *adj.* ŭm-ch'im han 음침한

dismay *n.* nol-la-um 놀라움; *v.t.* nol-la-ge ha-da 놀라게하다

dismiss *v.t.* joch'-a-nae-da 쫓아내다

dismount *v.* nae-ri-da 내리다

disobedience *n.* sun-jong-ch'i an-hŭm 순종치않음

disobedient *adj.* sun-jong ha-ji an-nŭn 순종하지않는

disobey *v.t.* myŏng-yŏng-ŭl kŏ-yŏk ha-da 명령을거역하다

disorder *n.* mu-jil-sŏ 무질서

dispatch *n.* p'a-gyŏn 파견;   *v.t.* p'a-gyŏn ha-da 파견하다

disperse *v.* hŭt'-da 흗다

display *n.* chĭl-lyŏl 진렬; *v.* na-t'a-nae-da 나타내다

disposal *n.* ch'ŏ-ch'i 처치

dispose *v.t.* ch'ŏ-ri ha-da 처리하다

disposition *n.* sŏng-jil 성질

dispute *n.* mal ta-t'um 말다룸; *v.t. & i.* mal-ta-t'um ha-da 말다룸하다

disregard *v.t.* mu-si ha-da 무시하
다

disrespect *n.* sil-lye 실례

disrespectful *adj.* mu-rye han 무
례한

dissatisfy *v.t.* pul-man ha-ge ha-
da 불만하게하다

dissipate *v.t.* he-p'i-ssŭ-da 헤피쓰
다; *v.i.* pang-t'ang ha-da 방탕하
다

dissipated *adj.* pang-t'ang han 방
탕한

dissipation *n.* pang-t'ang 방탕

dissolve *v.t.* nok-da 녹다

distance *n.* kŏ-ri 거리

distant *adj.* mŏn 먼

distasteful *adj.* sir-hŭn 싫은

distinct *adj.* myŏng-baek han 명백
한

distinctly *adv.* pun-myŏng ha-ge
분명하게

distinguish *v.t.* ku-byŏl ha-da 구
별하다

distinguished *adj.* i-rŭm-nan 이
름난

distort *v.* wi-gok ha-da 위곡하
다

distract *v.* kyon-je ha-da 견제하
다

distress *n.* koe-ro-um 피로움

distribute *v.t.* na-nu-da 나누다

distribution *n.* pun-bae 분배

district *n.* ku-yŏk 구역

disturb *v.t.* pang-hae ha-da 방해하다

ditch *n.* to-rang 도랑

dive *n.* cham-su 잠수; *v.i.* mul-e dwi-yŏ tŭl-da 물에뛰여들다

divest *v.t.* pak-t'al ha-da 박탈하다

divide *v.t.* na-nu-da 나누다

divine *adj.* sŏng-sŭ-rŏ-un 성스러운

division *n.* ku-bun 구분; (mathematics) che-pŏp 제법; (army) sa-dan 사단

divorce *n.* i-hon 이혼; *v.* i-hon ha-da 이혼하다

dizzy *adj.* ŏ-ji-rŏ-un 어지러운

do *v.* ha-da 하다

docile *adj.* sun han 순한

dock *n.* (pier) pu-du 부두; (law) p'i-go-sŏk 피고석

dockyard *n.* cho-sŏn-so 조선소

doctor *n.* (medical) ŭi-sa 의사; (degree) pak-sa 박사; *v.* ch'i-ryo ha-da 치료하다

doctrine *n.* kyo-ri 교리

document *n.* mun-sŏ 문서

dodge *v.* sal-jak p'i ha-da 살짝피하다

doe *n.* am-no-ru 암노루

dog *n.* kae 개

doleful *adj*· sŭl-p'ŭn 슬픈

doll *n*· (plaything) kak-ssi 각씨;
(figurine) in-hyŏng 인형

dollar *n*· pul 불

dolmen *n*· ko-in tol 고인돌

dome *n*· tung-gŭn chi-bung 둥근지
붕

domestic *adj*· (household) ka-jŏng-
ŭi 가정의; (national) kuk-nae-
ŭi 국내의

dominate *v.t*· chi-bae ha-da 지배
하다

dominion *n*· chu-gwon 주권

donkey *n*· tang-na-gwi 당나귀

doom *n*· un-su 운수; *v.t*· un-ŭl
chŏng ha-da 운을정하다

door *n*· mun 문; d. bell *n*· ch'o-
in-chong 초인종

dormitory *n*· ki-suk-sa 기숙사

dose *n*· han ch'ŏp 한첩; *v*· yak-ŭl
chu-da 약을주다

dot *n*· chŏm 점; *v.i*· chŏm jik-da
점찍다

double *adj*· tu kop-ŭi 두곱의; *v*·
kop-ŭ-ro ha-da 곱으로하다

doubt *n*· ŭi-sim 의심; *v*· ŭi-sim
ha-da 의심하다

doubtful *adj*· ŭi-sim-sŭ-rŏ-un 의
심스러운

doubtfully *adv*· ŭi-sim-sŭ-rŏp-ge
의심스럽게

doubtless *adv.* mul-lon 물론

dove *n.* pi-dul-gi 비둘기

down *adv.* & *adj.* a-rae 아래; *prep.* mit'-e 밑에

downcast, be, *v.* nak-sim ha-da 낙심하다

downstairs *n.* a-rae-ch'ǔng 아래층

down-town *n.* si-nae 시내

downward *adv.* a-rae jok-e 아래쪽에

dowry *n.* chi-ch'am-gǔm 지참금

doze *v.i.* chol-da 졸다

dozen *n.* yǒl-tul 열둘

draft *n.* (rough copy) ch'o-an 초안; (depth) pae-su-ryang 배수량; *v.* (military) ip-dae-sik-hi-da 입대식히다

drag *v.t.* gǔl-da 끌다

dragon *n.* yong 용

dragonfly *n.* cham-ja-ri 잠자리

drain *n.* pae-su 배수; *v.* pae-su ha-da 배수하다

drake *n.* sut-o-ri 숫오리

drama *n.* kǔk 극

dramatic *adj.* kǔk-jǒk 극적

draught *n.* t'ǔm-pa-ram 틈바람

draw *v.t.* gǔl-da 끌다; *v.* (pictures) kǔ-ri-da 그리다

drawback *n.* pul-li 불리

drawer *n.* sǒr-hap 설합

drawing *n.* kŭ-rim 그림; **d. room**
n. ŭng-chŏp-sĭl 웅접실

dread *n.* mu-sŏ-um 무서움; *v.t.*
mu-sŏ-wo ha-da 무서워하다

dreadful *adj.* mu-sŏ-un 무서운

dream *n.* gum 꿈; *v.t.* gum gu-da
꿈꾸다

dreary *adj.* ŭm-ul han 음울한

dredge *v.* p'a-nae-da 파내다

dredger *n.* chun-sŏl sŏn 준설선

dress *n.* ot 옷; *v.* (someone else)
ip-hi-da 입히다; (oneself) ip-da
입다

drift *v.* p'yo-ryu ha-da 표류하다

drill *n.* song-got 송곳; (practice)
yŏn-sŭp 연습; *v.* (hole) ku-nyŏng
dul-da 구녕뚫다; *v.t.* (practice)
yŏn-sŭp si-k'i-da 연습시키다

drink *v.t.* ma-si-da 마시다; *n.* han
chan 한잔

drip *v.i.* mul pang-ŭl-i dŏr-ŏ-ji-da
물방을이떨어지다

drive *v.t.* mol-da 몰다; *v.* (car)
un-jŏn ha-da 운전하다

driver *n.* un-jŏn-su 운전수

drizzle *n.* i-sŭl-pi 이슬비

droop *v.* su-kŭ-rŏ-ji-da 수그러지
다; (flower) si-dŭl-da 시들다

drop *v.t.* dŏ-rŏ-t'ŭ-ri-da 떨어드리
다; *v.i.* dŏ-rŏ-ji-da 떨어지다 「다

drown *v.* mul-e ba-ji-da 물에빠지

drowsy *adj.* chol-um-o-nun 졸음
오는

drug *n.* yak 약; *v.* yak-ŭl mŏk-i-
da 약을먹이다

drum *n.* puk 북

drummer *n.* ko-su 고수

drunkard *n.* chu-jŏng-gun 주정군

drunkenness *n.* sul-ch'wi 술취

dry *v.t.* mal-li-da 말리다; *v.i.* ma-
rŭ-da 마르다; *adj.* ma-rŭn 마른

duck *n.* o-ri 오리

due *adj.* kap'-a-ya-man ha-nŭn 갚
아야만하는; *adv.* pa-ro 바로

dull *adj.* tun han 둔한

duly *adv.* pa-rŭ-ge 바르게

dumb *adj.* pŏng-ŏ-ri-ŭi 벙어리의

dumb-bell *n.* a-ryŏng 아령

duplicate *n.* tŭng-pon 등본; *v.* tu-
t'ong-ŭ-ro man-dŭl-da 두롱으로
만들다

duration *n.* chi-sok 지속

during *prep.* ……ha-nŭn-dong-an
……하는동안

dusk *n.* hwang-hon 황혼

dust *n.* mŏn-ji 먼지; *v.i.* mŏn-ji
t'ŏl-da 먼지털다

dust-bin *n.* ssŭ-re-gi t'ong 쓰레기
통

duster *n.* ch'ong-ch'ae 총채

dusty *adj.* mŏn-ji t'u-sŏng-ŭi 먼
지루성의

dutiable *adj.* se-gŭm i-nŭn 세금있
는

dutiful *adj.* ch'ung-sŏng-sŭ-rŏ-un
충성스러운

duty *n.* ŭi-mu 의무; (customs) se-
gŭm 세금

dwarf *n.* nan-jaeng-i 난쟁이

dwell *v.i.* sal-da 살다

dye *v.t.* mul-dŭr-i-da 물들이다;
n. mul-kam 물감

dyke *n.* duk 뚝; *v.* duk-ŭl ssa-da
뚝을쌓다

dysentery *n.* i-jil 이질

〔 E 〕

each *adj.* kak-kak-ŭi 각각의; *pron.*
kak-ja 각자

eager *adj.* yŏl-jung ha-nŭn 열중하
는

eagerly *adv.* yŏl-sĭm-hi 열심히

eagerness *n.* yŏl-sĭm 열심

eagle *n.* sol-gae-mi 솔개미

ear *n.* kwi 귀; **e. ache** *n.* kwi-
pyŏng 귓병

early *adj.* i-rŭn 이른; *adv.* il-ji-
gi 일찌기

earn *v.t.* pol-da 벌다; *v.* (get,
gain) ŏt-da 얻다

earnest *adj.* chŏng-sŏng doen 성성
됨

earnestly *adv.* chǐn-jŏng-ǔ-ro 진
정으로

earnings *n.* su-ip 수입

earring *n.* kwi-ko-ri 귀고리

earth *n.* chi-gu 지구

earthen *adj.* hǔk-ǔi 흙의

earthenware *n.* chil kǔ-rǔt 질그
릇

earthly *adj.* se-sang-ǔi 세상의

earthquake *n.* chi-jin 지진

earthworm *n.* chi-rŏng-i 지렁이

ease *n.* p'yŏn-an 편안; *v.t.* an-sǐm
si-k'i-da 안심시키다

easel *n.* hwa-ga 화가

easily *adv.* swip-ge 쉽게

east *n.* tong-jok 동쪽; *adv.* tong-
ǔ-ro 동으로; **Far E.** kǔk-tong 극
동; **E. Asia** tong-a 동아

Easter *n.* pu-hwal-che 부활제

eastern *adj.* tong-jok-ǔi 동쪽의

eastward *adj.* tong-jok 동쪽

easy *adj.* swi-un 쉬운

easy-chair *n.* al-lak ǔi-ja 안락의
자

eat *v.* mŏk-da 먹다; (honorific)
chap-su-si-da 잡수시다

eaves *n.* chǐp ch'ŏ-ma 집처마

ebb *n.* ssŏl-mul 썰물; *v.i.* mul-i
ssŏ-da 물이써다

ebony *n.* hǔk-dan 흑단

echo *n.* pan-hyang 반향

eclipse *n.* (sun) hae mŏk-ŭm 해먹음; (moon) tal mŏk-ŭm 달먹음

economical *adj.* kyŏng-je-jŏk 경제적

economics *n.* kyŏng-je-hak 경제학

economize *v.* kyŏng-je ha-da 경제하다

economy *n.* kyŏng-je 경제

ecstasy *n.* mu-han han chŭl-gŏum 무한한즐거움

edge *n.* ka-sang-sa-ri 가상사리

edit *v.t.* p'yŏn-jǐp ha-da 편집하다

editor *n.* chu-gan 주간

educate *v.t.* kyo-yuk ha-da 교육하다

education *n.* kyo-yuk 교육

educational system kyo-yuk che-do 교육제도

eel *n.* paem chang-ŏ 뱀장어

effect *n.* kyŏl-gwa 결과; *v.* si-haeng ha-da 시행하다

effective *adj.* yu-hyo han 유효한

efficiency *n.* nŭng-yul 능률

effort *n.* no-ryŏk 노력

egg *n.* al 알; (of hen) tal-gyal 달걀

egg-plant *n.* ka-ji 가지

eight *n.* & *adj.* yŏ-dŏl 여덟

eighteen *n.* & *adj.* yŏl yŏ-dŏl 열여덟

eighty *n.* yŏ-dŭn 여든

either *adj.* ŏ-nŭ-gŏt-i-dŏn-ji 어느 것이던지; **either……or** na……na 나……나

ejaculate *v.t. & i.* we-ch'i-da 웨치다

elapse *v.i.* chi-na-ka-da 지나가다

elastic *n.* ko-mu gŭn 고무끈; *adj.* t'an-sŏng i-nŭn 탄성있는

elbow *n.* p'al-kum-ch'i 팔꿈치; *v.t. & i.* dŏ-mil-da 떠밀다

elder *adj.* son-u-ŭi 손우의; *n.* no-in 노인; (of church) chang-no 장로; **e. brother** (male's) hyŏng-nĭm 형님; **e. brother** (female's) op-ba 옵바; **e. sister** *n.* (male's) nu-nĭm 누님; **e. sister** (female's) hyŏng-nĭm 형님

elderly *adj.* na-i-ga chi-gŭt han 나이가지긋한

eldest daughter *n.* k'ŭn dal 큰딸; **e. son** *n.* k'ŭn a-dŭl 큰아들

elect *v.t.* sŏn-gŏ ha-da 선거하다

election *n.* sŏn-gŏ 선거

electric *adj.* chŏn-gi 전기

electric fan *n.* sŏn-p'ung-gi 선풍기

electric power house *n.* pal-chŏn-sŏ 발전서　　　　　　「기사

electrician *n.* chŏn-gi ki-sa 전기

electricity *n.* chŏn-gi 전기

element *n.* yo-so 요소

elementary *adj.* ki-bon-jŏk 기본적

elementary school *n.* so hak-kyo
소학교

elephant *n.* k'o-gi-ri 코끼리

elevate *v.t.* ol-li-da 올리다

elevator *n.* sung-kang-gi 승강기

eleven *n.* yŏl-ha-na 열하나

elf *n.* chŏk-ŭn yo-jŏng 적은요정

eliminate *v.* ŏp-sae-da 없새다

elm *n.* nŭ-rŭm na-mu 느름나무

eloquent *adj.* mal chal ha-nŭn 말
잘하는

else *adv.* kŭ pak-e 그밖에; **or e.**
hok 혹

elsewhere *adv.* ta-rŭn-de 다른데

embankment *n.* che-bang 제방

embark *v.* (board) t'a-da 타다;
(start) si-jak ha-da 시작하다

embarrass *v.* kŏ-buk ha-ge ha-da
거북하게하다

embassy *n.* tae-sa-gwan 대사관

embrace *n.* p'o-ong 포옹; *v.t.* gyŏ-
an-da 껴안다

embroider *v.t.* su no-ta 수놓다

embroidery *n.* su 수

emerald *n.* e-me-ral-dŭ 에메랄드

emerge *v.* na-o-da 나오다

emergency *n.* wi-gŭp 위급

emigrate *v.i.* & *v.t.* i-min ha-da
이민하다

eminence *n.* nop'-ŭn-de 높은데

eminent *adj.* dwi-ŏ-na-nŭn 뛰어나
는

emotion *n.* chŏng-sŏ 정서

emperor *n.* hwang-je 황제

emphasize *v.* kang-jo ha-da 강조
하다

empire *n.* che-guk 제국

employ *v.t.* ssŭ-da 쓰다

employee *n.* chong-ŏp-won 종업원

employer *n.* chu-in 주인

employment *n.* chik 직

empress *n.* hwang-hu 황후

empty *adj.* pin 빈; *v.* pi-u-da 비
우다

enable *v.* ……hal-su-it-ge ha-da
……할수있게하다

enchant *v.* hwang-hol ha-ge ha-da
황홀하게하다

enclose *v.t.* tul-lŏ ssa-da 둘러싸다

encounter *v.t.* man-na-da 만나다

encourage *v.* chang-yŏ ha-da 장려
하다

encouragement *n.* chang-yŏ 장려

end *n.* gŭt 끝; *v.t. & i.* mat-ch'u-
da 맞추다

endear *v.t.* kwi-yŏp-ge ha-da 귀엽
게하다

endeavour *n.* no-ryŏk 노력; *v.t.*
him-ssŭ-da 힘쓰다

ending *n.* gŭt 끝

endless *adj.* gŭt ŏp-nŭn 끝없는

endorse v. po-jŭng ha-da 보증하다
endow v.t. ki-gŭm-ŭl chu-da 가금
을주다
endurance n. ch'am-ŭl-sŏng 참을성
endure v. ch'am-da 참다
enemy n. chŏk 적
energy n. him 힘
engage in v. chong-sa ha-da 종사
하다
engaged, to be, (to marry) v. yak-
hon ha-da 약혼하다
engagement n. yak-hon 약혼
engine n. ki-gwan 기관
engineer n. ki-sa 기사
England n. yŏng-guk 영국
English adj. (language) yŏng-ŏ 영
어
Englishman n. yŏng-guk sa-ram
영국사람
enjoy v.t. chŭl-gi-da 즐기다
enjoyment n. hyŏng-nak 형락
enlarge v. k'ŭ-ge ha-da 크게하다
enlist v. (in army) kun-dae-e tŭl-
da 군대에들다; (in a cause) to-
ŭm-ŭl pat-da 도움을받다
enmity n. chŏk-ŭi 적의
enormous adj. kwang-dae han 광
대한
enough adj. nŏk-nŏk han 넉넉한;
adv. nŏk-nŏk ha-ge 넉넉하게; n.
nŏk-nŏk 넉넉

enrage *v.t.* sŏng-nae-ge ha-da 성
내게하다

enroll *v.t.* (in school) ip-hak ha-da
입학하다

ensign *n.* (flag) ki 기; (navy) hae-
gun so-wi 해군소위

ensure *v.* po-jŭng ha-da 보증하다

enter *v.t. & i.* tŭr-ŏ-ka-da 들어가
다

enterprise *n.* sa-ŏp 사업

entertain *v.t.* tae-jŏp ha-da 대접
하다

entertaining *adj.* chae-mi i-nŭn 재
미있는

entertainment *n.* chŭp-dae 접대

enthusiasm *n.* yŏl-sĭm 열심

enthusiastic *adj.* yŏl-gwang-jŏk
열광적

entice *v.t.* goe-i-da 꾀이다

entire *adj.* wan-jŏn han 완전한

entirely *adv.* chŏn-hyŏ 전혀

entitle *v.t.* ch'ing-ho-rŭl chu-da 칭
호를주다

entrance *n.* ip-jang 입장; (door)
ip-ku 입구

entreat *v.t.* kan-ch'ŏng ha-da 간청
하다

entrust *v.* pu-t'ak ha-da 부탁하다

enumerate *v.t.* he-a-ri-da 헤아리
다

envelop *v.* pong ha-da 봉하다

envelope *n.* pong-t'u 봉투

envious *adj.* saem-nae-nŭn 샘내는

environment *n.* hwan-gyŏng 환경

envy *n.* pu-rŏ-um 부러움; *v.t.* pu-rŏ-wo ha-da 부러워하다

epidemic *n.* yu-haeng pyŏng 유행병

Episcopalian Church *n.* kam-dok kyo 감독교

equal *adj.* kat-ŭn 같은; **be e. to** *v.* tong-dŭng ha-da 동등하다

equality *n.* tae-dŭng 대등

equally *adv.* dok kat-chi 똑같이

equator *n.* chŏk-do 적도

equip *v.t.* ka-chu-da 갖추다

equipment *n.* sŏl-bi 설비

equivalent *adj.* kap' kat'-ŭn 값같은

era *n.* si dae 시대

erase *v.t.* chi-u-da 지우다

eraser *n.* chi-u-gae 지우개

erect *adj.* kot-ŭn 곧은; *v.t.* se-u-da 세우다

err *v.i.* kŭ-rŭ-ch'i-da 그르치다

errand *n.* sĭm-bu-rŭm 심부름

error *n.* t'ŭl-lĭm 틀림

erupt *v.i.* t'ŏ-jŏ-na-da 터져나다

eruption *n.* (volcano) pun hwa 분화; (rash) pal-jin 발진

escape *n.* to-mang ka-da 도망가다; *n.* to-mang 도망

especially *adv.* t'ŭk-pyŏl-hi 특별히

essay *n.* non-mun 논문

essential *adj.* pon-jil-jŏk 본질적;
n. pon-jil 본질

establish *v.t.* sŏl-lip ha-da 설립하
다

establishment *n.* sŏl-lip 설립

estate *n.* (property) chae-san 재산

esteem *n.* chon-gyŏng 존경; *v.t.*
chon-gyŏng ha-da 존경하다

estimate *v.* p'yŏng-ga ha-da 평가
하다; *n.* (of cost) kyŏn-jŏk 견적

et cetera tŭng 등

eternal *adj.* yŏng-gu han 영구한

eternity *n.* yŏng-won 영원

ether *n.* e-t'e-rŭ 에테르

ethics *n.* yul-li hak 윤리학

etiquette *n.* ye-pŏp 예법

Europe *n.* ku-ra-p'a 구라파

European *adj.* ku-ra-p'a-ŭi 구라파
의; *n.* ku-ra-p'a sa-ram 구라파
사람

evacuate *v.* dŏ-na-ka-da 떠나가다

evacuation *n.* ch'ŏl-gŏ 철거

evangelist *n.* pok-ŭm chŏn-do-ja
복음전도자

evaporate *v.* kim na-da 김나다

eve *n.* chŏn nal pam 전날밤

even *adj.* p'an-p'an han 판판한;
adv. pi-rok 비록

evening *n.* chŏ-nyŏk 저녁

event *n.* kyŏng-u 경우

ever *adv.* hang-sang 항상

everlasting *adj.* yŏng-gu han 영구
한

evermore *adv.* hang-sang 항상

every *adj.* kak 각

everybody *n.* mo-dŭn sa-ram 모든
사람

everyday *adj.* mae-il 매일

everyone *n.* mo-dŭn sa-ram 모든
사람

everything *n.* mo-du 모두

everywhere *adv.* ŏ-de-dŭn-ji 어데
든지

evidence *n.* chŭng-gŏ 증거

evident *adj.* myŏng-baek han 명백
한

evil *adj.* ak-han 악한; *n.* ak 악

exact *adj.* chŏng-hwak han 정확한

exactly *adv.* gok 꼭

exaggerate *v.* kwa-jang ha-da 파
장하다

exaggeration *v.* kwa-jang 과장

examination *n.* si-hŏm 시험

examine *v.t.* si-hŏm ha-da 시험하
다

example *n.* mo-bŏm 모범

exceed *v.t.* nŏm-da 넘다

exceedingly *adv.* tae-dan-hi 대단히

excel *v.* nat-da 낫다

excellent *adj.* hul-lyung han 훌륭
한

except *prep.* ······rŭl che ha-myŏn
······를제하면

exception *n.* ye-oe 예외

exceptional *adj.* t'ŭk-pyŏl-han 특
별한

exchange *v.t.* kyo-hwan ha-da 교
환하다; *n.* kyo-hwan 교환

excite *v.* sŏn-dong ha-da 선동하다

excitement *n.* hŭng-bun 흥분

exclaim *v.* we-ch'i-da 웨치다

exclamation *n.* we-ch'im 쉐침

excursion *n.* won-jok 원족

excuse *n.* ku-sil 구실; *v.t.* yong-
sŏ ha-da 용서하다

execute *v.t.* (carry out) sil-haeng
ha-da 실행하다; *v.* (punish) sa-
hyŏng ha-da 사형하다

execution *n.* (performance) chĭp-
haeng 집행; (punishment) sa-
hyŏng chĭp-haeng 사형집행

executioner *n.* sa-hyŏng chĭp-haeng-
ja 사형집행자

executive *n.* sĭl-haeng-ja 실행자

exercise *n.* un-dong 운동; *v.* un-
dong ha-da 운동하다

exert *v.t.* (him-ŭl) nae-da (힘을)
내다

exertion *n.* chĭl-lyŏk 진력

exhaust *v.t.* p'i-p'e ha-ge ha-da
피페하게하다; *n.* kong-gi bae-gi
공기빼기

exhaustion *n.* p'i-p'e 피폐

exhibit *v.t.* po-i-da 보이다; *n.* ch'ul-p'um 출품

exhibition *n.* chŏl-lam hoe 전람회

exile *n.* ch'u-bang 추방; (person) ch'u-bang-in 추방인

exist *v.i.* it-da 있다

existence *n.* chon-jae 존재

exit *n.* ch'ul-gu 출구

expand *v.* hwak-jang ha-da 확장 하다

expect *v.t.* pa-ra-da 바라다

expectation *n.* ki-dae 기대

expedition *n.* won-jŏng 원정

expel *v.* joch-a-nae-da 쫓아내다; (from school) t'oe-hak si-k'i-da 퇴학시키다

expense *n.* pi-yong 비용

expensive *adj.* pi-ssan 비싼

experience *n.* kyŏng-hŏm 경험; *v.t.* kyŏng-hŏm ha-da 경험하다

experiment *n.* sil-hŏm 실험

expert *adj.* ik-suk han 익숙한; *n.* chŏn-mun-ga 전문가

explain *v.t.* sŏl-myŏng ha-da 설명 하다

explanation *n.* sŏl-myŏng 설명

explode *v.* p'ok-bal ha-da 폭발하 다

exploit *n.* kong-jŏk 공적; *v.t.* i-yong ha-da 이용하다

exploration *n.* t'am-hŏm 탐험

explore *v.* t'am-hŏm ha-da 탐험하 다; (mentally) t'am-sa ha-da 탐 사하다

explorer *n.* t'am-hŏm-ga 탐험가

explosion *n.* p'ok-bal 폭발

export *n.* su-ch'ul ha-da 수출하다; *n.* su-ch'ul-p'um 수출품

expose *v.* pal-gyŏn ha-da 발견하 다

express *v.* (show) p'yo-hyŏn ha-da 표현하다; *n.* (car) kŭp-haeng-yŏl ch'a 급행렬차

expression *n.* p'yo-hyŏn 표현

extend *v.* (time) nŭl-i-da 늘이다; (make large) p'yŏl-ch'i-da 펼치 다

extensive *adj.* nŏlb-ŭn 넓은

extent *n.* nŏlb-i 넓이

exterior *adj.* pa-kat-ŭi 바깥의

extinguish *v.* gŭ-da 끄다

extra *adj.* tŏ 더; *n.* (newspaper) ho-oe sin-mun 호외신문

extract *v.t.* bop-da 뽑다; *n.* ch'u-rĭm 추림

extraordinary *adj.* t'ŭk-pyŏl han 특별한

extravagant *adj.* koeng-jang han 굉장한

extreme *n.* & *adj.* kŭk-tan-ŭi 극단 의

eye *n.* nun 눈
eyebrow *n.* nun-sŏp 눈섭
eyelash *n.* sok nun-sŏp 속눈섭
eyelid *n.* nun tu-dŏng 눈두덩
eyesight *n.* al-lyŏk 안력

〔 F 〕

fable *n.* tong-hwa 동화
face *n.* ŏl-gul; 얼굴; *v.t.* ······ŭl
tae ha-da ······을대하다
facility *n.* yong-i 용이
fact *n.* sa-sïl 사실
faction *n.* tang-p'a 당파
factory *n.* kong-jang 공장
faculty   *n.*   chae-nŭng   재능;
(school) 직원
fade *v.i.* si-tŭl-da 시들다
fail *v.* sil-p'ae ha-da 실패하다
failure *n.* sil-p'ae 실패
faint *adj.* hŭi-mi han 희미한; *v.i.*
ki-jŏl ha-da 기절하다
faintness *n.* ki-jŏl 기절
fair *n.* chang 장; *adj.* a-rŭm-da-
un 아름다운; (just) kong-p'yŏng
han 공평한
fairly *adv.* kong-jŏng ha-ge 공정
하게; (rather) pi-gyo-jok 비교적
fairy *n.* yo-jŏng 요정
faith *n.* mi-dŭm 믿음
faithful *adj.* ch'ung-sïl han 충실한
faithfulness *n.* ch'ung-sïl 충실

faithless *adj.* sín-ŭi-ga ŏp-nŭn 신의가없는

fall *v.* dŏr-ŏ-ji-da 떨어지다; *n.* ch'u-rak 추락; (autumn) ka-ŭl 가을; **f. in** *v.* ba-ji-da 빠지다

false *adj.* kŏ-jĭt-ŭi 거짓의

falsehood *n.* kŏ-jĭt 거짓

fame *n.* myŏng-sŏng 명성

famed *adj.* i-rŭm nan 이름난

familar *adj.* ch'ĭn han 친한

family *n.* ka-jok 가족

famine *n.* ki-gŭn 기근

famous *adj.* yu-myŏng han 유명한

fan *n.* pu-ch'ae 부채; *v.t.* pu-ch'i-da 부치다

fanciful *adj.* kong-sang han 공상한

fancy *n.* kong-sang 고상; *v.t.* sang-sang ha-da 상상하다

far *adj.* mŏn 먼; *adv.* mŏl-li 멀리; **how f.** ŏl-man-k'ŭm 얼만큼; **from f.** mŏl-li-sŏ-put-t'ŏ 멀리서붙터; **so f.** i-man-k'ŭm 이만큼; **f.-sighted** *adj.* sŏn-gyŏn it-da 선견있다

fare *n.* ĭm-gŭm 임금

farewell *n.* chŏn-byŏl 전별

farm *n.* nong-jang 농장

farmer *n.* nong-bu 농부

farm-hand *n.* mŏ-sŭm 머슴

farmhouse *n.* nong-ga 농가

farming *n.* nong-sa 농사
farmyard *n.* nong-jang 농장
farther *adj.* tŏ mŏn 더먼
farthest *adv.& adj.* che-il mŏn
제일먼
fascinate *v.* hol-li-ge ha-da 홀려게
하다
fashion *n.* yu-haeng 유행; *v.t.* …
…ro man-dŭl-da ……로만들다
fast *adj.* (quick) ba-lŭn 빠른;
adv. (tight) ŏk-sen 억센; *v.* tan-
sĭk ha-da 단식하다
fasten *v.t.* tong-yŏ mae-da 동여
매다
fasting *n.* tan-sĭk 단식
fat *adj.* sal-jĭn 살진; *n.* chi-bang
지방
fatal *adj.* un-myŏng-ŭi 운명의
fate *n.* un-myŏng 운명
father *n.* a-bŏ-ji 아버지; **f.-in-
law** (man's) chang-in 장인; **f.-
in-law** (woman's) si-a-bŏ-ji 시
아버지
fatigue *n.* p'i-gon 피곤
fault *n.* (defect) kyŏl-jŏm 결점
favor *n.* tŏk-t'aek 덕택
favorite *adj.* ma-ŭm-e tŭ-nun 마
음에드는
fawn *n.* sae-ki no-ru 새끼노루
fear *n.* mu-sŏ-um 무서움; *v.* mu-
sŏ-wo ha-da 무서워하다

feast *n.* chan-ch'i 잔치

feat *n.* kong-jŏk 공적

feather *n.* kit 깃

feature *n.* mo-yang 모양

February *n.* i wol 이월

fee *n.* sak 삯

feeble *adj.* yak han 약한

feed *v.t.* mŏk-i-da 먹이다; *n.* (for chickens) mo-i 모이; (for cattle, horses) gol 꼴; (for dogs & cats) pap 밥

feel *v.* man-jyŏ po-da 만져보다; (with senses) nŭ-ki-da 느끼다; *n.* nŭ-kim 느낌

feeling *n.* kam-jŏng 감정

fellow *n.* nom 놈

felt *n.* chŏn 전

female *n.* yŏ-ja 여자; *adj.* (used as prefix for aminals) am 암; (for people) yŏ 여

fence *n.* ul-t'a-ri 울타리

ferment *v.* pal-hyo ha-da 발효하다

fern *n.* ko-sa-ri 고사리

ferry *n.* na-ru 나루; *v.* pae-ro kŏn-nŭ-da 배로건느다; **f.-boat** *n.* yŏl-lak sŏn 열락선; (river) na-ru pae 나루배

ferryman *n.* sa-gong 사공

fertile *adj.* pi-ok han 비옥한

fertilizer *n.* kŏ-rŭm 거름

festival *n.* chan-ch'i 잔치

fetch *v.t.* ka-ji-rŏ-ka-da 가지러가다

fetter *n.* sa-sŭl 사슬; *v.* sa-sŭl-lo mae-da 사슬로매다

fever *n.* yŏl 열

few, be, *v.* chŏk-da 적다

fibre *n.* sŏm-yu 섬유

fiction *n.* so-sŏl 소설

field *n.* tŭl 들; **dry f.** pat 밭

field-hospital *n.* ya-jŏn pyŏng-won 야전병원

field-marshal *n.* won-su 원수

fierce *adj.* sa-na-un 사나운

fifteen *n.* yŏl-ta-sŏt 열다섯

fifty *n.* swin 쉰

fig *n.* mu-hwa-gwa 무화과

fight *v.* ssa-u-da 싸우다; *n.* ssa-um 싸움

figure *n.* (numeral) su-cha 수짜

file *v.* ta-tŭm-da 다듬다; (papers) goe-ŏ tu-da 꿰어두다; *n.* chul 줄; (of men) yŏl 열; (for papers) chong-i ki-u-gae 종이끼우개

fill *v.* ch'ae-u-da 채우다

film *n.* p'il-lŭm 필름

filter *v.* kŏ-rŭ-da 거르다

filth *n.* pu-jong-mul 부정물

fin *n.* chi-nŭ-rŏ-mi 지느러미

final *adj.* ma-ji-mak 마지막

finance *n.* chae-jŏng 재정

find *v.t.* ŏt-da 얻다; *v.* (something lost) ch'at-da 찾다

fine *n.* pŏl-gŭm 벌금; *v.* pŏl-gŭm-ŭl kwa ha-da 벌금을과하다; *adj.* ko-un 고운

finger *n.* son-ka-rak 손가락

finger-nail *n.* son-t'op 손톱

finish *v.t.* ma-ch'i-da 마치다

fir *n.* chon na-mu 전나무

fire *n.* pul 불; *v.* (from job) hae-go ha-da 해고하다; (a gun) sso-da 쏘다; (set on fire) Pul no-ta 불놓다; **make a f.** pul p'i-u-da 불피우다

fire-alarm *n.* hwa-jong 화종

fire-brigade *n.* so-bang-dae 소방대

fire-cracker *n.* p'ok-juk 폭죽

fire-drill *n.* so-bang yŏn-sŭp 소방연습

fire-engine *n.* so-bang ch'a 소방차

fire-escape *n.* so-bang sa-ta-ri 소방사다리

firefly *n.* kae-tong pŏ-le 개똥버레

fireman *n.* so-bang su 소방수

firewood *n.* chang-jak 장작

firm *n.* hoe-sa 회사; *adj.* tŭn-tŭn han 튼튼한

first *adv* ch'ŏt-chae 첫째

fish *n.* mul ko-gi 물고기; *v.* ko-gi chap-da 고기잡다;

fisherman *n.* ŏ-bu 어부

fishing-boat *n.* ŏ-sŏn 어선

fishing-line *n.* nak-si chul 낚시 줄

fishing-rod *n.* nak-si-dae 낚시대

fishing-village *n.* ŏ-ch'on 어촌

fist *n.* chu-mŏk 주먹

fit *adj.* mat-nŭn 맞는; *v.*······e mat-da ······에맞다; *n.* pal-jak 발작

five *n. & adj.* ta-sŏt 다섯

fix *v.* su-ri ha-da 수리하다

flag *n.* ki 기; **national f.** kuk ki 국기

flail *n.* to-ri-kae 도리깨

flake *n.* jok 쪽

flame *n.* pul got 불꽃

flannel *n.* p'ŭl-lae-nel 플래넬

flap *v.i* na-p'ul na-p'ul ha-da 나풀나풀하다; *v.* (birds) hwae-chi-da 홰지다; *n.* (envelope) (pong-t'u) hyŏ (봉루) 혀

flash *v.* pŏn-chŏk-i-da 번쩍이다; *n.* sŏm-gwang 섬광

flat *adj.* p'ŏn-p'ŏn han 편편한; *n.* bang-ku 빵꾸

flat-iron *n.* ta-ri-mi 다리미

flatten *v.t.* p'ŏn-p'ŏn ha-ge ha-da 편편하게하다

flatter *v.t. & i.* al-lang kŏ-ri-da 알랑거리다

flattery *n.* a-ch'ŏm 아첨
flavor *v.* cho-mi ha-da 조미하다;
  n. mat 맛
flaw *n.* kyŏl-jŏm 결점
flax *n.* sam 삼
flea *n.* pyŏ-ruk 벼룩
flee *v.* to-mang ha-da 도망하다
fleece *n.* yang-mo 양모
fleet *n.* ham-dae 함대
flesh *n.* (meat & fish) ko-gi 고
  기; (people) sal 살
flexible *adj.* kup-hil-su i-nŭn 굽
  힐수있는
flight *n.* to-mang 도망; (airplane)
  pi-haeng 비행
fling *v.t.* tŏn-ji-da 던지다
flint *n.* pu-sit-tol 부싯돌
flit *v.i.* na-ra ta-ni-da 나라다니다
float *n.* (buoy) pu-p'yo 부표; *v.*
  dŭ-da 뜨다
flock *n.* de 떼; *v.* mo-i-da 모이
  다
flog *v.t.* mae dae-ri-da 매때리다
flood *n.* hong-su 홍수; *v.* pŏm-
  ram ha-da 범람하다
floor *n.* ma-ru 마루
flounder *n.* (fish) nŏp-ch'i 넙치
flour *n.* mil ka-ru 밀가루
flourish *v.i.* mu-sŏng ha-da 무성
  하다
flow *v.* hŭ-rŭ-da 흐르다

flower *n.* got 꽃; **f.-pot** *n.* hwa-bun 화분

fluent *adj.* yu-ch'ang han 유창한

fluid *n.* yu-dong-mul 유동물

flush *v.* ssis-ŏ-nae-ri-da 씻어내리다; (be red) pulk-ŏ-ji-da 붉어지다

flute *n.* p'i-ri 피리

fly *n.* p'a-ri 파리; *v.i.* (bird) nal-da 날다; *v.t.* (kite) nal-li-da 날니다

flyer *n.* pi-haeng-sa 비행사

fly-paper *n.* p'a-ri yak-chong-i 파리약종이

foal *n.* mang-a-ji 망아지

foam *n.* kŏ-p'um 거품

fodder *n.* gol 꼴

foe *n.* won-su 원수

fog *n.* an-gae 안개

fold *n.* chu-rŭm 주름; *v.t.* chŏp-da 접다

foliage *n.* uk-ŏ-jin ip' 욱어진잎

follow *v.* da-rŭ-da 따르다

follower *n.* pu-ha 부하

folly *n.* ŏ-ri-sŏk-ŭm 어리석음

fond *adj.* cho-a-sŏ 좋아서

fondly *adv.* sa-rang-sŭ-rŏp-ge 사랑스럽게

food *n.* ŭm-sik 음식

fool *n.* ŏ-ri-sŏk-ŭn-ja 어리석은자; *v.t.* sok-i-da 속이다

foolish *adj*. ŏ-ri-sŏk-ŭn 어리석은
foot *n*. pal 발; (measure) cha 자
football *n*. ch'uk-gu 축구
footpath *n*. so-ro kil 소로길
footprint *n*. cha-ch'wi 자취
footstep *n*. pal so-ri 발소리
for *prep*······ŭl ŭi-ha-ya ···을의하야;
　(on account of) dae-mun-e 때문
　에
forbid *v.t*. kŭm ha-da 금하다
force *n*. him 힘; *v.t*. ŏk-ji-ro···
　···ha-ge ha-da 억지로······하게하다
forcibly *adv*. kang-je-ro 강제로
ford *n*. mul yat-ŭn-de 물얕은데;
　v. kŏr-ŏ kŏn-ne-da 걸어건네다
forecast *v.t*. ye-ch'ŭk ha-da 예측
　하다; *n*. ye-sang 예상
forefathers *n*. cho-sang 조상
forefinger *n*. tul chae son-ka-rak
　둘째손가락
forehead *n*. ap'-i-ma 앞이마
foreign *adj*. oe-kuk-ŭi 외국의
foreigner *n*. oe-kuk-in 외국인
foreleg *n*. ap'-pal 앞발
foremost *adj*. maen ch'ŏ-ŭm-ŭi 맨
　처음의
forenoon *n*. o-jŏn 오전
foresee *v*. ye-ji ha-da 예지하다
forest *n*. sal-lim 산림
foretell *v.t*. ye-ŏn ha-da 예언하다
forever *adv*. hang-sang 항상

forge *n.* tae-jang-gan 대장간; *v.*
(steel) pyŏ-ru-da 벼루다 ;
(counterfeit) wi-jo ha-da 위조
하다

forgery *n.* wi-jo 위조

forget *v.* i-ta 잊다

forgetful *adj.* chal it-nŭn 잘잊는

forgive *v.t.* yong-sa ha-da 용사하
다

fork *n.* p'o-o-k'u 포오크; (in the
road) kal-lae kil 갈래길

forlorn *adj.* chŏk-mak han 적막한

form *n.* mo-yang 모양; *v.t.* hyŏng-
t'ae-rŭl i-ru-da 형태를이루다

formal *adj.* (in form) hyŏng-sik
형식

formation *n.* tae-hyŏng 대형

former *adj.* i-jŏn-ŭi 이전의

formula *n.* kong-sik 공식

fort *n.* sŏng 성

fortification *n.* ch'uk-sŏng 축성

fortified area *n.* yo-saek chi-dae
요색지대

fortify *v.* ch'uk-sŏng ha-da 축성
하다

fortnight *n.* po-rŭm 보름

fortress *n.* ch'uk-sŏng 축성

fortunate *adj.* un-su cho-ŭn 운수
좋은

fortune *n.* un-su 운수

forty *n.* ma-hŭn 마흔

forward *adj·* ap'-ŭi 앞의; *adv.* ap'-ŭ-ro 앞으로; *v.* ch'e-song ha-da 체송하다

foster- *adj·* su-yang 수양

foul *adj·* tŏ-rŏ-un 더러운; *n.* kyu-ch'ŭk ŭi-pan 규측의반

found *v.* ch'ang-nip ha-da 창립하다

foundation *n·* ki-ch'o 기초

founder *n·* sŏl-lip-ja 설립자

foundry *n.* chu-jo 주조

fountain *n.* saem 샘

fountain-pen *n·* man-nyŏn-p'il 만년필

four *n·* net 넷

fourteen *n·* yŏl-net 열넷

fowl *n.* tak 닭

fox *n.* yŏ-u 여우

fragment *n.* gae-jĭn cho-gak 깨진 조각

fragrance *n.* hyang-gi 향기

frail *adj·* yak han 약한

frame *n.* t'ŭl 틀; *v.* t'ŭl-e pak-da 틀에박다

framework *n.* cho-jĭk 조직

frank *adj·* sol-jĭk han 솔직한

frantic *adj·* mi-ch'ĭn 미친

fraud *n.* hyŏp-jap 협잡

freckle *n.* chuk-ŭn gae 죽은깨

free *adj·* cha-yu-ŭi 자유의; *v.* sŏk-bang ha-da 석방하다

freedom *n.* cha-yu 자유

freeze *v.* ŏl-da 얼다

freight *n.* hwa-mul 화물; **f. boat** *n.* hwa-mul-sŏn 화물선; **f. car** *n.* hwa-mul-ch'a 화물차

frequent *adj.* pin-bŏn han 빈번한

fresh *adj.* saeng 생

fret *v.t.* ae-t'ae-u-da 애태우다; *v.i.* tap-dap ha-da 답답하다

friction *n.* ma-ch'al 마찰

Friday *n.* kŭm-yo-il 금요일

friend *n.* ch'in-gu 친구

friendless *adj.* pŏt-ŏp-nŭn 벗없는

friendly *adj.* pŏt-ĭn 벗인

friendship *n.* u-jŏng 우정

fright *n.* nol-lam 놀람

frighten *v.t.* gam-jak nol-la-ge ha-da 깜작놀라게하다

frog *n.* kae-gu-ri 개구리

from *prep.* ······ro pu-t'ŏ ······로부터

front *n.* ap' 앞

frontier *n.* kuk kyŏng 국경

frost *n.* sŏ-ri 서리

frown *v.* ji-p'u-ri-da 찌푸리다

frozen *adj.* ŏr-ŭn 얼은

frugal *adj.* kŏm-so han 검소한

fruit *n.* kwa-sil 과실

fry *v.t.* p'ŭ-ra-i ha-da 프라이하다

frying-pan *n.* p'ŭ-ra-i nam-bi 프라이남비

fulfil *v.t.* i-ru-da 이루다

fuel *n.* yŏl-lyo 연료

full *adj*. ch'an 찬; *adv*. kat-tŭk
자득; **f. moon** *n*. mang-wol 망
월

fun *n*. chang-nan 장난

fund *n*. cha-gŭm 자금

funeral *n*. chang-ye 장례

funnel *n*. (boat) kul-tuk 굴뚝;
(Pouring) gal-dae 깔대

funny *adj*. u-sŭ-un 우스운

fur *n*. t'ŏl 털

furious *adj*. mi-ch'ĭn-dŭt sŏng
naen 미친듯성낸

furl *v.t*. kam-da 감다

furlough *n*. hyu-ga 휴가

furnace *n*. su-nal-lo hwa-dŏk 수난
로화덕

furnish *v.t*. kong-gŭp ha-da 공급
하다

furnishings *n*. chang-ch'i-mul 장
치물

furniture *n*. ka-gu 가구

furrow *n*. (Pat') kol (밭) 골

furry *adj*. t'ŏl ka-juk kat'-ŭn 털가
죽같은

further *adj*. tŏ mŏn 더먼; *adv*.
tŏ mŏl-li 더멀리

furtive *adj*. sal-sal ha-nŭn 살살하
는

fury *n*. kyŏk-no 격노

fuse *n*. (electric) hyu-jŭ 휴즈;
(ordnance) sin-gwan 신관

fuss *n.* so-dong 소동; *v.i.* dŏ-dŭl-
da 떠들다

futile *adj.* hŏt 헛

future *n.* chang-nae 장래; *adj.*
chang-nae-ŭi 장래의

〔 **G** 〕

gaiety *n.* k'wae-hwal 쾌활

gaily *adv.* k'wae-hwal-hi 쾌활히

gain *v.* ŏt-da 얻다; *n.* i-dŭk 이득

gait *n.* kŏr-ŭm kŏr-i 걸음걸이

gale *n.* kang p ung 강풍

gallant *adj.* hul-lyung han 훌륭한

gallery *n.* hoe-rang 회랑

gallon *n.* kael-lon 갤론

gallop *n.* (mal-ŭi) dwim pak-jil
(말의) 뜀박질; *v.t. & i.* dwim
pak-jil-lo ka-da 뜀박질로가다

galvanized iron *n.* ham-sŏk 함석

gamble *v.* to-bak ha-da 도박하다

game *n.* yu-hŭi 유희

gangway *n.* nal-ta-ri 날다리

gap *n.* t'ŭm-sae 틈새

garage *n.* cha-dong-ch'a ch'a-go 자
동차차고

garbage *n.* hŏ-sŏp ssŭ-re-gi 허섭
쓰레기

garden *n.* dŭl 뜰

gardener *n.* chŏng-won-sa 정원사

garlic *n.* ma-nŭl 마늘

garment *n.* ot 옷

garrison *n.* su-bi-dae 수비대

garter *n.* tae-nim 대님

gas *n.* gae-ssŭ 깨쓰

gasoline *n.* hwi-bal-yu 휘발유

gasp *v.* hŏl-tŏk kŏ-ri-da 헐떡거리다

gate *n.* mun 문

gather *v.* mo-ŭ-da 모으다; (come together) mo-i-da 모이다; (sewing) chu-rŭm-ŭl chap-da 주름을 잡다

gathering *n.* chip-hoe 집회

gay *adj.* k'wae-hwal han 쾌활한

gaze *v.* pa-ra-po-da 바라보다

gear *n.* gi-yŏ 끼여; (equipment) pi-p'um 비품

gem *n.* po-sŏk 보석

gender *n.* sŏng 성

genealogy *n.* chok-po 족보

general *n.* chang-gun 장군; *adj.* il-ban-jŏk 일반적; **g. election** *n.* ch'ong sŏn-gŏ 총선거

generate *v.* saeng-gi-ge ha-da 생기게하다; (electricity) pal-chŏn ha-da 발전하다

generation *n.* il-dae 일대

generosity *n.* kwan-dae 관대

generous *adj.* kwan-dae han 관대한

genius *n.* ch'ŏn-jae 천재

gentle *adj.* on-hwa han 온화한

gentleman *n.* sin-sa 신사

gentlewoman *n.* suk-nyŏ 숙녀

gently *adv.* on-hwa ha-ge 온화하게

genuine *adj.* chin-jŏng han 진정한

geographical *adj.* chi-ri hak jŏk 지리학적

geography *n.* chi-ri hak 지리학

geometry *n.* ki-ha hak 기하학

German *adj.* tok-il-ŭi 독일의; *n.* tok-il sa-ram 독일사람

Germany tok-il 독일

gesture *n.* mom-jit 몸짓

get *v.* (acquire) ŏt-da 얻다; **g. up** *v.* ir-ŏ-na-da 일어나다

ghost *n.* kwi-sin 귀신

giant *n.* kŏ-in 거인

giddy *adj.* ŏ-chil-ŏ-chil han 어찔어찔한

gift *n.* sŏn-mul 선물

gifted *adj.* chae-nung-i i-nŭn 재능이있는

gigantic *adj.* kŏ-dae han 거대한

giggle *v.* k'il-k'il ut-da 킬킬웃다

gild *v.t.* kŭm-ŭl ip-hi-da 금을입히다

gill *n.* (fish) ŏ-ga-mi 어가미

ginger *n.* saeng-gang 생강

ginko *n.* ŭn-haeng na-mu 은행나무

ginseng *n.* in-sam 인삼

gipsy *n.* chip-ssi 집씨

giraffe *n.* ki-rin 기린

girder *n.* tŭl-bo 들보

girl *n.* so-nyŏ 소녀

give *v.t.* chu-da 주다; **g. up** *v.* nae-pŏ-ri-da 내버리다

glacier *n.* ping-ha 빙하

glad *adj.* ki-pŭn 기쁜

gladden *v.t.* ki-pŭ-ge ha-da 기쁘 게하다

gladness *n.* ki-pŭm 기쁨

glance *v.* ŏl-p'it po-da 얼핏보다; *n.* il-pyŏl 일별

gland *n.* sŏn 선

glare *v.* pŏn-chŏk-pŏn-chŏk pit na-da 번쩍번쩍빛나다; *adj.* (light) pŏn-chŏk-pŏn-chŏk han 번쩍번쩍 한

glass *n.* yu-ri 유리; (drinking) yu-ri-chan 유리잔

glassware *n.* yu-ri ki-gu 유리기구

gleam *n.* mi-gwang 미광; *v.* pan-chak pit na-da 반짝빛나다

glee *n.* hwal-lak 환락

glimmer *v.* pan-chak-ban-chak pit na-da 반짝반짝빛나다

glimpse *n.* pyŏl-kyŏn 별견

glisten *v.i.* pŏn-chŏk-bŏn-chŏk pit na-da 번쩍번쩍빛나다

glitter *v.i.* pan-chak-ban-chak pit na-da 반짝반짝빛나다

globe *n.* chi-gu 지구

gloom *n.* ŏ-dum 어둠

glorify *v.* yŏng-gwang-ŭl tol-li-da 영관을돌리다

glorious *adj.* yŏng-gwang-sŭ-rŏ-un 영광스러운

glory *n.* yŏng-gwang 영광

glove *n.* chang-gaP 장갑

glow *v.i.* paek-yŏl ha-da 백열하다

glue *n.* pu-re p'ul 부레풀

gnat *n.* ha-ru-sa-ri 하루사리

gnaw *v.* mur-ŏ dŭt-da 물어뜯다

go *v.i.* ka-da 가다; **g. across** kŏn-nŭ-da 건느다; **g. abroad** yang-haeng ha-da 양행하다; **g. back and forth** wat-da kat-da 왔다갔다; **g. down** nae-ryŏ ka-da 내려가다; **g. out** (light) gŏ-ji-da 꺼지다; **g. up** ol-lŏ ka-da 올너가다; **g. without saying** mul-lon i-da 물론이다

goal *n.* mok-p'yo 목표

goat *n.* yŏm-so 염소

gobble *v.t.* a-gwi-a-gwi mŏk-da 아귀아귀먹다

go-between *n.* chung-gae in 중개인

god *n.* sĭn 신; **God** *n.* ha-na-nĭm 하나님

goddess *n.* yŏ-sĭn 여신

godliness *n.* kyŏng-gŏn 경건

gold *n. & adj* kŭm 금

golden *adj* kŭm pich-ŭi 금빛의

goldfish *n.* kŭm-pung-ŏ 금붕어

golf *n.* gol-p'ŭ 꼴프

gong *n.* ching 징

good *n.* pok-ni 복리; *adj* choh-ŭn 좋은; **g. day** al-lyŏng ha-sim-ni-ka 안녕하십니가; **g. morning** al-lyŏng-hi chu-mu-sŏss-ŭm-ni-ka 안녕히주무셨읍니가; **g. night** al-lyŏng-hi chu-mu-sip-si-yo 안녕히주무십시요; **good-bye** *n.* chak-byŏl 작별; *greet.* al-lyŏng-hi ka-sip-si-yo 안녕히가십시요

goodness *n.* tŏk 덕

goods *n.* mul-gŏn 물건

goose *n.* kŏ-wi 거위; **wild g.** ki-rŏ-gi 기러기

gorgeous *adj.* ch'al-lan han 찬란한

gorilla *n.* ko-ril-la 고릴라

gospel *n.* pok-ŭm 복음

gossip *n* chap-dam 잡담; *v.* chap-dam ha-da 잡담하다

gourd *n.* pak 박

govern *v.* chi-bae ha-da 지배하다

government *n.* chŏng-bu 정부

governor *n.* chi-sa 지사

grab *v.* put-chap-da 붙잡다

grace *n.* ŭn-hye 은혜; (before meals) ki-do 기도

graceful *adj.* u-mi han 우미한

gracious *adj.* kan-gok han 간곡한

grade *n.* tŭng-gŭp 등급; (in school) hak nyŏn 학년; *v.* (mark) tŭng-gŭp-ŭl chu-da 등급을주다; *v.* (level) p'yŏng-hi tak-da 평히닥다

gradual *adj.* chŏm-ch'a-ŭi 접차의

graduate *n.* chor-ŏp-saeng 졸업생; *v.t.* chor-ŏp ha-da 졸업하다

graduation *n.* chor-ŏp sik 졸업식

grain *n.* kok-sik 곡식

grammar *n.* mun pŏp 문법

grammatical *adj.* mun pŏp sang 문법상

gramophone *n.* ch'uk-ŭm-gi 축음기

granary *n.* kok-ch'ang 곡창

grand *adj.* chang-ŏm han 장엄한

granddaughter *n.* son-nyŏ 손녀

grandeur *n.* chang-ŏm 장엄

grandfather *n.* hal a-bŏ-ji 할아버지

grandmother *n.* hal mŏ-ni 할머니

grandson *n.* son-ja 손자

grand-stand *n.* t'ŭk-pyŏl kwal-lak sŏk 특별관락석

granite *n* hwa-gang-sŏk 화강석

grant *v.t.* sŭng-nak ha-da 승낙하다

grape *n.* p'o-do 포도; **g.-vine** *n.* p'o-do tŏng-k'ul 포도덩쿨

grasp *v.* chap-da 잡다

grasping *adj.* yok-sĭm-i sen 욕심이센

grass *n.* p'ul 풀

grasshopper *n.* myŏ-tu-gi 메뚜기

grate *v.* chul-p'an-e kal-da 줄판에갈다

grateful *adj.* ko-map-ge saeng-gak ha-nŭn 고맙게생각하는

grater *n.* chul-p'an 줄판

gratify *v.* man-jok si-k'i-da 만족시키다

gratitude *n.* kam-sa 감사

grave *n.* mu-dŏm 무덤; *adj.* chung-dae han 중대한

gravel *n.* cha-kal 자갈

gravely *adv.* chang-ŏm ha-ge 장엄하게

grave-stone *n.* myo-bi 표비

graveyard *n.* myo-ji 표지

gravity *n.* chang-jung 장중; (weight) chung-yŏk 중력

graze *v.i.* p'ul-ŭl mŏk-da 풀을먹다

grease *n.* ki-rŭm 기름; (lubricating) kŭ-ri-i-sŭ 그리이스; *v.* ki-rŭm pal-lŭ-da 기름발르다

great *adj.* k'ŭn 큰; g.-grandchild *n.* chŭng-son-ja 승손자; g.-grandfather *n.* chŭng-cho-bu 승조부; g.-grandmother *n.* chŭng-cho-mo 승조모

greatness *n.* wi-dae 위대

Greece *n.* hŭi-rap 희랍

greed *n.* yok-sĭm 욕심

greedy *adj.* yok-sĭm man-ŭn 욕심 많은

green *adj.* ch'o-rok saek 초록색; **be g.** *v.* (unripe) sŏl-da 설다

greenhouse *n.* on-sil 온실

greet *v.t.* in-sa ha-da 인사하다

greeting *n.* in-sa 인사

grey *adj.* hoe-saek 회색

grief *n.* sŏr-ŭm 설음

grim *adj.* ŏm-han 엄한

grieve *v.* sŏr-ŏ-wo ha-da 설어워하다

grime *n.* dae 때

grind *v.t.* kal-da 갈다

grindstone *n.* mae tol 매돌

grip *v.t.* goak put'-chap-da 꽉불잡다; *n.* p'a-ak 파악

grit *n.* mɔ-rae al 모래알

groan *n.* sin-ŭm 신음; *v.t.* sin-ŭm ha-da 신음하다

grocer *n.* sik-yo-p'um chang-sa 식료품장사

groceries *n.* sik-yo-p'um 식료품

groom *n.* sil-lang 신랑; (horse) ma-bu 마부

grope *v.* tŏ-dŭm-da 더듬다

ground *n.* dang 땅; **g.-floor** *n.* a-rae-ch'ŭng 아래층

group *n.* mu-ri 무리

grove *n.* sup' 숲

grow *v.* cha-ra-da 자라다; (cultivate) chae-bae ha-da 재배하다

growl *v.* ǔ-rǔ-rǒng kǒ-ri-da 으르 렁거리다

growth *n.* saeng-jang 생장

grub *n.* pǒl-gǒ-ji 벌거지

gruel *n.* chuk 죽

grumble *n.* t'u-dǒl-dae-gi 투덜대 기; *v.i.* t'u-dǒl kǒ-ri-da 투덜거 리다

guarantee *v.* po-jǔng ha-da 보증 하다; *n.* po-jǔng 보증

guarantor *n.* po-jǔng in 보증인

guard *n.* kyǒng-bi 경비; *v.t.* chik'i-da 지키다

guess *v.t.* ch'u-ch'ǔk ha-da 추측하 다; *n.* ch'u-ch'ǔk 추측

guest *n.* son-nim 손님

guide *n.* al-lae-ja 안내자; *v.* in-do ha-da 인도하다

guide-book *n.* yǒ-haeng al-lae-sǒ 여행안내서

guilt *n.* choe 죄

guilty *adj.* choe i-nǔn 죄있는

gulf *n.* man 만

gull *n.* kal-mae-gi 갈매기

gun *n.* ch'ong 총

gunner *n.* p'o-su 포수

gunpowder *n.* hwa-yak 화약

gush *v.i.* t'ŏ-jyŏ na-o-da 터져나오
다

gust *n.* il-jǐn-ŭi pa-ram 일진의바
람

gutter *n.* to-rang 도랑

gutteral *adj.* hu-ŭm 후음

gymnasium *n.* ch'e-yuk-gwan 체
육관

gymnastics *n.* ch'e-jo 체조

gyroscope *n.* hoe-jŏn-ŭi 회전의

〔 **H** 〕

habit *n.* pŏ-rŭt 버릇

habitable *adj.* sal-su i-nŭn 살수
있는

hack *v.* cha-rŭ-da 자르다

haggard *adj.* su-ch'ŏk han 수척한

hail *n.* ssar-ak nun 쌀악눈; *v.i.*
ssar-ak-nun-i na-ri-da 쌀악눈이
나리다; *v.* (call) pul-ŭ-da 불으다

hair *n.* mŏ-ri-t'ŏl 머리털

hair-brush *n.* mŏ-ri sol 머리솔

half *n.* & *adj.* pan 반

half-brother *n.* i-bu hyŏng-je 이
부형제

half-hearted *adj.* yŏl-i ŏp-nŭn 열
이없는

half-mast *n.* pan ki-ŭi 반기의

half-moon *n.* pan-dal 반달

half-sister *n.* i-bu cha-mae 이부
자매

half-way *adv.* chung-do-ŭi 중도의

hall *n.* (auditorium) kang-dang 강당; (corridor) hol 홀; **City H.** si-ch'ŏng 시청

halt *v.* mŏm-ch'u-da 멈추다; (military command) chŏng-ji 정지

halve *v.* tŭng-bun ha-da 등분하다

ham *n.* haem 햄

hammer *n.* ma-ch'i 마치; *v.* ma-ch'i-jil ha-da 마치질하다

hand *n.* son 손; *v.t.* nae-yŏ chu-da 내여주다; **to lend a h.** to-a chu-da 도아주다; **to have on h.** chun-bi-hae it-da 준비해있다

hand-bag *n.* so ka-bang 소가방

hand-cart *n.* ku-ru-ma 구두마

hand-cuff *n.* su-gap 수갑

handful *n.* han-chum 한줌

handicap *n.* pul-li han cho-gŏn 불리한조건

handkerchief *n.* son-su-gŏn 손수건

handle *n.* son-jab-i 손잡이; *v.t.* cho-jong ha-da 조종하다

hand-shake *n.* ak-su 악수

handsome *adj.* a-rŭm da-un 아름다운

handy *adj.* p'yŏl-li han 편리한

hang *v.t.* kŏl-da 걸다; *v.i.* kŏl-yŏ it-da 걸여있다

hangar *n.* kyŏk-nap-go 겨납고
happen *v.i.* ir-ŏ-na-da 일어나다
happily *adv.* chŭl-gŏp-ge 즐겁게
happiness *n.* haeng-bok 행복
happy *adj.* haeng-bok han 행복한
harbor *n.* hang-gu 항구
hard *adj.* kut-ŭn 굳은; *adv.* ae-ssŏ-sŏ 애써서
hardly *adv.* kan-sin-hi 간신히
hardship *n.* ko-cho 고초
hardy *adj.* kut-sen 굳센
hare *n.* t'o-ki 토끼
harm *n.* hae 해; *v.t.* hae ha-da 해하다
harness *n.* ma-gu 마구
harp *n.* ha-a-p'ŭ 하아프; (Korean) kŏ-mun-go 거문고
harrow *n.* soe-sŭ-rang 쇠스랑; *v.t.* soe-sŭ-rang-jil-ŭl ha-da 쇠스랑질을하다
harsh *adj.* kŏ-ch'il-ŭn 거칠은
harshly *adv.* kŏ-ch'il-ge 거칠게
harvest *n.* ch'u-su 추수; **poor h.** hyung-nyŏn 흉년; **good h.** p'ung-nyŏn 풍년; **h. time** *n.* ch'u-su-gi 추수기
haste *n.* kŭp-ham 급함
hasten *v.* ba-rŭ-ge ha-da 빠르게하다
hastily *adv.* kŭp-hi 급히
hasty *adj.* kŭp-han 급한

hat *n.* mo-ja 모자

hatch *v.* al-ŭl ga-da 알을까다

hatchet *n.* to-ki 도끼

hate *v.t.* mi-wo ha-da 미워하다

hateful *adj.* mi-un 미운

hatred *n.* mi-um 미움

haughty *adj.* kŏ-man han 거만한

haul *v.* gŏl-da 끌다

haunch *n.* hŏ-ri 허리

haunt *v.t.* ch'ul-mol ha-da 출몰하다

have *v.* (hold, possess) it-da 있다; (be endowed with) kat-da 갖다

havoc *n.* p'a-goe 파괴

hawk *n.* mae 매

hawthorn *n.* a-ga-wi na-mu 아가위나무

hay *n.* kŏn-ch'o 건초

haystack *n.* kŏn-cho tŏ-mi 건초더미

haze *n.* a-ji-raeng-i 아지랭이

hazel *n.* kae-am na-mu 개암나무

hazy *adj.* an-gae kin 안개낀

he *pron.* kŭ-i 그이

head *n.* mŏ-ri 머리

head office *n.* pon-bu 본부

headache, to have a, *v.* mŏ-ri a-p'ŭ-da 머리아프다

head-land *n.* kot 곶

head-light *n.* hə-dŭ-ra-it' 헤드라일

headline *n.* che-mok 제목

headquarters *n.* sa-ryŏng-bu 사령부; **general h.** ch'ong sa-ryŏng-bu 총사령부

heal *v.* ko-ch'i-da 고치다

health *n.* kŏn-gang 건강

healthy *adj.* kŏn-gang han 건강한

heap *n.* tŏ-mi 더미; *v.t.* ssah-a-ol-li-da 쌓아올리다

hear *v.t.* tŭt-da 듣다

heart *n.* sim-jang 심장

heart-broken *adj.* pi-t'ong-hae ha-nŭn 비통해하는

heart-burn *n.* chil-t'u 질투

heart-disease *n.* sim-jang-pyŏng 심장병

heart-failure *n.* sim-jang ma-bi 심장마비

hearth *n.* nal-lo 난로

heartily *adv.* chin-sim-ŭ-ro 진심으로

heartless *adj.* mu-jŏng-han 무정한

hearty *adj.* kan-jil han 간질한

heat *n.* yŏl 열; *v.t.* te-u-da 데우다

heater *n.* hi-i-t'a 히이타

heathen *adj.* i-kyo-ŭi 이교의

heave *v.t.* (throw) tŏn-ji-da 던지다; *v.* (pull) chab-a gŭl-da 잡아끌다

heaven *n.* ha-nŭl 하늘

heavy *adj.* mu-gŏ-un 무거운; **to be h.** *v.* mu-gŏp-da 무겁다

hedge *n.* ul-t'a-ri 울타리

heedful *adj.* cho-sim-sŏng i-nŭn 조심성있는

heedless *adj.* pu-ju-ŭi han 부주의한

heel *n.* pal-gum-ch'i 발꿈치

heifer *n.* am-song-a-ji 암송아지

height *n.* nop'-i 높이; (person) k'i 키

heighten *v.t.* nop'-i-da 높이다

heir *n.* sa-ja 사자

heiress *n.* yŏ-ja sang-sok-in 여자상속인

helicopter *n.* he-ri-k'op-t'ŏ 헤리코터

hell *n.* chi-ok 지옥

hello (a call) yŏ-bo-se-yo 여보세요; (a greeting) al-lyŏng ha-sim-ni-ka 안녕하십니가

helm *n.* k'i 키

helmet *n.* ch'ŏl-mo 철모

help *v.* to-wa chu-da 도와주다; *n.* to-um 도움

helper *n.* to-wa chu-nŭn sa-ram 도와주는사람

helpful *adj.* to-ŭm-i doe-nŭn 도움이되는   「어찌할수없는

helpless *adj.* ŏ-chi-hal-su ŏp-nŭn

hem *n.* sŏn 선; *v.* sŏn tu-ru-da 선두르다

hemisphere *n.* pan-gu 반구

hemp *n.* sam 삼

hen *n.* am-tak 암탉

hence *adv.* (from now) i-je pu-t'ŏ 이제부터; (therefore) ku-rŏ-mu-ro 그러므로

hen-coop *n.* tak-jang 닭장

her *pron.* ku-yŏ-ja 그여자

herb *n.* san na-mul 산나물

herd *n.* ka-ch'uk-ui de 가축의떼

herdsman *n.* mok-ja 목자

here *adv.* yŏ-gi-e 여기에

hereafter *adv.* i-da-um-e 이다음에

heredity *n.* yu-jŏn 유전

heritage *n.* sang-sok 상속

hermit *n.* un-dun-ja 은둔자

hero *n.* yŏng-ung 영웅

heroic *adj.* yŏng-ung-da-un 영웅다운

heroine *n.* yŏ-jang-bu 여장부

heron *n.* wae-ga-ri 왜가리

herring *n.* ch'ŏng-ŏ 청어

herself *pron.* ku yŏ-ja cha-sin 그여자자신

hesitate *v.i.* chu-jŏ ha-da 주저하다

hew *v.t.* jik-da 찍다

hide *n.* ka-juk 가죽

hide *v.* kam-ch'u-da 감추다;(oneself) sum-da 숨다

high *adj.* nop'-ŭn 높은; *adv.* nop'-i 높이; **h. seas** *n.* kong-hae 공해

highly *adv.* kŭk-do-ro 극도로

highway *n.* tae-ro 대로

hill *n.* ŏn-dŏk 언덕; (military) ko chi 고지

hinder *v.t.* pang-hae ha-da 방해하다

hindrance *n.* pang-hae 방해

hinge *n.* tol jŏ-gwi 돌쩌귀; *v.* (on) ⋯⋯yŏ ha-e tal-li-da ⋯⋯여하에달리다

hint *n.* am-si 암시; *v.* am-si-rŭl chu-da 암시를주다

hire *n.* sak 삯; *v.* ko-yong ha-da 고용하다

hiss *n.* swi-i ha-nŭn so-ri 쉬이하는소리; *v.i.* swi-i so-ri nae-da 쉬이소리내다

historian *n.* yŏk-sa-ga 역사가

history *n.* yŏk-sa 역사

hit *v.t.* mat-ch'i-da 맞치다

hitch *v.* (horse to cart) me-u-da 메우다; (tie) mae-da 매다

hither *adv.* i-ri-ro 이리로

hitherto *adv.* yo-t'ae ga-ji 여태까지

hive *n.* pŏl-chip 벌집

hives *n.* tu-dŭ-re-gi 두드레기

hoard *n.* ch'uk-jŏk 축적; *v.* ch'uk-jŏk ha-da 축적하다

hoarse *adj.* mok-swin 목쉰

hobby *n.* ki-ho il 기호일

hoe *n.* kwaeng-i 괭이

hog *n.* twae-ji 돼지

hoist *v.t.* ol-li-da 올리다

hold *v.* put-chap-da 붓잡다; *n.* (ship) sŏn-j'ang 선창

hole *n.* ku-mŏng 구멍

holiday *n.* hyu-il 휴일

Holiness Church *n.* sŏng-gyŏl kyo 성결교

hollow *adj.* pin 빈; *v.t.* tŏng pi-ge ha-da 덩비게하다; *n.* ku-mŏng 구멍

hollyhock *n.* ch'ok-kyu hwa 촉규화

holy *adj.* sin-sŏng han 신성한

home *n.* ka-jŏng 가정

homely *adj.* maep-si ŏp-nŭn 맵시 없는

homesickness *n.* hyang-su 향수

hone *n.* sut-tol 숫돌; *v.* kal-da 갈다

honest *adj.* chŏng-jik han 정직한

honesty *n.* chŏng-jik 정직

honey *n.* gul 꿀

honeymoon *n.* sin-hon yŏ-haeng 신혼여행

honor *n.* myŏng-ye 명예; *v.* chon-gyŏng ha-da 존경하다

honorable *adj*. myŏng-ye-su-rŏ-un 명예스러운

hood *n*. ch'ŏ-nŭi 처늬

hoof *n*. kup 굽

hook *n*. kal-gu-ri soe 갈구리쇠; *v*. kal-gu-ri soe-ro ch'ae-u-da 갈 구리쇠로채우다

hoop *n*. t'e 테

hop *v.i.* gae-gŭm dwi-da 깨금뛰 다

hope *n*. hŭi-mang 희망; *v*. pa-ra-da 바라다

hopeful *adj*. hŭi-mang i-nŭn 회망 있는

hopeless *adj*. hŭi-mang-i ŏp-nŭn 희망이없는

horizon *n*. chi-p'yŏng 지평

horizontal *adj*. su-p'yŏng-ŭi 수평 의; **h. bar** *n*. su-p'yŏng-mok 수평목

horn *n*. bul 뿔; (bugle) na-p'al 나팔

hornet *n*. mal-pŏl 말벌

horoscope *n*. ku-sŏng 구성

horrible *adj*. mu-sŏ-un 무서운

horror *n*. kong-p'o 공포

horse *n*. mal 말

horse chestnut *n*. il-gop-ip' na-mu 일곱잎나무

horsefly *n*. tŭng-ae 등애

horseman *n*. ki-su 기수

horse-power *n.* ma-ryŏk 마력
horse-radish *n.* yang-gat 양갓
horseshoe *n.* mal-p'yŏn-ja 말편자
hose *n.* ho-o-sŭ 호오스
hospitable *adj.* hu-dae ha-nŭn 후
대하는
hospital *n.* pyŏng-won 병원
hospitality *n.* kwan-dae 관대
host *n.* chu-in 주인; (great number) ta-su 다수
hostage *n.* ĭn-jĭl 인질
hot *adj.* (temperature) dŭ-gŏ-un
뜨거운; (taste) mae-un 매운
hotel *n.* ho-t'el 호텔
hotspring *n.* on-ch'ŏn 온천
hound *n.* sa-nyang kae 사냥개
hour *n.* si-gan 시간; (o'clock) si
시
house *n.* chĭp 집
household *n.* han chip-an 한집안
housekeeper *n.* ka-jŏng-bu 가정
부
housewife *n.* chu-bu 주부
hovel *n.* o-mak sa-ri 오막사리
how *adv.* ŏ-dŏ-ke hae-sŏ 어떻게해
서
however *conj.* kŭ-rŏ-na 그러나
howl *v.* ul-da 울다
hue *n.* (color) saek 색
hug *v.t.* gyŏ-an-da 껴안다
huge *adj.* kŏ-dae 거대

hull *n.* gŏp-jil 껍질; *v.* gŏp-dae-gi-rŭl pŏt-ki-da 껍데기를벗기다; *v.* (rice) pe-jit-da 배꼈다; *n.* (ship) sŏn-ch'e 선체

hum *v.i.* ing-ing kŏ-ri-da 잉잉거리다

human *n.* ĭn-gan 인간

humble *adj.* kyŏm-son han 겸손한

humid *adj.* sŭp-gi man-nŭn 습기많는

humor *n.* ik-sal 익살

hump *n.* hŭk 혹   「등이

hunchback *n.* gop-sa-dŭng-i 꼽사

hundred *n.* paek 백

hunger *n.* chu-rĭm 주림

hungry *adj.* chu-rĭn 주린; **to be h.** *v.* pae-ko-p'ŭ-da 배고프다

hunt *n.* sa-nyang 사냥; *v.* sa-nyang ha-da 사냥하다; **h. for** *v.* ch'at-da 찾다

hunter *n.* sa-nyang-gun 사냥군

hunting *n.* sa-nyang 사냥

hurl *v.t.* him-gŏt tŏn-ji-da 힘껏던지다

hurrah *n.* man-se 만세!

hurry *v.* kŭP-hi……ha-da 급히……하다

hurt *v.t.* sang ha-ge ha-da 상하게하다; *n.* sang-ch'ŏ 상처

husband *n.* nam-p'yŏn 남편

husbandry *n.* nong-ŏp 농업

hush v· cho-yong ha-ge ha-da 조용
하게하다

hut n· o-du-mak chip 오두막집

hydrant n· so-hwa su-do gok-ji
소화수도꼭지

hydrogen n· su-so 수소

hydroplane n· su-sang pi-haeng-gi
수상비행기

hymn n· ch'an-mi-ga 찬미가

〔 I 〕

I pron· na 나

ice n· ŏ-rŭm 얼음; **i· box** ŏr-ŭm-
jang 얼음장; **i· cream** a-i-sŭ-
k'ŭ-rim 아이스크림; **i·-house**
ping-sil 빙실; **i·-water** ŏ-rŭm-
mul 어름물

iceberg n· ping-san 빙산

icicle n· ko-dŭ-rŭm 고드름

idea n· saeng-gak 생각

ideal n· & adj· i-sang (ŭi) 이상
(의)

identification n· p'yo-sik 표식;
i· card chŭng-myŏng-sŏ 증명서

identify v· sik-pyŏl ha-da 식별하
다

idiom n· suk-ŏ 숙어

idiot n· pa-bo 바보

idle adj· ke-ŭ-rŭn 게으른; (not
working) nol-go i-nŭn 놀고있는;
v.t· & i· ke-ŭ-rŭ-da 게으르다

idleness *n.* ke-ŭ-rŭm 게으름

idler *n.* ke-ŭ-rŭn sa-ram 게으른 사람

idol *n.* u-sang 우상

if *conj.* man-il……ha-myŏn 마일 ……하면

ignorance *n.* mu-sik 무식

ignorant *adj.* mu-sik han 무식한

ignore *v.t.* mu-sik ha-da 무식하다

ill *adv.* na-pŭ-ge 나쁘게; **to be i.** *v.* pyŏng nat-da 병낫다

ill-bred *adj.* pŏ-rŭt ŏp-nŭn 버릇 없는

illegal *adj.* pul pŏp-ŭi 불법의

illiteracy *n.* mun-maeng 문맹

illiterate *n.* mun-maeng-ja 문맹자

illness *n.* pyŏng 병

ill-treatment *n.* hak-dae 학대

illustrate *v.* (example) ye-ro sŏl-myŏng ha-da 예로설명하다; (picture) kŭ-rim-ŭl nŏt-ta 그림을넣다

illustration *n.* sŏl-myŏng 설명

image *n.* sang 상

imaginary *adj.* sang-sang-jŏk in 상상적인

imagination *n.* sang-sang 상상

imagine *v.* sang-sang ha-da 상상하다

imitate *v.t.* mo-bang ha-da 모방하다

imitation *n.* mo-bang 모방

immediate *adj.* chŭk-si-ŭi 즉시의

immediately *adv.* chŭk-si 즉시

immense *adj.* mak-tae han 막대한

immigrant *n.* nae-ji i-ju-ja 내지이주자

immigrate *v.* i-ju ha-yŏ o-da 이주하여오다

immodest *adj.* yam-jŏn ha-ji mot han 얌전하지못한

immoral *adj.* pu-to-dŏk-ŭi 부도덕의

immortal *adj.* pul myŏl-ŭi 불멸의

immovable *adj.* pu-dong-ŭi 부동의

imp *n.* tok-ka-bi 독가비

impartial *adj.* kong-p'yŏng han 공평한

impatient, to be, *v.* ch'am-ŭl sŏng ŏp-da 참을성없다

imperative *adj.* myŏng-yŏng-jŏk 명령적

imperfect *adj.* pul wan-jŏn han 불완전한

imperial *adj.* che-guk-ŭi 제국의

imperialism *n.* che-guk chu-ŭi 제국주의

impersonate *v.* ŭi-in-hwa ha-da 의인화하다

impertinent *adj.* kŏn-bang jin 건방진

implement *n·* yŏn-jang 연장; *v·*
sil-haeng ha-da 실행하다

implication *n·* am-si 암시

implore *v.t·* kan-ch'ŏng ha-da 간
청하다

imply *v·* am-si ha-da 암시하다

impolite *adj·* mu-re han 무례한

import *v·* su-ip ha-da 수입하다

importance *n·* chung-yo 중요

important *adj·* chung-yo han 중요
한

impossible *adj·* pul ka-nŭng han
불가능한

impress *v.t·* in-sang-ŭl chu-da 인
상을주다

impression *n·* in-sang 인상

impressive *adj·* in-sang-jŏk 인상
적

imprison *v.t·* t'u-ok ha-da 투옥하
다

improper *adj·* pu-dang han 부당한

improve *v·* kae-sŏn ha-da 개선하다

improvement *n·* kae-sŏn 개선

imprudence *n·* kyŏng-sol 경솔

imprudent *adj·* kyŏng-sol han 경
솔한

impudent, to be, *v·* pŏn-bŏn-sŭ-
rŏp-da 뻔뻔스럽다

impulse *n·* ch'ung-dong 충동

impulsive *adj·* ch'ung-dong-jŏk-in
충동적인

impulsively *adv.* ch'ung-dong-jŏk-ŭ-ro 충동적으로

impure *adj.* pul sun han 불순한

impurity *n.* pul sun 불순

in *prep.*······e ······에

inability *n.* mu-nŭng 무능

inaccurate *adj.* pu chŏng-hwak han 부정확한

inactive *adj.* hwal-bal ha-ji an-ŭn 활발하지않은

inadequate *adj.* pu-ch'ung-bun han 부충분한

inattention *n.* pu-ju-ŭi 부주의

inaugurate *v.* ch'wi-ĭm-sĭk-ŭl ha-da 취임식을하다

inauguration *n.* ch'wi-ĭm-sĭk 취임식

incapable *adj.*······hal su-ga ŏp-nŭn ······할수가없는

incendiary *n.* (arsonist) pang-hwa-pŏm-in 방화범인; *n.* (bomb) pang-hwa-t'an 방화탄; *adj.* Pang-hwa-ŭi 방화의

incense *n.* hyang 향

incentive *n.* cha-gŭk 자극

incessant *adj* gŭn'-im ŏp-nŭn 끊임없는

inch *n.* in-ch'i 인치

incident *n.* sa-gŏn 사건

inclination *n.* kyŏng-sa 경사

incline *v.t.* ki-ul-da 기울다;

v. (be disposed to) ma-ŭm-i ssol-li-da 마음이쏠리다

include *v.* p'o ham ha-da 포함하다

incoherent *adj.* cho-ri ŏp-nŭn 조리없는

income *n.* su-ip 수입

incomplete *adj.* pul-wan-jŏn han 불완전한

inconsiderate *adj.* kyŏng-hŭl han 경흘한

inconsistent *adj.* mo-sun doe-nŭn 모순되는

inconvenience *n.* pul-p'yŏn 불편

inconvenient *adj.* pul p'yŏn han 불편한

incorrect *adj.* t'ŭl-lin 틀린

increase *v.* chŭng-ga ha-da 증가하다; *n.* chŭng-ga 증가

incredible *adj.* mid-ŭl-su ŏp-nŭn 믿을수없는

incurable *adj.* kot-ch'il-su ŏp-nŭn 곳칠수없는

indebted *adj.* pu-ch'ae-ga i-nŭn 부채가있는

indeed *adv.* ch'am-ŭ-ro 참으로

indefinite *adj.* pu-jŏng-ŭi 부정의

independence *n.* tong-nip 독립

independent *adj.* tong-nip-ŭi 독립의

indescribable *adj.* hyŏng-ŏn hal-su ŏp-nŭn 형언할수없는

indestructible *adj.* pul-myŏl-ŭi
불멸의

index *n.* saek-in 색인

India *n.* in-do 인도

indicate *v.t.* chi-si ha-da 지시하다

indifferent *adj.* mu-sĭm han 무심
한

indigestion *n.* so-hwa pul-lyang
소화불량

indignant *adj.* hwa-naen 화낸

indigo *n.* jok-pit 쪽빛

indirect *adj.* kan-jŏp-ŭi 간접의

indiscreet *adj.* pun-byŏn ŏp-nŭn
분변없는

indiscriminate *adj.* mu-ch'a-byŏl-
ŭi 무차별의

indispensible *adj.* ŏps-ŭl-su ŏp-
nŭn 없을수없는

indistinct *adj.* dok-dok ha-ji an-
ŭn 똑똑하지않은

individual *adj.* kae-in 개인

indolence *n.* yu-il 유일

indolent *adj.* ke-u-rŭn 게우른

indoor *adj.* chĭp-an 집안

indorse *v.* po-jŭng ha-da 보증하
다

induce *v.t.* kwon-yu ha-da 권유하
다

induct *v.* (into military) (kun-dae-
e) p'yŏn-ip ha-da (군쇄에) 편
입하다

induction *n.* yu-do 유도

industrial *adj.* san-ŏp-ŭi 산업의

industrious *adj.* pu-ji-rŏn-han 부지런한

industry *n.* san-ŏp 산업; (diligence) kŭn-myŏn 근면

inefficient *adj.* pi-nŭng-yul-jŏk 비능률적

inevitable *adj.* p'i ha-ji mot hal 피하지못할

inexcusable *adj.* yong-sŏ hal-su ŏp-nŭn 용서할수없는

inexperienced *adj.* kyŏng-hŏm-i ŏp-nŭn 경험이없는

infant *n.* ŏ-rĭn-a-i 어린아이

infantry *n.* po-byŏng 보병

infect *v.* chŏn-yŏm si-k'i-da 전염시키다

infection *n.* chŏn-yŏm 전염

inferior *adj.* dŏ-rŏ-ji-nŭn 떠러지는

infest *v.* hoeng-haeng ha-da 횡행하다

infinitive *n.* pu-jŏng pŏp 부정법

influence *n.* yŏng-hyang 영향; *v.t.* yŏng-hyang-ŭl gi-ch'i-da 영향을 끼치다

influenza *n.* yu-haeng-sŏ kam-gi 유행서감기

inform *v.t.* al-li-da 알리다

information *n.* po-do 보도

ingratitude *n·* mang-ŭn 망은
ingredient *n·* sŏng-bun 성분
inhabit *v·t·* sal-da 살다
inhabitant *n·* chu-min 주민
inherit *v·t·* kye-sŭng ha-da 계승
하다
inhospitable *adj·* pul ch'in-chŏl
han 불친절한
inject *v·* chu-sa ha-da 주사하다
injection *n·* chu-sa 주사
injure *v·t·* hae ha-da 해하다
injury *n·* sang hae 상해
injustice *n·* pu-jŏng 부정
ink *n·* ing-k'ŭ 잉크; **India i·** mŏk
먹
ink-stone *n·* pyŏ-ru 벼루
inland *n·* & *adj·* nae-ji 내지
inlay *v·* nu-gak ha-da 누각하다;
n· nu-gak 누각
inlet *n·* chŏk-ŭn man 적은만
inn *n·* yŏ-gwan 여관
innocent *adj·* kyŏl-baek han 결백한
innumerable *adj·* he-a-ril-su ŏp-
nŭn 헤아릴수없는
inoculate *v·t·* chŏp-jong ha-da 접종
하다
inoculation *n·* chŏp-jong 접종
inopportune *adj·* si-gi-rŭl no-ch'in
시기를노친
inquest *n·* ch'wi-jo 취조
inquire *v·* mut-da 묻다

inquiry *n.* sim-mun 심문

inquisitive *adj.* ho-gi-sim-i sen 호기심이센

inscribe *v.t.* sae-gi-da 새기다

inscription *n.* ki-myŏng 기명

insect *n.* kon-ch'ung 곤충

insecticide *n.* sal-ch'ung-je 살충제

insecure *adj.* an-jŏn ha-ji mot han 안전하지못한

insert *v.* chib-ŏ nŏt-ta 집어넣다

inside *n.* nae-myon 내면; *adv.* & *prep.* an-e 안에

insignia *n.* hwi-jang 휘장

insincere *adj.* sŏng-ŭi ŏp-nŭn 성의없는

insist *v.* chu-jang ha-da 주장하다

inspect *v.t.* kŏm-sa ha-da 검사하다

inspection *n.* kŏm-sa 검사

inspector *n.* kŏm-sa-ja 검사자

inspire *v.t.* ko-mu ha-da 고무하다

instalment *n.* pu-bun 부분; monthly i. wol-bu 월부

instance *n.* kyŏng-u 경우

instant *n.* sun-gan 순간

instantly *adv.* kot 곧

instead *adv.* tae-sin-e 대신에

instinctively *adv.* pol-lŭng-jŏk-ŭ-ro 본능적으로

institute *v.* sŏl-lip ha-da 설립하다; *n.* (meetings) kang-sŭp hoe 강습회

institution *n.* ki-gwan 기관

instruct *v.t.* ka-rŭ-ch'i-da 가르치
다

instruction *n.* chi-do 지도

instrument *n.* ki-gye 기계

insulate *v.t.* chŏl-yŏn ha-da 절연하
다

insult *v.t.* mo-yok 모욕

insurance *n.* po-hŏm 보험

insure *v.* po-jŭng ha-da 보증하
다

insurrection *n.* mo-ban 모반

integrity *n.* ch'ung-jik 충직

intelligence *n.* chi-hye 지혜; (military) chŏng-bo 정보

intelligent *adj.* ch'ong-myŏng han
총명한

intend *v.t.* ha-ryŏ-go saeng-gak ha-
da 하려고생각하다

intense *adj.* kyŏng-nyŏl han 격렬
한

intent *adj.* chŏn-sĭm ha-nŭn 전심
하는

intention *n.* ŭi-hyang 의향

intentionally *adv.* il-bu-rŏ 일부러

interest *n.* hŭng-mi 흥미; (money)
i-ja 이자

interesting *adj.* chae-mi i-nŭn 재
미있는

interfere *v.* kan-sŏp ha-da 간섭하
다

interior *n.* nae-bu 내부; *adj.* nae-bu-ŭi 내부의

internal *adj.* nae-bu-ŭi 내부의

international *adj.* kuk-je-jŏk 국제적

interpret *v.* t'ong-yŏk ha-da 통역하다

interpretation *n.* (analysis) hae-sŏk 해석; (translation) t'ong-yŏk 통역

interpreter *n.* t'ong-yŏk-ja 통역자

interrogate *v.t.* sim-mun ha-da 심문하다

interrogation *n.* sim-mun 심문

interrupt *v.t.* pang-hae ha-da 방해하다

interruption *n.* pang-hae 방해

interval *n.* sa-i 사이

interview *n.* hoe-gyŏn 회견

intimate *adj.* ch'in-mil han 친밀한 *v.t.* am-si ha-da 암시하다

intimidate *v.* ŭi-hyŏp ha-da 의협하다

into *prep.* an-ŭ-ro 안으로

intolerable *adj.* ch'am-ŭl-su ŏp-nŭn 참을수없는

intoxicated *adj.* ch'wi han 취한

intricate *adj.* pok chap han 복잡한

introduce *v.t.* so-gae ha-da 소개하다; *v.* (bring in) in-do ha-da 인도하다

introduction *n·* so-gae 소개; (in a book) sŏ-mun 서문

intuition *n·* chik-kak 직각

invade *v·t·* ch'im-ip ha-da 침입하다

invalid *n·* pyŏng-ja 병자

invalidate *v·* mu-hyo-ro ha-da 무효로하다

invasion *n·* ch'im-ip 침입

invent *v·t·* pal-myŏng ha-da 발명하다

invention *n·* pal-myŏng 발명

inventor *n·* pal-myŏng-ja 발명자

inventory *n·* sang-p'um cho-sa mong-nok 상품조사목록

invest *v·* (funds) t'u-ja ha-da 투자하다

investigate *v·t·* cho-sa ha-da 조사하다

investigation *n·* cho-sa 조사

investment *n·* t'u-ja 투자

invincible *adj·* chŏng-bok hal-su ŏp-nŭn 정복할수없는

invisible *adj·* po-i-ji an'-nŭn 보이지않는

invitation *n·* ch'o-dae 초대

invite *v·t·* ch'o-dae ha-da 초대하다

invoice *n·* song-jang 송장

involve *v·* yŏn-jwa si-k'i-da 연좌시키다

iris *n.* ch'ang-p'o 창포; (eye) hong-ch'ae 홍채

iron *n.* tae-ri-mi 대리미; *v.t.* tae-rŏ-da 대려다

iron *n.* ch'ŏl 철; (galvanized) ham-sŏk 함석

ironing *n.* tae-ri-mi-jil 대리미질

ironmonger *n.* ch'ŏl-mul-jŏn 철물전

irregular *adj.* (not proper) pul-kyu-ch'ŭk han 불규측한; (uneven) ko-ru-ji an-ŭn 고루지않은

irregulars *n.* pu-jŏng-gyu-gun 부정규군

irresponsible *adj.* mu-ch'aek-im han 무책임한

irrigate *v.* kwan-gae ha-da 관개하다

irrigation *n.* kwan-gae 관개

irritable *adj.* hwa chal nae-nŭn 화잘내는

island *n.* sŏm 섬

-ism *n.* chu-ŭi 주의

issue *n.* mun-je 문제; *v.t.* nae-da 네다; *v.i.* (come out) na-o-da 나오다

-ist *n.* chu-ŭi-ja 주의자

isthmus *n.* chi-hyŏp 지협

it *pron.* kŭ-gŏt 그것

itch *v.* ka-ryŏp-da 가렵다

item *n.* cho-mok 조목

itinerary *n.* sun-haeng 순행

itinerate *v.* sun-haeng ha-da 순행
하다

itself *p on.* sŭ-sŭ-ro 스스로

ivory *n.* sang-a 상아

ivy *n.* tam-jaeng-i 담쟁이

〔 **J** 〕

jack *n.* chaek-k'ŭ 잭크

jacket *n.* chŏ-go-ri 저고리

jade *n.* kyŏng-ok 경옥

jail *n.* ku-ryu-so 구류소

jam *n.* jaem 쨈; *v.* (passage) ka-
ro mak-da 가로막다; *v.* (radio)
pang-hae pang-song 바해방송;
v. (machinery) kŏl-li-da 걸니다

janitor *n.* chĭp chik-i 집직이

January *n.* chŏng-wol 정월

Japan *n.* il-bon 일본

Japanese *n.* il-bon sa-ram 일본사
람; *adj.* il-bon-ŭi 일본의

jar *n.* tok 독

jaundice *n.* hwang-dal 황달

javelin *n.* t'u-ch'ang 루창

jaw *n.* t'ok 턱

jealous *adj.* chil-t'u-sĭm i-nŭn 질
투심 있는

jeer *v.* cho-rong ha-da 조롱하다

jelly-fish *n.* hae p'a-ri 해파리

jeopardize *v.* ŭi-d'ae ha-ge ha-da
의태하게하다

jerk *v.* kap-ja-gi gŭl-da 잠짜기끌
다

jest *n.* nong-dam 농담; *v.i.* nong-
dam ha-da 농담하다

Jesus *n.* ye-su 예수

jet plane *n.* chet' pi-haeng-gi 젤비
행기

jetty *n.* pu-du 부두

Jew *n.* yu-t'ae sa-ram 유태사람

jewel *n.* po-sŏk 보석

jeweler *n.* po-sŏk-sang 보석상

jingle *v.* jŏl-lŏng jŏl-lŏng ɛo-ri na-
da 찔렁찔렁소리나다

job *n.* il-cha-ri 일자리

join *v.* kyŏl-hap ha-da 결합하다

joint *n.* (bending) kwan-jŏl 관절;
(connection) yŏn-gyol 연결, *adj.*
hap-dong 합동

joke *n.* nong-dam 농담; *v.t.* nong-
dam ha-da 농담하다

jolly *adj.* yu-k'wae han 유쾌한

jolt *v.* hŭn-dŭl-li-da 흔들이다; *n.*
tong-yo 동요

jostle *v.* mir-ŏ-je ch'i-da 밀어제치
다

jot down *v.* ssŏ noh-ta 써놓다

journaliat *n.* ki-ja 기자

journey *n.* yŏ-haeng 여행; *v.i.* yŏ-
haeng ha-da 여행하다

joy *n.* ki-pǔm 기쁨

joyful *adj.* ki-pǔn 기픈

judge *n.* chae-p'an-gwan 재판관;
   v. p'an-gyŏl ha-da 판결하다
judgment *n.* chae-p'an 재판
jug *n.* chu-jŏn-ja 주전자
jugular *n.* mok-e i-nŭn tae-dong-
   mæk 목에있는대동맥
juice *n.* chŭp 즙
July *n.* ch'il-wol 칠월
jump *v.* dwi-da 뛰다; *n.* to-yak
   도약
June *n.* yu-wol 유월
jungle *n.* sup' 숲
junior *n.* yŏn-so-ja 연소자; *adj.*
   yŏn-so-han 연소한
junk *n.* chang-k'ŭ sŏn 장크선
jurisdiction *n.* sa-pŏp-gwon 사법
   권
jury *n.* pae-sim-gwan 배심관
just *adv.* pa-ro 바로; *adj.* kong-
   pyŏn han 공변한
justice *n.* chŏng-ŭi 정의
justification *n.* chŏng-dang-hwa
   정당화
jut *v.* pul-ssuk na-o-da 불쑥나오다

〔 **K** 〕

kangeroo *n.* k'aeng-ga-ru-u 캥가
   루우
keel *n.* yong-gol 용골
keen *adj.* nal-k'a-ro-un 날카로운

keep *v.t.* (guard) chi-k'i-da 지키
다; *v.i.* (raise) ki-rŭ-da 기르다;
v. (retain) ka-ji-go it-da 가지고
있다

keep out ch'ul-ip-kŭm-ji 출입금지

keeper *n.* chi-k'i-nŭn sa-ram 지키
는사람

kennel *n.* kae-chĭp 개집

kernel *n.* haek 핵

kerosene *n.* tŭng-hwa-yong sŏk-yu
등화용석유

kettle *n.* chu-chŏn-ja 주전자

key *n.* yŏl-soe 열쇠

khaki *adj.* kun saek 군색

kick *v.* pal-lo ch'a-da 발로차다;
n. pal-lo ch'a-gi 발로차기

kid *n.* sae-ki yŏm-so 새끼염소

kidnap *v.* nap-je ha-da 납제하다

kidney *n.* sin-jang 신장

kill *v.t.* chuk-i-da 죽이다

killed in action chŏn-sa 전사

kiln *n.* ka-ma 가마

kilogram *n.* k'il-lo-gŭ-ram 킬로그
람

kilometer *n.* k'il-lo-me-t'a 킬로
메―타

kin *n.* ch'in-jok 친족

kind *n.* chong-jok 종족; *adj.* ch'in-
jŏl han 친절한

kindergarten *n.* yu-ch'i-won 유치
원

kindle v. pul sa-rŭ-da 불사르다

kindness n. ch'in-jŏl 친절

kindred n. il-ga 일가; adj. yu-sa
han 유사한

king n. wang 왕

kingdom n. wang-guk 왕국

kingfisher n. pi-ch'wi 비취

kiss n. ip-mat-ch'u-gi 입맞추기;
v.t. ip-mat-ch'u-da 입맞추다

kitchen n. pu-ŏk' 부엌

kite n. yŏn 연

kitten n. sae-ki ko-yang-i 새끼고
양이

knack n. su-jae 수재

knapsack n. pae-rang 배랑

knead v. pan-juk ha-da 반죽하다

knee n. mu-rŭp' 무릎

kneel v.i. mu-rŭp' gul-ta 무릎꿇다

knife n. k'al 칼

knight n. ki-sa 기사; v.t. ki-sa-
jĭk-ŭl chu-da 기사직을주다

knit v. ja-da 짜다

knitting n. dŭ-gae-jĭl 뜨개질

knob n. son-jab-i 손잡이

knock v. du-dŭ-ri-da 뚜드리다;
n. du-dŭ-ri-gi 뚜드리기

knot n. mae-dŭp 매듭; (nautical
mile) hae-ri 해리; v. mae-dŭp
chit-da 매듭짓다

know v. al-da 알다

knowledge n. chi-sik 지식

known *adj.* al-lyŏ-jyŏ i-nŭn 알려
저있는

knuckle *n.* son-ka-rak-ŭi ma-da
손가락의마다

Korea *n.* han-guk 한국; **Republic of K.** tae-han-min-guk 대한
민국

kumquat *n.* kŭm-gyul 금귤

〔 L 〕

label *n.* pu-jŏn 부전

labor *n.* no-dong 노동; *v.i.* il ha-
da 일하다

laboratory *n.* sil-hŏm sil 실험실

labor-union *n.* no-dong cho-hap
노동조합

lace *n.* re-i-sŭ 레이스

laces *n.* gŭn 끈

lack *n.* pu-jok 부족; *v.* ŏpt-da
없다; **be lacking** *v.* ……ga pu-
jok ha-da ……가부족하다

lacquer *n.* ot 옷

lad *n.* chŏlm-ŭn sa-ram 젊은사람

ladder *n.* sa-da-ri 사다리

lading, bill of, *n.* sŏn-ha-jŭng-
gwon 선하증권

ladle *n.* kuk-ja 국자

ladies and gentlemen *n.* sĭn-sa-
sung-nyŏ 신사숙녀

lady *n.* kwi-bu-ĭn 귀부인

lair *n.* chĭm-sŭng-ŭi cham-cha-ri 짐승의잠자리

laity *n.* sok-ĭn 속인

lake *n.* ho-su 호수

lamb *n.* ŏ-rĭn yang 어린양

lame *adj.* chŏl-lŭm pa-ri-ŭi 절름바리의

lament *v.* sŭl-p'ŭ-da 슬프다

lamp *n.* tŭng 등

lamplight *n.* tŭng-pul 등불

land *n.* dang 땅; (lot) t'o-ji 토지; *v.* sang-yuk ha-da 상륙하다

landlord *n.* (house) chu-in 주인; (property) chi-ju 지주

landmark *n.* chi-p'yo 지표

landowner *n.* t'o-ji so-yu-ja 토지소유자

landscape *n.* kyŏng-ch'i 경치

lane *n.* chob-ŭn kil 좁은길

language *n.* mal 말

lantern *n.* tŭng 등

lap *v.* (drink) halt'-da 핥다; (over) ssa-da 싸다; *n.* mu-rŭp' 무릎

lapse *v.* (backslide) t'a-rak ha-da 타락하다; (time) ki-han kyŏng-gwa ha-da 기한경과하다

large *adj.* k'ŭn 큰

lark *n.* chong-dal-sae 종달새

lasciviousness *n.* ho-saek-ka 호색가

lash *n.* ch'ae-chuk 채국; *v.* ch'ae-chuk ha-da 채국하다; (tie) gok ŏlg-ŏ mae-da 꼭얽어매다

lass *n.* so-nyŏ 소녀

last *v.* kye-sok ha-da 계속하다; *adj.* ch'oe-hu-ŭi 최후의; *adv.* ch'oe-hu-ro 최후로

latch *n.* pit-chang 빗장

late *adj.* nŭj-ŭn 늦은; (dead) ko 고; *adv.* nŭt-ge 늦게

lately *adv.* yo-sa-i 요사이

latest *adj.* ch'oe-gŭn-ŭi 최근의

latitude *n.* wi-do 위도

latrine *n.* pyŏn-so 변소

latter *n.* hu-ja 후자

laudable *adj.* ch'ing-ch'an hal man han 칭찬할만한

laugh *v.i.* ut-da 웃다; *n.* us-ŭm 웃음

laughter *n.* us-ŭm 웃음

launch *v.t.* (ship) chin-su ha-da 진수하다; *v.* (start) si-jak ha-da 시작하다; *n.* mo-t'a bo—t'ŭ 모타뽀―트

laundry *n.* bal-lae 빨래

laurel *n.* wol-gye na-mu 월계나무

lavatory *n.* hwa-jang-sĭl 화장실

law *n.* pŏm-yul 법률

lawn *n.* chan-dŭi-pat 잔듸밧

lawyer *n.* pyŏn-ho-sa 변호사

lax *adj.* tŭng-han han 둥한한

lay *v.* (egg) na-ta 낳다; (put) no-ta 놓다

layer *n.* (strata) chi-ch'ŭng 지층; (thickness) kyŏp 겹

layman *n.* sok-ĭn 속인

lazy, to be, *v.* ke-ŭ-rŭ-da 게으르다

lead *v.* in-do ha-da 인도하다

lead *n.* (metal) nap 납

leader *n.* chi-do-ja 지도자

leading *n.* chi-do 지도

leaf *n.* ip' 잎

leaflet *n.* bi-ra 삐라

league *n.* yŏn-maeng 연맹; **L. of Nations** kuk-je yŏn-maeng 국제연맹

leak *n.* sae-gi 새기; *v.* sae-da 새다

lean *adj.* yŏ-won 여윈; *v.* ki-ul-da 기울다; (on) ki-dae-da 기대다

leap *v.i.* dwi-da 뛰다; *n.* yak-do 약도

leap-year *n.* yun-yŏn 윤년

learn *v.* pae-u-da 배우다

learning *n.* hak-mun 학문

lease *n.* im-dae ke-yak 임대계약; *v.* im-dae ha-da 임대하다

least *adj.* ch'oe-so-ŭi 최소의; *adv.* ka-jang chŏk-ge 가장적게; **at l.** chŏk-ŏ-do 적어도

leather *n.* ka-juk 가죽

leave *v.* dŏ-na-ka-da 떠나가다;
n. hyu-ga 휴가

lecture *n.* kang-ŭi 강의; *v.i.* kang
ŭi ha-da 강의하다

lecturer *n.* kang-sa 강사

ledge *n.* si-rŏng 시렁

ledger *n.* chang-bu 장부

leek *n.* p'a 파

left *adj.* oen-p'yŏn-ŭ-ro 왼편으로;
n. oen-p'yŏn 왼편

left-handed oen-son-jab-i-ŭi 왼손
잡이의

left-wing *n.* chwa-ik 좌익

leg *n.* ta-ri 다리

legacy *n.* yu-san 유산

legal *adj.* pŏp-yul-sang-ŭi 법률상
의

legation *n.* kong-sa-gwan 공사관

legend *n.* chŏn-sŏl 전설

legible *adj.* il-gi swi-un 일기쉬운

legislation *n.* ip-pŏp 입법

legislator *n.* ip-pŏp-ja 입법자

legislature *n.* ip-pŏp-bu 입법부

legitimate *adj.* hap-pŏp-ŭi 합법의

leisure *n.* yŏ-ga 여가

leisurely *adv.* ch'ŏn-ch'on-hi 천천
히

lemon *n.* re-mŏn 레먼

lemonade *n.* re-mŏn-e-i 레먼에이

lend *v.t.* pil-lyŏ chu-da 빌려주다

length *n.* kŏ-ri 거리

lenient *adj.* nŏ-kŭ-rŏ-un 너그러운·

lens *n.* ren-sŭ 렌스·

Lent *n.* sa-sun-je 사순제

leopard *n.* p'yo-pŏm 표범

leper *n.* mun-dung-pyŏng hwan-ja
문둥병환자

leprosy *n.* mun-dung-pyŏng 문둥
병

less *adj.* po-da chŏg-ŭn 보다적은

lessen *v.t.* chŏk-ge ha-da 적게하다

lesson *n.* kyo-gwa 교과

lest *conj.* ······ha-ji an-to-rok
···하지않도록

let *v.* (allow) hŏ-rak ha-da 허락하
다; *v. aux.* ha-ge ha-da 하게하다

letter *n.* p'yŏn-ji 편지

letter-box *n.* p'yŏn-ji tong 편지동

lettuce *n.* sang-ch'i 상치

level *adj.* p'yŏng-p'yŏng han 평평
한

lever *n.* chi-re-dae 지레대

liable *adj.* ŭi-mu-rŭl chyŏ-ya hal
의무를저야할

liaison *n.* yŏl-lak 연락

liar *n.* kŏ-jit mal jaeng-i 거짓말쟁
이

libel *n.* pi-pang-mun 비방문

liberal *adj.* cha-yu-ro-un 자유로운

liberate *v.* hae-bang ha-da 해방하
다

liberty *n.* cha-yu 자유

library *n.* to-sŏ-gwan 도서관

licence *n.* myŏn-hŏ-jang 면허장;
v. (permit) in-ga ha-da 인가하다

lick *v.t.* halt'-da 핥다

lid *n.* du-kŏng 뚜껑

lie *n.* kŏ-jit-mal 거짓말; *v.i.* kŏ-
jit-mal-ŭl ha-da 거짓말을 하다;
(recline) nup-da 눕다

lieutenant *n.* (lst) chung-wi 중위;
(2nd) so-wi 소위; (navy) tae-wi
대위; (j.g., navy) chung-wi 중위;
l. colonel chung-yŏng 중영;
l. commander so-ryŏng 소령;
l. general chung-jang 중장

life *n.* saeng-myŏng 생명; (span
of) il-saeng 일생

life-boat *n.* ku-jo-sŏn 구조선

life-insurance *n.* saeng-myŏng po-
hŭm 생명보홈

life-preserver *n.* ho-sĭn-gi 호신기

lifework *n.* il-saeng-ŭi sa-ŏp 일생
의사업

lift *v.* ol-li-da 올리다; *n.* sŭng-
gang-gi 승강기

light *n.* pit 빛; **be l.** *v.* palk-da
밝다; *n.* (lamp) pul 불; *v.*
(light) pul-k'yŏ-da 불켜다; *v.*
(fire) pul-p'i-u-da 불피우다; *adj.*
ka-byŏ-un 가벼운

lighter *n.* (boat) chong-sŏn 종선;
(cigarette) ra-i-t'a 라이타

lighthouse *n.* tŭng-dae 등대

lightly *adv.* ka-byŏp-ge 가볍게

lightning *n.* pŏn-gaet pul 번갯불

like *v.t.* choh-a ha-da 좋아하다;
prep. ...... wa kach-i ......와같이;
be l. *v.* ......wa kat'-da ......와같
다

likely *adj.* (promising) yu-mang
han 유망한; *adv.* a-ma 아마

liken with, to *v.t.* ......e pi ha-da
......에비하다

likeness *n.* yu-sa 유사

likewise *adv.* ma-ch'yan-ga-ji-ro
마찬가지로

lilac *n.* chŏng-hyang hwa 정향화

lily *n.* paek-hap 백합; **l. of the
valley** ŭn-pang-ul-got 은방울꽃;
water l. yŏn 연; **tiger l.** na-ri
나리

limb *n.* ka-ji 가지

lime *n.* sŏk-hoe 석회

limestone *n.* sŏk-hoe sŏk 석회석

limit *v.* che-han ha-da 제한하다;
n. han-gye 한계

limitation *n.* che-han 제한

limp *v.* ta-ri chŏl-da 다리절다

line *n.* son 손; *v.t.* an-noh-da 안
놓다

linen *n.* pe 베

liner *n.* chŏng-gi hang-no sŏn 정
기항로선

linguist *n.* ŏ-hak-ja 어학자

lining *n.* an pat-hi-nŭn gŏt 안받히 는것

link *v.* yŏn-gyŏl ha-da 연결하다

lion *n.* sa-ja 사자

lioness *n.* am-sa-ja 암사자

lip *n.* ip-sul 입술

liquid *n.* aek-ch'e 액체

liquor *n.* sul 술

lisp *v.* hyŏ-rŭt toe-ch'ae-ji mot ha-da 혀를되채지못하다

list *v.* (boat) ki-ul-da 기울다; *n.* p'yo 표; *v.* myŏng-bu-e chŏk-da 명부에적다

listen *v.i.* tŭt-da 듣다

literal *adj.* kŭl-ja-dae-ro-ŭi 글자 대로의

literature *n.* mun-hak 문학

litre *n.* ri-t'ŏ 리터

litter *n.* (stretcher) kŏ-juk 거죽; (mess) nan-jap 난잡

little *adj.* (size) chŏg-ŭn 적은; (amount) chag-ŭn 작은; *n.* cho-kŭm 조금

live *v.i.* sal-da 살다

livelihood *n.* saeng-gye 생계

lively *adj.* k'wae-hwal han 쾌활한

liver *n.* kan 간

living *adj.* sar-a i-nŭn 살아있는; *n.* saeng-hwal 생활

lizard *n.* to-ma paem 도마뱀

load *n.* chim 짐; *v.t.* chim-ŭl sit-da 짐을싣다

loaf *n.* (bread) bang tŏng-ŏ-ri 빵 덩어리; *v.i.* nol-go chi-nae-da 놀고지내다

loan *n.* tae-kŭm 대금

lobster *n.* k'ŭn sae-u 큰새우

local *adj.* chi-bang-jŏk 지방적

locate *v.* (put) wi-ch'i-rŭl chŏng ha-da 위치를정하다; (find) wi-ch'i-rŭl ch'at'-da 위치를찾다

location *n.* wi-ch'i 위치

lock *n.* cham-ŭl soe 잠을쇠; *v.* cham-gi-da 잠기다; *n.* (water) su-mun 수문

lock-jaw *n.* chŏ-jak-kŭn kyŏng-nyŏn 저작근경련

locomotive *n.* ki-gwan ch'a 기관차

locust *n.* me-tu-gi 메뚜기

lodge *v.* suk-bak ha-da 숙박하다; *n.* cho-kŭ-man han chip 조그만한 집

lodging *n.* suk-bak 숙박

loft *n.* ta-rak pang 다락방

lofty *adj.* tae-dan-hi nop'-ŭn 대단히높은

log *n.* t'ong na-mu 통나무

logic *n.* nol-li 논리

loiter *v.* pae-hoe ha-da 배회하다

lonely *adj.* ssŭl-ssŭl han 쓸쓸한

lonesome *adj.* ssŭl-ssŭl han 쓸쓸한

long *adj.* kin 긴; *adv.* kil-ge 길게; *v.i.* yŏl-mang ha-da 널망하다

longevity *n.* chang-su 장수

longitude *n.* kyŏng-do 경도

look *v.* (at) po-da 보다; *n.* il-gyŏn 일견

looking-glass *n.* kŏ-ul 거울

loom *n.* pe-t'ŭl 베틀; *v.t.* ŏ-ryŏm-p'us-i na-t'a-na-da 어렴풋이나타나다

loop *n.* tul-le 둘레

loop-hole *n.* ba-jyŏ-nal pang-do 빠져날방도

loose *adj.* hŏl-gŏ-wo-jin 헐거워진; *v.t.* nŭt-ch'u-da 늦추다

loosen *v.* nŭt-ch'u-da 늦추다

loot *n.* yak-t'al-p'um 약탈품

Lord *n.* (deity) chu-nim 주님; (noble) im-gŭm 임금

lordship *n.* chu-gŭn 주근

lose *v.* irh-ŏ pŏ-ri-da 잃어버리다; (fail to win) chi-da 지다

loss *n.* son-sil 손실

lot *n.* che-bi 제비; (house) t'o-ji 토지

lotion *n.* ssit-nŭn yak 씻는약

lottery *n.* kyŏng-p'um bop-gi 경품뽑기

lotus *n.* yŏn 연

loud *adj.* so-ri-ga k'ŭn 소리가큰

louse *n.* i 이

love *n.* sa-rang 사랑; *v.t.* sa-rang ha-da 사랑하다

lovely *adj.* i-pŭn 이쁜

low *adj.* naj-ŭn 낮은

lower *v.t.* nat-ch'u-da 낮추다

lowly *adj.* pi-ch'ŏn han 비천한

loyal *adj.* ch'ung-sŏng-ŭi 충성의

lubricate *v.t.* ki-rŭm-ŭl ch'i-da 기름을치다

luck *n.* un 운

luckily *adv.* ta-haeng-ŭ-ro 다행으로

lucky *adj.* un-i cho-ŭn 운이좋은

luggage *n.* su-ha-mul 수하물

lukewarm *adj.* mi-ji-gŭn han 미지근한

lull *v.* chae-u-da 재우다; *n.* chin-jŏng 진정

lullaby *n.* cha-jang-ga 자장가

lumber *n.* chae-mok 재목

luminous *adj.* pit'-na-nŭn 빛나는

lump *n.* tŏng-ŏ-ri 덩어리

lunar *adj.* tal-ŭi 달의

lunatic *n.* mi-ch'ĭn sa-ram 미친사람

lunch *n.* chŏm-sĭm 점심

lung *n.* p'ye 폐

lust *n.* saek-yok 색욕

luxury *n.* sa-ch'i 사치

lye *n.* chaem-mul 잼물

lying *adj.* (false) kŏ-jit-mal ha-nŭn 거짓말하는; (down) ka-ro nup-nŭn 가로눕는

〔 M 〕

macaroni *n.* ma-k'a-ro-ni 마카로니

machine *n.* ki-gye 가계

machinery *n.* ki-gye 기계

mackerel *n.* ko-dŭng-ŏ 고등어

mad *adj.* mi-ch'in 미친

madman *n.* mi-ch'in sa-ram 미친사람

magazine *n.* chap-ji 잡지

magic *n. & adj.* yo-sul 요술

magician *n.* ma-sul-sa 마술사

magistrate *n.* ch'i-an-p'an-sa 치안판사

magnanimous *adj.* a-ryang i-nŭn 아량있는

magnet *n.* cha-sŏk 자석

magnetic *adj.* cha-sŏk-ŭi 자석의

magnificent *adj.* chang-dae han 장대한

magnify *v.t.* hwak-dae ha-da 확대하다

magnolia *n.* mok-nan 목란

magpie *n.* ga-ch'i 까치

maiden *n.* so-nyŏ 소녀

maidservant *n.* yŏ-ha-in 여하인

mail *n.* u-p'yŏn 우편; *v.t.* Pu-ch'i-da 부치다

mail box *n.* u-ch'e t'ong 우체통

maim *v.t.* pyŏng-sĭn-ŭ-ro man-dŭl-da 병신으로만들다

main *adj.* chu-yo han 주요한

mainland *n.* tae-ryuk 대륙

mainly *adv.* chu-ro 주로

maintain *v.t.* (insist) chu-jang ha-da 주장하다; (keep-up) yu-ji ha-da 유지하다

majesty *n.* chon-ŏm 존엄

major *n.* (Army) yuk-gun so-ryŏng 육군소령; *adj.* ŭ-tŭm-in 으뜸인; **m. general** yuk-gun so-jang 육군소장

majorty *n.* tae-da-su 대다수

make *v.* man-dŭl-da 만들다

maker *n.* man-dŭ-nŭn sa-ram 만드는사람

makeshift *n.* cham-chŏng-jók su-dan 잠정적수단

malady *n.* pyŏng 병

malaria *n.* hak-jĭl 학질

male *n.* nam-ja 남자; *adj* (of animals) su 수

malice *n.* ak-ŭi 악의

maltreat *v.t.* hak-dae ha-da 학대하다

man *n.* sa-ram 사람; (male) nam-ja 남자

manage v. chi-bae ha-da 지배하다

management n. kwal-li 관리

manager n. chi-bae-in 지배인

Manchuria n. man-ju 만주

mandate n. myŏng-yŏng 명령;
(trusteeship) sin-t'ak t'ong-ch'i
신탁롱지

mane n. kal-gi 갈기

manger n. ku-yu 구유

manifest n. chŏk-ha-mul mong-
nok 적하물목록

mankind n. in-nyu 인류

manner n. t'ae-do 태도

manners n. ye-jŏl 예절

manoeuver n. ch'aeng-yak 책략;
(military) ki-dong yŏn-sŭp 기동
연습

mansion n. chŏ-t'aek 저택

mantis n. tang-nang 당랑

manufacture n. che-jo 제조; v.t.
che-jo ha-da 제조하다

manufacturer n. che-jo-ja 제조
자

manure n. kŏ-rŭm 거름; v.t. kŏ-
rŭm-ŭl chu-da 거름을주다

manuscript n. won-go 원고

many adj. man'-ŭn 많은

map n. chi-do 지도

maple n. tan-p'ung 단풍

mar v.t. sang ha-ge ha-da 상하게
하다

marathon *n.* (race) ma-ra-son 마라손

marble *n.* tae-ri-sŏk 대리석

March *n.* sam-wol 삼월

march *n.* haeng-jin 행진; *v.t.* haeng-jin ha-da 행진하다

mare *n.* am-mal 암말

margin *n.* ka-jang cha-ri 가장자리

marine *adj.* pa-da-ŭi 바다의; **m. products** *n.* hae-san-mul 해산물

mariner *n.* hae-won 해원

Marines *n.* hae-byŏng-dae 해병대

mark *n.* p'yo 표; *v.t.* p'yo-rŭl put'-i da 표를붙이다

market *n.* si-jang 시장; **m.-place** si-jang 시장

marking *n.* P'yo han gŏt 표한것

marksman *n.* sa-gyŏk-su 사격수

marmalade *n.* ma-a-mŏl-le-i-dŭ 마아멀레이드

marriage *n.* kyŏl-hon 결혼

marry *v.* kyŏl-hon ha-da 결혼하다; (for man) chang-ga tŭl-da 장가들다; (for woman) si-chip ka-da 시집가다

marsh *n.* nŭp' 늪

marshal *n.* (military title) won-su 원수

martial *adj.* kun-sa-ŭi 군사의; **m. law** *n.* kye-ŏm-yŏng 계엄령

martyr *n.* sun-gyo-ja 순교자
marvel *n.* ki-gŭi han il 기괴한일
marvellous *adj.* ki-gŭi han 기괴한
mascot *n.* ma-sŭ-k'o-t'ŭ 마스코트
masculine *adj.* nam-sŏng-jŏk 남성적
mask *n.* ka-myŏn 가면
mason *n.* sŏk-gong 석공
mass *n.* (quantity) tae-ryang 대량 (bulk) pu-p'i 부피; (group) chĭp-dan 집단
Mass *n.* mi-sa 미사
massacre *n.* hak-sal 학살
massive *adj.* pu-p'i-ga k'ŭn 부피가큰
mast *n.* tot-dae 돛대
master *n.* chu-in 주인
masterpiece *n.* kŏl-jak 걸작
mat *n.* (straw) kŏ-jŏk 거적; (bamboo) tae-ja-ri 대자리
match *n.* sŏng-nyang 성냥; (athletic) kyong-gi 경기; *v.* …wa al-mat-da ……와알맞다; **m.-box** *n.* sŏng-nyang-gap 성냥잡
mate *n.* (marriage) pae-p'il 배필; (companion) tong-mu 동무
material *n.* chae-ryo 재료; *adj.* mul-chil-ŭi 물질의
maternity hospital *n.* san-kwa pyŏng-won 산과병원

mathematics *n.* su hak 수학

matter *n.* mul-jil 물질; *v.i.* sang-gwan-i it-da 상관이있다

mattress *n.* pang-sŏk 방석

mature *adj.* (things) ig-ŭn 익은; (people) sŏng-suk han 성숙한

maxim *n.* kyŏk-ŏn 격언

maximum *adj.* ch'oe-dae 최대

may *auxil.* ⋯⋯hae-do cho-ta ⋯⋯ 해도좋다

May *n.* o-wol 오월

maybe *adv.* a-ma 아마

mayor *n.* si-jang 시장

meadow *n.* p'ul-pat' 풀밭

meagre *adj.* mo-ja-ra-nŭn 모자라 는

meal *n.* sik-sa 식사

mean *adj.* pi-ru-han 비루한; (average) p'yŏng-gyun-ŭi 평균의

meaning *n.* dŭt 뜻

meantime *n. & adv.* kŭ-sa-i 그사 이

meanwhile *adv.* kŭ-sa-i 그사이

measles *n.* hong-yŏk 홍역

measure *n.* ch'i-su 치수; *v.t.* chae-da 재다; *v.* (weight) toe-da 되다

meat *n.* ko-gi 고기

mechanic *n.* ki-gye-gong 기계공

mechanical *adj.* ki-gye-jŏk 기계적

medal *n.* hun-jang 훈장

meddle *v.i.* kan-sŏp ha-da 간섭하다

mediate *v.* chung-jae ha-da 중재하다

medical *adj.* ŭi-sul-ŭi 의술의

medicine *n.* yak 약; (science) ŭi hak 의학

medium *adj.* chung-dŭng-ŭi 중등의

meek *adj.* pu-dŭ-rŏ-un 부드러운

meet *v.* man-na-da 만나다

meeting *n.* hoe 회

mellow *adj.* pu-dŭ-rŏ-un 부드러운

melodious *adj.* kok-jo a-rŭm-da-un 곡조아름다운

melody *n.* ŭm-yul 음율

melon *n.* ch'am-oe 참외

melt *v.t.* nog-i-da 녹이다; *v.i.* nok-da 녹다

member *n.* hoe won 회원; *n.* (suffix) ······won ······원

memorandum *n.* pi-mang-rok 비망록; (by note) kak-sŏ 각서

memorial *adj.* ki-nyŏm-ŭi 기념의

memory *n.* ki-ŏk 기억

menace *n.* wi-hyŏp 위협

mend *v.* ko-ch'i-da 고치다

mental *adj.* chŏng-sĭn-sang 정신상

mention *v.t.* ······ŭl mal ha-da ······을말하다

merchant *n.* chang-sa 장사

merciful *adj.* in-jŏng man-ŭn 인
정많은

mercury *n.* su-ŭn 수은

mercy *n.* cha-bi 자비

mere *adj.* tan-sun han 단순한

merely *adv.* tan-sun-hi 단순히

merit *n.* kong-jŏk 공적; *v.t.* ……
ŭl pad-ŭl-man ha-da ……을받을
만하다

merry *adj.* chŭl-gŏ-un 즐거운

message *n.* t'ong-sin 통신

messenger *n.* sa-ja 사자

mess hall *n.* sĭk-dang 식당

Messiah *n.* me-si-ya 메시야

messy *adj.* ŏ-ji-rŏ-un 어지러운

metal *n.* kŭm-sok 금속

meteor *n.* yu-sŏng 유성

meteorology *n.* ki-sang hak 기상
학

meter *n.* (measurer) kye-ryang-gi
계량기

method *n.* pang-bŏp 방법

Methodist Church *n.* kam-ni kyo
감리교

metre *n.* me-t'ŏ 메터

mew *v.* nya-ong ha-da 냐옹하다

microphone *n.* ma-i-k'ŭ 마이크

microscope *n.* hyŏn-mi-gyŏng 현
미경

mid-day *n.* chŏng-o 정오

middle *n.* ka-un-de 가운데

middle-class *n.* chung-yu 중류

midnight *n.* pam-jung 밤중

midsummer *n.* han yŏ-rŭm 한여름

midway *adv.* chung-gan 중간

midwife *n.* san-p'a 산파

might *n.* him 힘

mighty *adj.* him i-nŭn 힘있는

mild *adj.* on-sun han 온순한

mildew *n.* kom-paeng-i 곰팽이

mile *n.* ma-il 마일

military *adj.* kun-ŭi 군의; **m. attache** tae-sa-gwan pu-mu-gwan 대사관부무관; **m. use** kun-yong 군용

milk *n.* u-yu 우유; (mother's) chŏt 젖; *v.* u-yu-rŭl ja-da 우유를짜다

mill *n.* pang-at-gan 방앗간

millet *n.* chop-ssal 좁쌀

million *n. & adj.* paek-man 백만

mimeograph *v.* tŭng-sa ha-da 등사하다; **m. machine** *n.* tŭng-sa-gi 등사기   「다

mimic *v.* hyung-nae nae-da 흉내내

mince *v.* ta-ji-da 다지다

mind *n.* ma-ŭm 마음; *v.* chu-i ha-da 주이하다; (obey) mal-tŭt-da 말듣다

mine *pron.* nae-gŏt 내것; *n.* kwang-san 광산

miner *n.* kwang-bu 광부

mineral *n.* kwang-mul 광물

mingle *v.* sŏk-da 셖다

minimum *n.* ch'oe-so 최소

mining industry *n.* kwang-ŏp 광업

minister *n.* (church) mok-sa 목사; (govt.) tae-sĭn 대신

Ministry *n.* (suffix) ⋯⋯bu ⋯⋯부

minor *n.* so 소

minority *n.* so-su 소수

mint *n.* pak-ha 박하; (money) cho-p'ye-guk 조폐국; *v.* ton-ŭl man-dŭl-da 돈을만들다

minus *prep.* ⋯⋯ŭl bae-go ⋯⋯을 빼고

minute *adj.* kŭk-hi chag-ŭn 극히 작은; *n.* il-bun 일분

minutes *n.* (meeting) hoe-rok 회록

miracle *n.* ki-jŏk 기적

mirror *n.* kŏ-ul 거울

mirth *n.* chŭl-gŏ-um 즐거움

miscellaneous *adj.* ka-ji kak-saek-ŭi 가지각색의

mischief *n.* chang-nan 장난

mischievous *adj.* chang-nan ha-nŭn 장난하는

misdeed *n.* na-pŭn haeng-sil 나쁜 행실

miser *n.* in-saek-han sa-ram 인색한사람

miserable *adj.* pul-sang-han 불상한

misery *n.* ko-saeng 고생

misfortune *n.* pul-haeng 불행

misjudge *v.* o-sĭm ha-da 오심하다

mislay *v.* it-da 잊다

misprint *n.* o-sĭk 오식

miss *v.t.* no-ch'i-da 놓지다

Miss *n.* (only used in addressing letters) yang 양

missing (in action) haeng-bang pul-myŏng 행방불명

mission *n.* sa-myŏng 사명; (church) sŏn-gyo-hoe 선교회

missionary *n.* sŏn-gyo-sa 선교사

mist *n.* an-gae 안개

mistake *v.t.* t'ul-li-da 틀리다

mistaken *adj.* t'ŭl-lĭn 틀린

mister *n.* ······ssi ······씨

mistletoe *n.* ki-saeng-mok 기생목

mistrust *v.* ŭi-sĭm ha-da 의심하다

misunderstand *v.t.* o-hae ha-da 오해하다

mix *v.* sŏk-da 셖다

mixture *n.* hon hap 혼합

moan *n.* sin-ŭm 신음; *v.* sin-ŭm ha-da 신음하다

moat *n.* mot 못

mob *n.* p'ok-do 폭도

mobile *adj.* um-jig-i-nŭn 움직이는

mock *v.t.* hŭi-rong ha-da 회롱하다; *adj.* kŏ-jĭs-ŭi 거짓의

model n. (pattern) p'yo-bon 표본;
(ideal) mo-bŏm 모범; v. Pon-
dŭ-da 본뜨다

moderate adj. on-gŏn han 온건한

moderation n. chung-yong 중용

moderator n. (Presbyterian)
ch'ong-hoe-jang 총회장

modern adj. hyŏn-dae-ŭi 현대의

modest adj. kyŏm-son han 겸손한

modesty n. kyŏm-son 겸손

modify v. su-jŏng ha-da 수정하다

moist adj. ch'uk-ch'uk han 축축한

moisture n. sŭp-gi 습기

mole n. ki-mi 기미; (animal) tu-
dŏ-jwi 두더쥐

moment n. sun-gan 순간

monarch n. che-wang 제왕

monarchy n. wang-guk 왕국

monastery n. su-do-won 수도원

Monday n. wol-yo-il 월요일

money n. ton 돈; **m.-order** n.
wi-ch'e 위체

monitor n. kam-dok-ja 감독자

monk n. su-do-sŭng 수도승

monkey n. won-sung-i 원숭이

monoplane n. tan-yŏp pi-haeng-gi
단엽 비행기

monopoly n. tok-jŏm 독점

monotonous adj. tan-jo-ro-un 단조
로운

monster n. koe-mul 괴물

month *n.* tal 달

monthly *adj.* tal-ma-da-ŭi 달마다
의

monument *n.* pi-sŏk 비석

mood *n.* ki-bun 기분

moon *n.* tal 달

moonlight *n.* tal-Pit 달빛

moor *n.* hwang-ya 황야; *v.t.*
chŏng-bak ha-da 정박하다

mop *n.* kŏl-le 걸레

moral *adj.* to-dŏk-sang-ŭi 도덕상
의; *n.* kyo-hun 교훈

morale *n.* (military) sa-gi 사기;
(civilian) ki-p'ung 기풍

morality *n.* to-dŏk 도덕

more *adj.* tŏ man-ŭn 더많은; *adv.*
tŏ man-i 더많이

moreover *adv.* kŭ-wi-e 그위에

morning *n.* a-ch'im 아침

morsel *n.* han-ip 한입

mortal *adj.* chuk-ŭl 죽을; *n.* sa-
ram 사람

mortar *n.* hoe 회; (gun) pak-
kyŏk-p'o 박격포

mortgage *n.* chŏ-dang 저당

mosquito *n.* mo-gi 모기; **m. net**
n. mo-gi-jang 모기장

moss *n.* i-ki 이끼

most *adj.* ka-chang man-ŭn 가장
많은

moth *n.* chom 좀

mother *n.* ŏ-mŏ-ni 어머니; **m.-country** pon-guk 본국; **m.-in-law** (for woman) si-ŏ-mŏ-ni 시어머니; (for man) chang-mo 장모; **m.-of-pearl** *n.* chin-ju-cha-gae 진주자개

motion *n.* un-dong 운동

motive *n.* tong-gi 동기

motor *n.* pal-dong-gi 발동기; **m.-cycle** cha-dong cha-jŏn-gŏ 자동자전거

motto *n.* p'yo-ŏ 표어

mould *n.* kom-p'ang-i 곰팡이

mound *n.* ŏn-dŏk 언덕

mount *v.t.* o-rŭ-da 오르다

mountain *n.* san 산; **m. range** san mæk 산맥

mountainous *adj.* san-i man-ŭn 산이많은

mourn *v.* æ-do ha-da 애도하다

mourner *n.* hoe-jang-ja 회장자

mourning *n.* æ-do 애도

mouse *n.* sæng-chwi 생쥐

moustache *n.* su-yŏm 수염

mouth *n.* ip 입

move *v.* um-jĭg-i-ge ha-da 움직이게하다

movement *n.* un-dong 운동

moving *adj.* um-jĭk-in 움직인; **m.-picture** *n.* hwal-tong sa-jĭn 활동사진

mow *v.t.* p'ul-ŭl pi-da 풀을비다

much *adj.* man-ŭn 많은; *adv.*
man-i 많이

mucus *n.* chŏm-aek 점액

mud *n.* chĭn-hŭk 진흙

muddy *adj.* chĭn-hŭk t'u-sŏng-i-ŭi
진흙투성이의

mug *n.* k'ŭn ch'a-chan 큰찻잔

mulberry *n.* byong na-mu 뽕나무

mule *n.* no-sae 노새

multiplication *n.* kop-sem 곱셈

multiply *v.t.* kop ha-da 곱하다

multitude *n.* mu-ri 무리

mumps *n.* i-ha-sŏn-yŏm 이하선염

municipal *adj.* to-si-ŭi 도시의

munition *n.* kun-su-p'um 군수품

murder *n.* sal-ĭn 살인; *v.t.* sal-
hae ha-da 살해하다

murderer *n.* sal-ĭn-ja 살인자

murmur *n.* sok-sak-im 속삭임;
v. sok-sak-i-da 속삭이다

muscle *n.* kŭn yuk 근육

museum *n.* pak-mul-gwan 박물관

mushroom *n.* pŏ-sŏt 버섯

music *n.* ŭm-ak 음악

musical *adj.* ŭm-ak-jŏk 음악적

musician *n.* ŭm-ak-ga 음악가

muslin *n.* me-rin-sŭ 메린스

must *auxil.* ······hae ya ha-da ······
해야하다

mustard *n.* ke-ja 계자

mute *adj.* pŏng-ŏ-ri-ŭi 벙어리의

mutilate *v.* chŏl-dan ha-da 절단하
다

mutiny *n.* p'ok-dong 폭동; *v.*
p'ok-dong-ŭl ir-ŭ-k'i-da 폭동을
일으키다

mutter *v.* sok-sak-i-da 속삭이다

mutton *n.* yang-ko-gi 양고기

mutual *adj.* sang-ho-ŭi 상호의

muzzle *n.* kul-le 굴레

my *pron.* na-ŭi 나의

mystery *n.* sĭn-bi 신비

myth *n.* sĭn-hwa 신화

〔 N 〕

nail *v.t.* mos-ŭl pak-da 못을박다;
n. mot 못; (finger) son-t'op 손
톱

naked *adj.* ot pŏs-ŭn 옷벗은

name *n.* i-rŭm 이름; *v.t.* i-rŭm
chit-da 이름짓다

namely *adv.* chŭk 즉

nap *v.i.* chol-da 졸다; *n.* chol-gi
졸기

napkin *n.* naep'-k'in 냅킨

narcotic *n.* ma-ch'wi-je 마취제

narrate *v.t.* mal ha-da 말하다

narration *n.* i-ya-gi 이야기

narrative *n.* i-ya-gi 이야기

narrow *adj.* chob-ŭn 좁은

nasturtium *n.* hal-lyŏn 한련

nasty *adj.* tŏ-rŏ-un 더러운

nation *n.* na-ra 나라

national *adj.* kuk-ga-ŭi 국가의;
n. kuk-min 국민; n. **anthem** kuk-
ga 국가; n. **defence** kuk-bang
국방; n. **script** (writing) kuk-
mun 국문

nationalism *n.* kuk-ga chu-ŭi 국
가주의

nationality *n.* kuk-jŏk 국적

native *adj.* ch'ŏn-bu-ŭi 천부의;
n. t'o-in 토인; n. **land** pon-
guk 본국; (Korean term for home
area) ko-hyang 고향

natural *adj.* cha-yŏn 자연

naturalization *n.* kwi-hwa 귀화

naturally *adv.* cha-yŏn-i 자연이

nature *n.* cha-yŏn 자연

naughty *adj.* pu-ryang han 부량한

naval *adj.* hae-gun-ŭi 해군의

navigate *v.* hang-haeng ha-da 항행
하다

navigation *n.* hang-hae 항해

navy *n.* hae-gun 해군

neap tide *n.* so-jo-su 소조수

near *adj.* ka-ka-un 가까운; *adv.*
ka-ka-i 가까이; *prep.* ……ka-
kap-ge ……가깝게

Near East *n.* kŭn-dong 근동

nearsighted *adj.* kŭn-si-ŭi 근시
의

nearly *adv.* kŏ-ŭi 거의

neat *adj.* mal-ssuk han 말쑥한

necessary *adj.* p'ir-yo han 필요한

necessity *n.* p'ir-yo-p'um 필요품

neck *n.* mok 목

necklace *n.* mok kŏ-ri 목거리

necktie *n.* nek-t'a-i 넥타이

need *n.* p'ir-yo 필요; *v.* p'ir-yo ha-da 필요하다

needle *n.* pa-nŭl 바늘

needlework *n.* pa-nŭ-jil 바느질

negative *n.* (film) won-p'an 원판; *adj.* so-gok-jŏk 소극적

neglect *v.* ke-ŭl-li ha-da 게을리하다

negotiate *v.* tam-p'an ha-da 담판하다

negotiation *n.* tam-p'an 담판

negro *n.* hŭk-in 흑인

neigh *v.* ŭl-da 울다

neighbor *n.* i-ut sa-ram 이웃사람

neighborhood *n.* kŭn-ch'ŏ 근처

neither ……nor *adv.* ……do-a-ni-yo do……do-a-ni-da ……도아니요 또……도아니다

nephew *n.* cho-k'a 조카

nerve *n.* sĭn-gyŏng 신경

nervous *adj.* sĭn-gyŏng-ŭi 신경의

nervousness *n.* sĭn-gyŏng-jil 신경질

nest *n.* po-gŭm cha-ri 보금자리

net *n.* kŭ-mul 그물; *adj.* (business) sun-i-ik 순이익

network *n.* ……mang ……망; **communications** n. kyo-t'ong-mang 교통망

neutral *adj.* chung-nĭp-ŭi 중립의

never *adv.* kyŏl-k'o……a-ni-da 결코……아니다

never mind! *inter.* kŏk-jŏng-mar-a-ra 걱정말아라 !

nevertheless *conj.* kŭ-rŏm-e-do 그렇에도

new *adj.* sae-ro-un 새로운

new year *n.* sae hae 새해; **New Year's Day** sŏl nal 설날

newly *adv.* sae-ro-i 새로이

news *n.* so-sik 소식

newspaper *n.* sin-mun 신문

next *adj.* ta-ŭm-ŭi 다음의

nice *adj.* cho-ŭn 좋은

nickel *n.* ni-k'el 니켈

nickname *n.* pyŏl-myŏng 별명

niece *n.* cho-k'a dal 조카딸

night *n.* pam 밤; **n. soil** in-bun 인분; **n.-gown** cha-ri-ot 자리옷; **n.-mare** *n.* mu-sŏ-un gum 무서운꿈

nimble *adj.* mĭn-ch'ŏp han 민첩한

nine *n. & adj.* a-hop 아홉

nineteen *n. & adj.* yŏl-a-hop 열아홉

ninety *n.* & *adj.* a-hŭn 아흔

no *adj.* ŏp-nŭn 없는; *adv.* a-ni-o
아니오

noble *adj.* ko-gwi-han 고귀한

nobleman *n.* kwi-jok 귀족

nobody *pron* a-mu-do……a-ni-da
아무도……아니다

nod *v.i.* gŭ-dŏk-i-da 끄덕이다; *n.*
gŭ-dŏk-ĭm 끄덕임

noise *n.* so-ri 소리

noisy *adj.* sĭ-kŭ-rŏ-un 시끄러운

nominal *n.* i-rŭm-man-ŭi 이름만의

nominate *v.t.* chi-myŏng ha-da 지
명하다

non-commissioned-officer *n.* ha-
sa-gwan 하사관

none *pron* a-mu-gŏt-do……ant-da
아무것도……않다

nonsense *n.* mu-ŭi-mi 무의미

non-stop *adj* chŭk-t'ong 즉통

noodles *n.* kuk-su 국수

nook *n.* ku-sŏk 구석

noon *n.* o-jŏng 오정

noose *n.* ol-ga-mi 올가미

nor *conj* …do do-han …a-ni-da
……도또한……아니다

normal *adj.* po-t'ong-ŭi 보통의;
n. school *n.* sa-bŏm hak-kyo 사
범학교

north *n.* & *adj.* puk 북; **n. pole**
n. puk-kŭk 북극

nose *n.* k'o 코

nostril *n.* k'ot ku-nyŏng 콧구녕

not *adv.* ⋯⋯a-ni ⋯⋯아니

notable *adj.* ko-myŏng han 고명한

notary *n.* kong-jŭng-in 공증인;
   (Korean "writer" who performs
   many of the functions of a notary)
   tae-sŏ-in 대서인

note *n.* (musical) ŭm-bu 음부;
   (memo) pi-mang-gi 비망기; *v.*
   (see) chu-ŭi ha-da 주의하다; *v.*
   (write) ki-rŏk ha-da 기럭하다;
   n.-book kong-ch'aek 공책; **n.-
   paper** *n.* p'yŏn-ji-ji 편지지

nothing *n.* a-mu-gŏt-do⋯⋯a-ni-da
   아무것도⋯⋯아니다;   *adv.* cho-
   kŭm-do⋯⋯ant-da 조금도⋯⋯않다

notice *n.* (notification) t'ong-ji 통
   지;   (warning) chu-ŭi 주의;
   v.t. ar-a-ch'ae-da 알아채다

notify *v.t.* t'ong-ji ha-da 통지하다

notion *n.* saeng-gak 생각

notorious *adj.* na-pŭn p'yŏng-p'an
   i-nŭn 나쁜평관있는

noun *n.* myŏng-sa 명사;   **abstract
   n.** ch'u-sang myŏng-sa 추상명사;
   common n. po-t'ong myŏng-sa
   보통명사;   **proper** n. ko-yu
   myŏng-sa 고유명사

nourish *v.t.* ka-ku-da 가꾸다

novel *n.* so-sŏl 소설

novelist *n.* so-sŏl-ga 소설가

November *n.* sĭp-ĭl-wol 십일월

novice *n.* sĭn-ch'ul-nae-gi 신출내기

now *adv.* i-je 이제; *n.* chĭ-kŭm 지금; *conj.* han-i-sang 한이상

nowhere, to be, *v.* a-mu-de-do-ŏp-da 아무데도없다

nude *adj.* pŏl-gŏ pŏs-ŭn 벌거벗은

nuisance *n.* pang-hae 방해

nullify *v.t.* hyo-ryŏk ŏp-ge ha-da 효력없게하다

number *n.* (figure) su cha 수자; (series) pŏn-ho 번호; (suffix) pŏn 번; (house) pŏn-ji 번지

numerous *adj.* su-ga man-ŭn 수가 많은

nun *n.* yŏ-sŭng 여승

nurse *n.* a-ma 아마; (hospital) kan-ho-bu 간호부; *v.* (hospital) kan-ho ha-da 간호하다; *v.* (give suck) chŏs-ŭl chu-da 젖을주다; **wet n.** yu mo 유모

nut *n.* kyŏn-gwa 견과; (of bolt) na-t'ŭ 나트

nutrition *n.* yŏng-yang 영양

〔 O 〕

oak *n.* ch'am na-mu 참나무

oar *n.* no 노

oasis *n.* sa-mak-jung-ŭi ok-ji 사막 중의옥지

oat *n.* kwi-ri 귀리

oath *n.* maeng-sŏ 맹서

obedience *n.* sun-jong 순종

obedient *adj.* sun-jong han 순종한

obey *v.t.* pok-jong ha-da 복종하다

obituary *n.* (sĭn-mun-chi-ŭi) pu-go-ran (신문지의) 부고란

object *n.* (aim) mok-jŏk 목적; (item) mul-ch'e 물체; *v.* pan-dae ha-da 반대하다

objection *n.* pan-dae 반대

objective *adj.* kaek-gwan-jŏk 객관적

obligation *n.* ŭi-mu 의무

oblige *v.* (compel) ŏk-ji-ro ha-ge ha-da 억지로하게하다; (please) hae chu-da 해주다

oblong *n.* chang-bang-hyŏng 장방형

obscure *adj.* hŭi-mi-han 회미한; *v.* hŭi-mi ha-ge ha-da 회미하게하다

observance *n.* chun-su 준수

observation *n.* kwan-ch'al 관찰

observatory *n.* ch'ŏn-mun-dae 천문대

observe *v.* (see) kwan-ch'al ha-da 관찰하다; (obey) chun-su ha-da 준수하다

obstacle *n.* chang-ae 장애

obstetrics *n.* san-gwa hak 산과학

obstruct *v.* pang-hae ha-da 방해
하다

obtain *v.t.* ŏt-da 얻다

obvious *adj.* myŏng-baek han 명백
한

occasion *n.* si-gi 시기

occasionally *adj.* i-da-gŭm 이따
금

occident *n.* sŏ-yang 서양

occupation *n.* (work) chig-ŏp 직업;
(military) chŏm-yŏng 점령

occupy *v.t.* chŏm-yŏng ha-da 점령
하다

occur *v.* ir-ŏ-na-da 일어나다

ocean *n.* tae-yang 대양

o'clock *n.* ……si ……시

octave *n.* che-p'al-ŭm 제팔음

October *n.* si-wol 시월

octopus *n.* mun-ŏ 문어

odd *adj.* (not even) ki-su-ŭi 기수
의; (strange) i-sang han 이상한

odds *n.* is-ŭm-jik han il 있음직한
일

odor *n.* hyang-gi 향기

of *prep.* (poss.) ……ŭi ……의;
(made of) ……ro doen ……로된

off *prep.* ……e sŏ ……에서

offence *n.* choe 죄; (attack) kong-
gyŏk 공격

offend *v.t.* kam-jŏng na-ge ha-da
감정나게하다

offer *v.t.* che-ch'ul ha-da 제출하다; *n.* che-an 제안 「금

offering *n.* (church) hŭn-gŭm 흔금

office *n.* (room) sa-mu-sïl 사무실; (section) sŏ 서

official *adj.* kong-mu-ŭi 공무의

often *adv.* kak-kŭm 각금

oil *n.* ki-rŭm 기름; *v.t.* ki-rŭm-ŭl ch'i-da 기름을치다; *n.* (lubricating) mo-bi-ru 모비루

oilpaper *n.* yu-ji 유지

oily *adj.* ki-rŭm gi i-nŭn 기름까 있는

ointment *n.* yŏn-go 연고

old *adj.* (person) nŭlg-ŭn 늙은; (thing) hŏn 헌

Old Testament *n.* ku-yak 구약

olden *adj.* ye-nal-ŭi 옛날의

older brother *n.* (boy) hyŏng-nïm 형님; (girl) o-pa 오빠

older sister *n.* (girl) hyŏng-nïm 형님; (boy) nu-nïm 누님

olive *n.* kam-nam 감람

Olympics *n.* o-rim-p'ik kyŏng-gi 오림픽경기

omen *n.* chïng-jo 징조

omit *v.t.* bae-not-da 빼놓다

on *prep.* ……wi e ……위에

once *adv.* han-bŏn 한번

one *adj.* han 한; *n.* ha-na 하나

oneself *pron.* cha-gi 자기

onion *n.* yang-p'a 양파

only *adj.* yu-il han 유일한; *adv.* ta-man 다만

onward *adv.* a-p'ŭ-ro 앞으로

open *v.t.* yŏl-da 열다; *adj.* yŏl-lin 열린

opening *n.* (beginning) si-jak 시작; (meeting) kae-hoe 개회; (open space) ku-nyŏng 구녕

opera *n.* o-p'e-ra 오페라

operate *v.i.* (machines) un-jŏn ha-da 운전하다; *v.t.* su-sul ha-da 수술하다

operation *n.* (hospital) su-sul 수술; (military) chak-jŏn 작전

operator *n.* ki-gwan-su 기관수

opinion *n.* ŭi-gyŏn 의견

opium *n.* a-p'yŏn 아편

opponent *n.* pan-dae-ja 반대자

opportunity *n.* ki-hoe 기회

oppose *v.t.* pan-dae ha-da 반대하다

opposite *adj.* chŏng-pan-dae-ŭi 정반대의

opposition *n.* pan-dae 반대

oppress *v.t.* ap-pak ha-da 압박하다

optimism *n.* nak-ch'ŏn-ju-ŭi 낙천주의

or *conj.* hog-ŭn 혹은

oral *n.* ku-du 구두

orange n. kyul 귤; adj. o-ren-ji pit 오렌지빛

orchard n. kwa-su-won 과수원

orchestra n. kwan-hyŏn ak-dae 관현악대

ordain v.t. (religious) sŏng-jik-e im-myŏng ha-da 성직에임명하다

order n. (command) myŏng-yŏng 명령; (arrangement) sun-sŏ 순서; v. (command) myŏng-yŏng ha-da 명령하다; v. (goods) chu-mun ha-da 주문하다

orderly adj. tan-jŏng han 단정한; n. chong-jol 종졸

ordinance n. pŏm-yŏng 법령

ordinary adj. po-t'ong ŭi 보통의

ordnance n. pyŏng-gi 병기

ore n. kwang-sŏk 광석

organization n. (system) cho-jik 조직; (outfit) ki-gwan 기관

organ n. (music) or-gan 올간; (of body) nae-jang 내장

orient n. tong-yang 동양

origin n. kŭn-won 근원

original adj. won-si-ŭi 원시의

ornament n. ch'i-jang 치장

orphan n. ko-a 고아

ostensible adj. kŏt-ŭ-ro-man-ŭi 겉으로만의

ostrich n. t'a-jo 타조

other adj. ta-rŭn 다른

ought *auxil*. gok……yŏ-ya-man
han-da 꼭……여야만한다

ounce *n*. on-sŭ 온스

our *ron* u-ri-dŭl-ŭi 우리들의

out *adv*. pak-e 밖에

outbreak *n*. pal-saeng 발생

outcry *n*. ko-ham 고함

outdoors *adv*. pak-e-sŏ 밖에서

outer *adj*. |pa-kat-jok-ŭi 바깥쪽
의

outfit *n*. chun-bi 준비

outline *n*. yun-gwak 윤곽; *v.t.*
yun-gwak-ŭl kŭ-ri-da 윤곽을그
리다

outlook *n*. hyŏng-se 형세

outpost *n*. chŏn-ch'o 전초

outright *adv*. chŏn-hyŏ 전혀; *adj*.
ch'ŏl-jŏ-jŏk 철저적

outside *n. & adj*. pak-at 밖앗;
adv. & prep. pak-e 밖에

oval *adj*. tal-gyal mo-yang-ŭi 달
걀모양의

oven *n*. sot' 솥

over *prep*. ……ŭi wi-e ……의위에;
adv. kŏn-nŏ-sŏ 건너서

overalls *n*. chag-ŏp-bok 작업복

overboard *adv*. pae-pak-ŭ-ro 배밖
으로

overcoat *n*. oe-t'u 외투

overcome *v.t.* i-gi-da 이기다

overflow *v*. nŏm-ch'i-da 넘치다

overhang *v.* ······ŭi wi-e tal-li-da
······의위에달려다

overhead *adv.* mŏ-ri wi-e 머리위
에; *adj.* mŏ-ri-wi-ŭi 머리위의

overhear *v.t.* yŏt tŭt-da 옆듣다

overlook *v.t.* mot-po-da 못보다

overseer *n.* kam-dok-ja 감독자

overshoe *n.* tŏt sin 덧신

oversight *n.* (omission) mot po-go
chi-nam 못보고지남

overtake *v.t.* da-ra ka-da 따라가
다

overturn *v.* twi-jib-ŏ not-da 뒤집
어놓다

owe *v.t.* pich-ŭl chi-da 빚을지다

owing *adj.* kap'-ŏ-ya hal 갚어야할

owl *n.* ol-bae-mi 올빼미

own *adj.* cha-gi cha-sĭn 자기자신;
v. ka-ji-da 가지다

owner *n.* im-ja 임자

ox *n.* hwang-so 황소

ox-cart *n.* u-ch'a 우차; (popularly
called)ma-ch'a 마차

oxygen *n.* san-so 산소

oyster *n.* kul 굴

〔 P 〕

pace *n.* han kŏr-ŭm 한걸음; *v.*
kŏr-ŭm-ŭ-ro chae-i-da 걸음으로재
이다

pacific *adj*. p'yŏng-on han 평온한

Pacific Ocean *n*. tae p'yŏng yang
대평양

pack *n*. chim 짐; *v.t*. chim-ŭl
ssa-da 짐을싸다

package *n*. so-p'o 소포

packing *n*. chim-ssa-gi 짐싸기

pad *v.t*. sok-ŭl ch'ae-u-da 속을채
우다; *n*. po-ryo 보료; (animal)
pal-pa-dak-sal 발바닥살

padded clothes *n*. som ot 솜옷

padding *n*. ch'ae-u-gi 채우기

paddle *n*. no 노; *v*. no-ro chŏt-
da 노로젓다

paddy-field *n*. non 논

padlock *n*. cha-mŭl-soe 자물쇠

page *n*. p'e-i-ji 페이지; *v*. pul-lŏ
chu-da 불너주다

pagoda *n*. t'ap 탑

pail *n*. pa-ge-ssŭ 바게쓰

pain *n*. a-p'ŭm 아픔

painful *adj*. a-p'ŭn 아픈

paint *n*. p'eng-ki 펭끼; *v*. ch'il
ha-da 칠하다; (pictures) kŭ-ri-
da 그리다

painter *n*. p'eng-ki-jaeng-i 펭끼쟁
이

painting *n*. (picture) kŭ-rŭm 그림

pair *n*. han-ssang 한쌍

palace *n*. tae-gwol 대궐

palate *n*. ip-ch'ŏn-jŏng 입천정

pale *adj*. ch'ang-paek han 창백한

pallbearer *n*. kwan-ŭl tŭ-nŭn sa-ram 관을드는사람

palm *n*. son pa-dak 손바닥; (tree) ya-ja na-mu 야자나무

pamphlet *n*. p'am-p'ül-let' 팜플렡

pan *n*. nam-bi 남비

pancake *n*. p'aen-k'ek 팬켘

pane *n*. yu-ri ch'ang 유리창

panel *n*. kŏng-p'an 경관

panic *n*. tang-hwang 당황

panorama *n*. p'a-no-ra-ma 파노라마

pansy *n*. go-ka-o-rang-k'ae got 꼬까오랑깨꽃

pant *v*. hŏ-dŏk kŏ-ri-da 허덕거리다

panther *n*. pŏm 범

pants *n*. pa-ji 바지

paper *n*. chong-i 종이; **p.-mill** *n*. che-ji kong-jang 제지공장

parachute *n*. nak-ha-san 낙하산

parade *n*. haeng-yŏl 행렬; *v.t.* & *i*. haeng-yŏl ha-da 행렬하다

paradise *n*. nak-won 낙원

paragraph *n*. tan 단

parallel *adj*. p'yŏng haeng-ŭi 평행의; *n*. wi-do-sŏn 위도선

paralysis *n*. ma-bi 마비

parapet *n*. nan-gan 난간

parasite *n*. ki-saeng-mul 기생물

parasol *n.* yang-san 양산

parcel *n.* so-p'o 소포

parch *v.t.* pa-chak ma-rü-da 바짝
마르다

pardon *n.* yong-sŏ 용서; *v.* yong-
sŏ ha-da 용서하다

parenthesis *n.* kwal-ho 괄호

parents *n.* pu-mo 부모

parish *n.* kyo-gu 교구

park *n.* kong-won 공원

parliament *n.* kuk-hoe 국회

parlor *n.* ŭng-jŏp-sil 응접실

parole *n.* sŏn-sŏ 선서

parrot *n.* aeng-mu 앵무

part *n.* pu-bun 부분; *v.* (from)
dŏ-na-da 떠나다; (divide) na-nu-
da 나누다

partial *adj.* pu-bun-jŏk 부분적

participate *v.* ch'am-ga ha-da 참
가하다

participle *n.* pun-sa 분사

particle *n.* p'a-t'i-kŭl 파리끌

particular *adj.* t'ŭk-su han 특수
한; *n.* (particulars) sa-hang 사항

particularly *adv.* t'ŭk-hi 특히

parting *n.* chak-byŏl 작별

partition *n.* ku-bun 구분

partizan (guerilla) *n.* yu-gyŏk-dae
유격대

partly *adv.* pu-bun-jŏk-ŭ-ro 부분
적으로

partner *n.* cho-hap-won 조합원
partnership *n.* cho-hap 조합
party *n.* chan-ch'i 잔치; (political) chŏng-dang 정당
pass *n.* ko-gae 고개; (military) p'a-sŭ 파스; *v.* chi-na-ka-da 지나가다
passage *n.* t'ong-no 통로
passenger *n.* sŭng-gaek 승객
passerby *n.* chi-na-ka-nŭn sa-ram 지나가는사람
passing *adj.* chi-na-ka-nŭn 지나가는
passion *n.* yŏl-jŏng 열정
passionate *adj.* yŏl-jŏng-jŏk 열정적
passive *adj.* su-dong-jŏk 수동적
passport *n.* yŏ-haeng-gwon 여행권
password *n.* am-ho mal 암호말
past *adj.* chi-na-kan 지나간; *n.* kwa-gŏ 과거; *prep.* chi-na-sŏ 지나서
paste *n.* p'ul 풀
pasteboard *n.* ma-bun-ji 마분지
pastime *n.* nol-ŭm 늘음
pastry *n.* kwa-ja 과자
pasture *n.* mok-jang 목장
pat *n.* sal jak dae-rim 살짝때림; *v.* ssŭ-da-dŭm-da 쓰다듬다
patch *n.* ki-un cho-gak 기운조각; *v.* kip-da 깁다
patent *n.* t'ŭk-hŏ 특허

path *n*. kil 길

patience *n*. in-nae 인내

patient *adj*. kyŏn-dil-sŏng i-nŭn 견딜성있는; *n*. pyŏng-ja 병자

patriot *n*. ae-guk-ja 애국자

patriotic *adj*. ae-guk-ŭi 애국의

patriotism *n*. ae-guk-sĭm 애국심

patrol *n*. chŏng-ch'al 정찰; *v*. chŏng-ch'al ha-da 정찰하다

patron *n*. hu-won-ja 후원자

pattern *n*. pon 본

pauper *n*. pin-min 빈민

pause *n*. hyu-sik 휴식; *v.i.* swi-da 쉬다 .

pave *v.t.* p'o-jang ha-da 포장하다

pavement *n*. p'o-jang 포장

pavilion *n*. ch'ŏn mak 천막

paw *n*. pal 발

pawn *n*. chol-pyŏng 졸병; *v.t.* chŏn-dang chap-da 전당잡다

pay *n*. kŭm-yo 급료; *v*. kap'-da 갚다

paymaster *n*. hoe-gye-won 회계원

payment *n*. chi-bul 지불

pea *n*. k'ong 콩

peace *n*. p'yŏng-hwa 평화

peaceful *adj*. t'ae-p'yŏng han 태평한

peach *n*. pok-sung-a 복숭아

peacock *n*. kong-jak 공작

peak *n*. gok-dae-gi 꼭대기

peal *n.* chong-so-ri 종소리
peanut *n.* dang k'ong 땅콩
pear *n.* pae 배
pearl *n.* chin-ju 진주
peasant *n.* nong-bu 농부
peat *n.* i-dan 이단
pebble *n.* cha-gal 자갈
peck *v.* jo-da 쪼다
peculiar *adj.* i-sang han 이상한
pedal *n.* pal-p'an 발판
peddler *n.* haeng-sang-in 행상인
pedestal *n.* chu-ch'u-dae 주추대
pedestrian *n.* po-haeng-ja 보행자
peel *n.* gŏp-jil 껍질; *v.t.* gŏp-jil pŏt-gi-da 껍질벗기다
peep *n.* yŏt pom 엿봄; *v.i.* yŏt po-da 엿보다
peer *v.i.* cha-se-hi po-da 자세히보다
peevish *adj.* sin-gyŏng-jil-in 신경질인
peg *n.* na-mu mot 나무못
pen *n.* (cage) u-ri 우리; (brush) put 붓; (steel) ch'ŏl-p'il 철필; (fountain) man-nyŏn-p'il 만년필
penalty *n.* pŏl 벌
pencil *n.* yŏn-p'il 연필
pendulum *n.* si-gye-ch'u 시계추
penetrate *v.* gwe-da 꿰다
penholder *n.* ch'ol-p'il-dae 철필대
peninsula *n.* pan-do 반도

penis *n.* cha-ji 자지

penitence *n.* nwi-u-ch'im 뉘우침

penmanship *n.* sŭp-ja 습자

penniless *adj.* han-p'un ŏp-nŭn 한
푼없는

pension *n.* yŏn-gŭm 연금

peony *n.* mo-ran 모란

people *n.* ĭn-mĭn 인민

pepper *n.* (black) ho-ch'u 호추;
(red) ko-ch'u 고추

peppermint *n.* pak-ha 박하

peppery *adj.* mae-un 매운

per cent *n.* paek-bun 백분

perch *v.* ol-la ant-da 올라앉다; *n.*
hwae 해

percussion *n.* ch'ung gyŏk 충격

perennial *adj.* kyŏng-yŏn-jŏk 경
년적

perfect *adj.* wan-jŏn han 완전한;
v.t. wan-sŏng ha-da 완성하다

perfectly *adv.* wan-jŏn hi 완전히

perform *v.t.* i-ru-da 이루다

performance *n.* su-haeng 수행

perfume *n.* hyang-gi 향기

perhaps *adv.* a-ma 아마; *inter.*
kŭl-ssi 글쎄

peril *n.* wi-hŏm 위험

period *n.* (dot) ma-ch'im-p'yo 마
침표; (time) si-dae 시대

periodical *n.* chŏng-gi-gan-haeng
chap-ji 정기간행잡지

periscope n. cham-mang-gyŏng 잠망경

perish v.t. myŏl-mang ha-da 멸망하다

permission n. hŭ-ga 허가

permit n. hŏ-ga chŭng 허가증; v. hŏ-rak ha-da 허락하다

perpendicular adj. su-jik 수직

perpetual adj. yŏng-sok han 영속한

perplex v.t. ŏ-chŏl-ji mo-rŭ-ge ha-da 어쩔지모르게하다

perseverance n. gut-gut ham 꿋꿋함

persevere v.i. ch'am-da 참다

persimmon n. kam 감; **dried p.** kok kam 곡감

persist v.i. ko-jip ha-da 고집하다

person n. sa-ram 사람

personal adj. cha-gi-ŭi 자기의

personnel n. in-won 인원; **p. office** in-sa-ch'ŏ 인사처

perspiration n. dam 땀

perspire v. dam-nae-da 땀내다

persuade v.t. kwon-go ha-da 권고하다

pertinent adj. chŏk-ch'ŏl han 적철한

pessimism n. yŏm-se 염세

pest n. na-pŭn pŏl-lŏ-ji 나쁜벌너지

pestilence *n.* huk-sa pyŏng 흑사병

pet *adj.* kwi-yŏ-un 귀여운; *n.* kwi-yŏ-un gŏt 귀여운것; *v.t.* kwi-ae ha-da 귀애하다

petal *n.* got ip' 꽃잎

petition *n.* t'an-won 탄원; *v.* t'an-won ha-da 탄원하다

petroleum *n.* sŏk-yu 석유

petticoat *n.* sok-ch'i-ma 속치마

petty *adj.* chŏk-ŭn 적은; **p. offi-cer** *n.* ha-sa 하사

pew *n.* chwa-sŏk 좌석

phantom *n.* to-kae-bi 도깨비

pharmacist *n.* yak-che-sa 약제사

pheasant *n.* gwong 꿩; (male) chaeng-ki 쟁끼; (female) ga-t'u-ri 까투리

phenomenon *n.* hyŏn-sang 현상

philanthropy *n.* pak-ae 박애

philosophy *n.* ch'ŏl hak 철학

phoenix *n.* pul-sa-jo 불사조

phone *n.* chŏn-hwa 전화; *v.* chŏn-hwa ha-da 전화하다

phonetic *adj.* ŭm-sŏng-ŭi 음성의

phonograph *n.* yu-sŏng-gi 유성기

phosphate *n.* in-san-yŏm 인산염

phosphorus *n.* in 인

photograph *n.* sa-jin 사진; *v.* sa-jin pak-da 사진박다

phrase *n.* suk-ŏ 숙어

physical *adj.* yuk-ch'e-ŭi 육체의;
p. education ch'e-yuk 체육; **p.
examination** sin-ch'e kŭm-sa 신
체금사; **p. science** *n.* cha-yŏn
kwa hak 자연과학

physician *n.* ŭi-sa 의사

physics *n.* mul-li hak 물리학

piano *n.* p'i-a-no 피아노

pick *n.* kok-kwaeng-i 곡괭이; *v.*
(flowers) da-da 따다

pickle *n.* kim-ch'i 김치

picnic *n.* won-jok 원족

picture *n.* kŭ-rĭm 그림

pie *n.* p'a-i 파이

piece *n.* han cho-gak 한조각

pier *n.* pu-du 부두

pierce *v.t.* dul-da 뚫다

pig *n.* twae-ji 돼지

pigeon *n.* pi-dul-gi 비둘기; **p.-
hole** *n.* kan-sa-ri 간사리

pile *n.* mu-de-gi 무데기; *v.* ssah-
ta 쌓다

pilgrim *n.* sun-ye-ja 순례자

pilgrimage *n.* sun-ye 순례

piling *n.* mal-tuk 말뚝

pill *n.* hwan-yak 환약

pillage *v.t.* yak-t'al ha-da 약탈하
다

pillar *n.* ki-dung 기둥

pillow *n.* pyŏ-gae 벼개; (wooden)
mok-ch'im 목침

pilot *n.* (plane) cho-jong-sa 조종
사; (ship) hyang-do 향도

pimple *n.* yŏ-dŭ-rŭm 여드름

pin *n.* p'in 핀; **safety p.** *n.* an-
jŏn p'in 안전핀; **hair p.** mŏ-ri
p'in 머리핀

pincers *n.* chip-gae 집개

pinch *v.t.* chip-da 집다

pine *n.* sol-na-mu 솔나무 「플

pineapple *n.* p'a-in-aɔ-p'ul 파인애

pink *adj.* pok-sa got pich-ŭi 복사
꽃빛의; *n.* pae-raeng-i got 패챙
이꽃

pioneer *n.* kae-ch'ŏk-ja 개척자

pious *adj.* sin-ang-sim man-ŭn 신
앙심많은

pipe *n.* tam-bae-dae 담뱃대

pirate *n.* hae-jŏk 해적

pistil *n.* am-sul 암술

pistol *n.* kwon-ch'ong 권총

piston *n.* p'i-sŭ-t'ŭn 피스튼

pit *n.* ham-jŏng 함정

pitch *n.* p'i-ch'wi 피취; *v.* tŏn-
ji-da 던지다; (set up) ch'i-da
치다

pitcher *n.* mul-pyŏng 물병;
(sports) p'it'-ch'wo 핕취

pitchfork *n.* soe-sŭ-rang 쇠스랑

piteous *adj.* pul-sang han 불상한

pity *n.* yŏn-min 연민; *v.* hi-yŏ-
gi-da 히여기ㅋ

place *n.* chang-so 장소; *v.t.* tu-da 두다

plague *n.* hŭk-sa-pyŏng 흑사병

plain *adj.* myŏng-baek han 명백한; *n.* p'yŏng-ya 평야

plan *n.* kye-hoek 계획; *v.t.* kye-hoek ha-da 계획하다

plane *n.* pi-haeng-gi 비행기; (carpenter) tae-p'ae 대패; *v.* tae-p'ae-jil ha-da 대패질하다

planet *n.* yu-sŏng 유성

plank *n.* nŏl-p'an-jak 널판짝

plant *n.* sik-mul 식물; *v.t.* sim-da 심다

plaster *n.* hoe 회; *v.t.* hoe-ch'il-ŭl ha-da 회칠을하다

plastic *adj.* p'ul-lae-sŭ-t'ik 풀래스틱

plate *n.* chŏp-si 접시

plateau *n.* ko-won 고원

platform *n.* yŏn-dan 연단; (station) sŭng-gang-jang 승강장

play *v.i.* nol-da 놀다; *v.t.* ······ha-da ······하다; *n.* yŏn-gŭk 연극

playground *n.* un-dong-jang 운동장

playmate *n.* chang-nan tong-mu 장난동무

plaything *n.* chang-nan kam 장난감

plead *v.* sŏl-bok ha-da 설복하다; (law) pyŏn-ho ha-da 변호하다

pleasant *adj.* yu-k'wae han 유쾌한

please *v.t.* chil-gŏp-ge ha-da 질겁게하다; (in Korean a suffix) …… chu-sip-si-yo ……주십시요

pleasing *adj.* yu-k'wae han 유쾌한

pleasure *n.* k'wae-rak 쾌락

plentiful *adj.* p'ung-bu han 풍부한

plenty *n.* p'ung-bu 풍부

pleurisy *n.* nŭk-mak-yŏm 늑막념

pliers *n.* chip-ge 집게

plod *v.i.* du-bŏk du-bŏk kŏt-da 뚜벅뚜벅걷다

plot *n.* mo-ryak 모략; (ground) t'ŏ 터; *v.t.* ŭm-mo ha-da 음모하다

plough, plow *n.* chaeng-gi 쟁기; *v.t.* kal-da 갈다

pluck *v.t.* dŭt-da 뜯다 「막다

plug *n.* ma-gae 마개; *v.t.* mak-da

plum *n.* o-yat 오얏

plumage *n.* kit 깃

plumbing *n.* su-do 수도

plumb-line *n.* ch'u-sŏn 추선

plump *adj.* sal-jin 살진

plunder *v.* yak-t'al ha-da 약탈하다

plunge *v.* tŭl-jin ha-da 들진하다

plural *n.* pok-su 복수

plus *prep.* tŏ-ha-yŏ 더하여

pneumonia *n.* p'ye-yŏm 페념

pocket *n.* ho chu-mŏ-ni 호주머니;
p.book chi-gap 지갑; p.money
chan-ton 잔돈 「자욱

pockmark *n.* ŏlk-ŭn cha-uk 얽은

pod *n.* gŏp-jil 껍질

poem *n.* si 시

poet *n.* si-in 시인

poetry *n.* si 시

point *n.* chŏm 점; *v.* son-ŭ-ro
ka-ri-ch'i-da 손으로가리치다

poison *n.* tok yak 독약; *v.* tok-ŭl
nŏ-ta 독을넣다

poke *v.t.* ssu-si-da 쑤시다

poker *n.* pu-ji-kaeng-i 부지깽이

polar *adj.* kŭk-ji-ŭi 극지의

pole *n.* chang-dae 장대; (plus)
yang-gŭk 양극; (minus) ŭm-gŭk
음극

police *n.* kyŏng-ch'al 경찰

policeman *n.* kyŏng-gwan 경관

police-station *n.* kyŏng-ch'al-sŏ
경찰서

policy *n.* chŏng-ch'aek 정책

polish *n.* tak-nŭn ki-rŭm 닦는기
름; *v.* tak-da 닦다

polite *adj.* kong-son han 공손한

politeness *n.* kong-son 공손

political *adj.* chŏng-ch'i-ŭi 정치의;
p. economy kyŏng-je hak 경제학;
p. party chŏng-dang 정당; p.
science chŏng-ch'i hak 정치학

politician *n.* chŏng-ch'i-ga 정치가
politics *n.* chŏng-ch'i 정치
poll *n.* t'u-p'yo 투표
pollen *n.* hoa-bun 화분
pond *n.* mot 못
ponder *v.* kip'-i saeng-gak ha-da 깊이생각하다
pontoon bridge *n.* pae ta-ri 배다리
pony *n.* chak-ŭn mal 작은말
pool *n.* p'ul 풀
poor *adj.* ka-nan han 가난한; **p. crop** hyung-jak 흉작
pope *n.* ro-o-ma kyo hwang 로오마교황
poplar *n.* p'o-p'ŭl-la 포플라
poppy *n.* yang-gwi-bi 양귀비
popular *adj.* (common) t'ong-sok-jŏk 통속적; (well liked) in-gi i-nŭn 인기있는
popularity *n.* in-gi 인기
population *n.* in-gu 인구
porcelain *n.* cha-gi 자기
porch *n.* mun-gan 문간
pore *n.* mo-gong 모공
pork *n.* twae-ji ko-gi 돼지고기
porridge *n.* chuk 죽
port *n.* hang-gu 항구
porter *n.* chim-kun 짐꾼
portion *n.* pae-dang 배당
portrait *n.* hwa-sang 화상

position *n.* wi-ch'i 위치

positive *adj.* chŏk-gŭk-jŏk 적극적

positively *adv.* (for sure) hwak-sil-hi 확실히

possess *v.t.* so-yu ha-da 소유하다

possession *n.* so-yu 소유

possessive *adj.* so-yu-ŭi 소유의

possible *adj.* ka-nŭng han 가능한

possibility *n.* ka-nŭng sŏng 가능성

possibly *adv.* (perhaps) a-ma 아마

post *n.* (mail) u-p'yŏn 우편; *v.t.* pu-ch'i-da 부치다; **parcel p.** so-p'o 소포

postage *n.* u-se 우세; **p.-stamp** u-p'yo 우표

postcard *n.* yŏp-sŏ 엽서

poster *n.* p'o-ssŭ-t'ŏ 포쓰터

postman *n.* pae-dal-bu 배달부

post-office *n.* u-p'yŏn-guk 우편국

postpone *v.t.* yŏn-gi ha-da 연기하다

postscript *n.* ch'u-baek 추백

posture *n.* t'ae-do 태도

pot *n.* sot' 솥; **chamber p.** yo-gang 요강

potato *n.* kam-ja 감자; **sweet p.** ko-gu-ma 고구마

potential *adj.* ch'am-jae-jŏk 참재적

pottery *n.* chil-kŭ-rŭt 질그릇

pouch *n.* chu-mŏ-ni 주머니

poultry *n.* ka-gŭm 가금

pounce *v.i.* ch'ae-ŏ ka-da 채어가다

pound *n.* kŭn 근; *v.t.* tu-dŭl-gi-da 두들기다

pour *v.* hŭl-li-da 흘리다

poverty *n.* ka-nan 가난

powder *n.* ka-ru 가루; (explosive) hwa-yak 화약

power *n.* kang-yak 강약; **electric p.** chŏl-lyŏk 전력; **horse p.** ma-ryŏk 마력; **p. house** pal-chŏn-so 발전소; **p. of attorney** wi-im-jang 위임장

powerful *adj.* him-sen 힘센

practical *adj.* sil-chi-jŏk 실지적

practice *n.* yŏn-sŭp 연습; (habit) sŭp-gwan 습관

practise *v.* yŏn-sŭp ha-da 연습하다

prairie *n.* k'ŭn ch'o-won 큰초원

praise *n.* ch'ing-ch'an 칭찬; *v.t.* ch'ing-ch'an ha-da 칭찬하다

prank *n.* chang-nan 작란

prawn *n.* sae-u 새우

pray *v.* (entreat) pil-da 빌다; (to God) ki-do ha-da 기도하다

prayer *n.* ki-do 기도

pre- (suffix in Korean) ……i-jŏn-ŭi ……이전의

preach v. chŏn-do ha-da 전도하다
preacher n. chŏn-do-sa 전도사
precaution n. cho-sim 조심
precede v.t. ap'-sŏ-da 앞서다
precedent n. chŏl-ye 전례
preceding adj. chŏn-ŭi 전의
precept n. kyŏk-ŏn 격언
precious adj. kwi-jung han 귀중한
precipice n. chŏl-byŏk 절벽
precise adj. chŏng-hwak han 정확
한
predestination n. ye-jŏng 예정
predicate n. sŏ-sul-bu 서술부
predict v. ye-ŏn ha-da 예언하다
preface n. sŏ-mun 서문
prefecture n. hyŏn 현
prefer v.t. cha-ra-ri……rŭl ch'wi
ha-da 차라리……를취하다
prefix n. chŏp-tu-ŏ 접두어
pregnant adj. ing-t'ae han 잉태한
prejudice n. p'yŏn-gyŏn 편견
preliminary adj. ch'o-bo-jŏk 초보
적
premier n. ch'ong-ni 총리
preparation n. chun-bi 준비
prepare v.t. chun-bi ha-da 준비하
다
preposition n. chŏn-ch'i-sa 전치사
Presbyterian n. chang-no kyo hoe-
won 장로교회원; adj. chang-no
kyo hoe-ŭi 장로교회의

presbytery *n.* tang-hoe 당회

prescribe *v.* kyu-jŏng ha-da 규정
하다

prescription *n.* ch'ŏ-bang 처방

presence *n.* chon-jae 존재

present *n.* & *adj.* hyŏn-jae (ŭi) 현
재 (의) ; *v.t.* chu-da 주다; *n.*
(gift) sŏn-mul 선물; **to be p.**
v. ch'ul-sŏk ha-da 출석하다

presently *adv.* ŏl-ma an-is-ŏ 얼마
안있어

preserve *v.t.* po-jon ha-da 보존하다

president *n.* (of country) tae-t'ong-
yŏng 대통령; **president of** ......
...... chang ......장

press *v.t.* nu-rŭ-da 누르다; *n.* sin-
mun 신문

pressure *n.* ap-yŏk 압력

presume *v.t.* ch'u-ch'ŭk ha-da 추
측하다

pretend *v.t.* ......ch'e ha-da ......체
하다

pretext *n.* ku-sil 구실

pretty *adj.* ko-un 고운

prevail *v.i.* i-gi-da 이기다

prevent *v.* pang-ji ha-da 방지하다

prevention *n.* ye-bang 예방; **fire
p.** pang-hwa 방화

previous *adj.* i-jŏn-ŭi 이전의

prey *v.* chap-ŏ mŏk-da 잡어먹다

price *n.* kap' 값

priceless *adj.* kwi-jung han 귀중한
prick *v.t.* ji-rŭ-da 찌르다
pride *n.* cha-rang 자랑; **p. oneself**
   v.t. cha-rang ha-da 자랑하다
priest *n.* sin-bu 신부; **Buddhist**
   p. chung 중
primary *adj.* pol-lae-ŭi 본래의;
   p. school so-hak-kyo 소학교
prime *adj.* ch'ŏt jae-ŭi 첫째의; **p.**
   minister kuk-mu-ch'ong-ni 국무
   총리
primer *n.* ip-mun-ch'aek 입문책
primitive *adj.* won-si-jŏk 원시적
prince *n.* wang-ja 왕자
princess *n.* wang-yŏ 왕녀
principal *adj.* che-il-ŭi 제일의;
   n. kyo-jang 교장
principle *n.* won-ch'ŭk 원측
print *v.t.* in-swae ha-da 인쇄하다
printer *n.* in-swae ŏp-ja 인쇄업자
printing *n.* in-swae 인쇄
prior *adj.* chŏn-ŭi 전의
priority *n.* u-sŏn-gwon 우선권
prison *n.* ka n-ok 감옥
prisoner *n.* choe-su 죄수; **p. of**
   war *n.* p'o-ro 포로
private *adj.* sa-sa-ŭi 사사의; *n.*
   pyŏng-jŏng 병정
privilege *n.* t'ŭk-gwon 득권
prize *n.* sang 상; *v.t.* so-jung-hi
   ha-da 소중히하다

probable *adj.* ······hal pŏp han ··· ···할법한

problem *n.* mun-je 문제

proceed *v.i.* chin-haeng ha-da 진행하다

proceedings *n.* ŭi-sa 의사

process *n.* pang-pŏp 방법

procession *n.* haeng-yŏl 행렬

proclaim *v.t.* sŏn-ŏn ha-da 선언하다

proclamation *n.* sŏn-ŏn 선언

procurator *n.* kŭm-sa 금사

procure *v.t.* ŏt-da 얻다

prodigal *adj.* nang-bi ha-nŭn 낭비하는

produce *v.t.* na-ta 낳다; *n.* san-ch'ul 산출

product *n.* saeng-san-mul 생산물

production *n.* saeng-san 생산

productive *adj.* pi-ok han 비옥한

profanity *n.* tok-sin-jŏk ŏn-haeng 독신적언행

profession *n.* chig-ŏp 직업

professor *n.* kyo-su 교수

proficient *adj.* nŭng-suk han 능숙한

profit *n.* i-ik 이익

program *n.* sun-sŏ 순서

progress *n.* chin-bo 진보; *v.i.* na-a ka-da 나아가다

progressive *adj.* chin-bo-jŏk 진보적

prohibit *v.t.* kŭm ha-da 금하다

project *n.* kye-hoek 계획; *v.t.*
(on screen) yŏng-sa ha-da 영사하
다; *v.* (jut out) pul-suk na-o-da
뿔숙나오다

prolong *v.t.* yŏn-jang ha-da 연장
하다

promenade *n.* san-po 산보

prominent *adj.* t'wi-ŏ-na-on 튀어
나온

promise *n.* yak-sok 약속; *v.t.*
yak-sok ha-da 약속하다

promote *v.t.* sŭng-jin si-k'i-da 승
진시키다

promotion *n.* sŭng-jin 승진

prompt *adj.* ba-rŭn 빠른; *v.* p'u-
ram-t'ŭ ha-da 푸람트하다

promptly *adj.* chae-ba-rŭ-ge 재빠
르게

pronoun *n.* tae-myŏng-sa 대명사

pronounce *v.* par-ŭm ha-da 발음하
다

pronunciation *n.* pa-rŭm 발음

proof *n.* chŭng-gŏ 증거; (of book)
kyo-jŏng 교정

propaganda *n.* sŏn-jŏn 선전

propeller *n.* p'u-ro-p'el-la 푸로펠
라

proper *adj.* chŏk-dang han 적당한

properly *adv.* chŏk-dang ha-ge 적
당하게

property *n.* so-yu 소유
prophecy *n.* ye-ŏn 예언
prophesy *v.* ye-ŏn ha-da 예언하다
prophet *n.* ye-ŏn-ja 예언자
proportion *n.* pi-ryul 비율
proposal *n.* che-ŭi 제의
propose *v.* che-ŭi ha-da 제의하다
prose *n.* san-mun 산문
prosecute *v.t.* ki-so ha-da 기소하다
prosecutor *n.* kŏm-sa 검사
prospect *n.* ye-sang 예상
prosper *v.* pŏn-ch'ang ha-da 번창하다
prosperity *n.* pŏn-ch'ang 번창
prosperous *adj.* pŏn-ch'ang han 번창한
prostitute *n.* ch'ang-yŏ 창녀
protect *v.t.* po-ho ha-da 보호하다
protection *n.* po-ho 보호
protector *n.* po-ho-ja 보호자
protege *n.* po-ho pat-nŭn ja 보호받는차
protest *v.* hang-ŭi ha-da 항의하다
Protestant *n.* sin-kyo-do 신교도
proud *adj.* cha-rang ha-nŭn 자랑하는
prove *v.* chŭng-myŏng ha-da 증명하다
proverb *n.* i-ŏn 이언
provide *v.* chun-bi ha-da 준비하다

province *n.* to 도
provisional *adj.* im-si-ŭi 임시의
provoke *v.* cha-gŭk ha-da 자극하다
prowl *v.* ka-man-i tor-a-ta-ni-da 가만 이돌아다니다
prudent *adj.* sin-jung han 신중한
pry *v.i.* yŏt po-da 엿보다
psalm *n.* si-p'yŏn 시편
psychology *n.* sim-ni hak 심리학
public *adj.* kong-jung-ŭi 공중의
publish *v.t.* ch'ul-p'an ha-da 출판하다
publisher *n.* ch'ul-p'an ŏp-ja 출판업자
publishing *n.* ch'ul-p'an 출판
pudding *n.* p'u-ding 푸딩
puddle *n.* mul ung-tŏng-i 물웅덩이
puff *n.* huk nae-pul-gi 훅내불기;
　v. huk nae-pul-da 훅내불다
pull *v.* gŭl-da 끌다
pulley *n.* hwal-ch'a 활차
pulp *n.* p'al-p'ŭ 팔프
pulpit *n.* sŏl-gyo-dan 설교단
pulse *n.* maek 맥
pump *n.* p'om-p'ŭ 폼프; *v.* p'om-p'ŭ-jil ha-da 폼프질하다
pumpkin *n.* ho-bak 호박
pun *n.* kyŏt-mal 곁말
punch *v.* (a hole) dul-ta 뚫다; (hit) t'a-gyŏk-ŭl chu-da 타격을주다

punctual *adj.* si-gan-ŭl chi-k'i-nŭn 시간을지키는

punctuality *n.* si-gan ŏm-su 시간엄수

punctuation *n.* ku-jŏl na-nu-gi 구절나누기

puncture *n.* bang-ku 빵꾸; *v.* bang-ku na-da 빵꾸나다

punish *v.t.* pŏl ha-da 벌하다

punishment *n.* hyŏng pŏl 형벌

pupil *n.* hak saeng 학생

puppet *n.* koe-roe 괴뢰

puppy *n.* kang-a-ji 강아지

purchase *v.t.* sa-da 사다; *n.* ku-ip 구입

pure *adj.* sun-su-han 순수한

purify *v.t.* chŏng-je ha-da 정제하다

purity *n.* sun-su 순수

purple *n. & adj.* cha saek 자색

purpose *n.* mok-jŏk 목적

purposely *adv.* il-bu-rŏ 일부러

purr *v.* ka-rŭng ka-rŭng ha-da 가릉가릉하다

purse *n.* chi-gap 지갑

purser *n.* sa-mu-jang 사무장

pursue *v.t.* da-ra ka-da 따라가다

pursuit *n.* ch'u-jŏk 추적

pus *n.* ko-rŭm 고름

push *n.* mil-gi 밀기; *v.* mil-da 밀다

put *v.* no-ta 놓다

puzzle *n.* nan-mun 난문; *v.* koe-rop-hi-da 괴롭히다

pyramid *n.* kŭm-ja-t'ap 금자탑

[Q]

quack *v.* wa-gŭl wa-gŭl dŏ-dŭl-da 와글와글떠들다

quail *n.* me-ch'u-ra-gi 메추라기

quaint *adj.* ki-myo han 기묘한

quake *v.i.* hŭn-dŭl-li-da 흔들이다

Quaker *n.* k'we-i-k'ŏ-ŏ kyo-do 퀘이커어교도

qualification *n.* cha-gyŏk 자격

qualify *v.* cha-gyŏk-ŭl ŏt-da 자격을얻다

quality *n.* p'um-jil 품질

quantity *n.* yang 양

quarantine *n.* kyŏng-ni 격리

quarrel *n.* chaeng-non 쟁론; *v.* chaeng-ron ha-da 쟁론하다

quarrelsome *adj.* ssa-u-gi cho-a ha-nŭn 싸우기좋아하는

quarry *v.* jo-a-nae-da 쪼아내다; *n.* ch'ae-sŏk-jang 채석장; (prey) mi-ki 미끼

quarter *n.* sa-bun-ji-il 사분지일

quartermaster *n.* (army)kun-su-gwan 군수관; (ship) cho-da-so 조타수

quarters *n.* suk-sa 숙사
quartz *n.* sŏk-yŏng 석영
quay *n.* pu-du 부두
queen *n.* yŏ-wang 여왕
queer *adj.* i-sang han 이상한
quest *n.* ch'at-gi 찾기
question *n.* chil-mun 질문; *v.t.*
   mut-da 묻다
quick *adj.* ba-rŭn 빠른
quickly *adj.* ba-rŭ-ge 빠르게
quicksilver *n.* su-ŭn 수은
quiet *adj.* ko-yo han 고요한; *n.*
   p'yŏng-on 평온
quietly *adv.* cho-yong-hi 조용히
quilt *n.* i-bul 이불
quince *n.* yang-mo-gwa 양모과
quinine *n.* kŭm-gye-rap 금계랍
quit *v.* kŭ-man-tu-da 그만두다
quite *adv.* gwae 꽤
quiver *n.* hwa-sil-t'ong 화살통;
   v.i. dŏl-da 떨다
quotation *n.* in-yong 인용
quote *v.* in-yong ha-da 인용하다

〔 R 〕

rabbit *n.* t'o-ki 토끼
rabies *n.* kwa-gyŏn-pyŏng 광견병
race *n.* kyŏng-ju 경주; *v.i.* kyŏng-
   ju ha-da 경주하다; *n.* (people)
   in-jong 인종
racial *adj.* in-jong-jŏk 인종적

rack *n.* sŏn-pan 선반

racket *n.* ra-k'et' 라켙; (din) ya-dan 야단

radiant *adj.* pit na-nŭn 빛나는; (radiating) pok-sa ha-nŭn 복사하는

radiate *v.* pok-sa ha-da 복사하다

radiator *n.* pok-sa ch'e 복사체

radio *n.* ra-di-o 라디오

radio-activity *n.* pang-sa-nŭng 방사능

radish *n.* mu 무

radium *n.* ra-di-um 라디움

raft *n.* de-mok 뗏목

rag *n.* kŏl-le cho-gak 걸레조각

rage *n.* kyŏk-bun 격분; *v.i.* kyŏk-bun ha-da 격분하다

ragged *adj.* nu-dŏ-gi-ŭi 누더기의

rags *n.* (ragged) nu-dŏ-gi 누더기

raid *n.* sŭp-gyŏk 습격; *v.* sŭp-gyŏk ha-da 습격하다

rail *n.* ch'ŏl-lo 철로

railing *n.* nan-gan 난간

railroad *n.* ch'ŏl-to 철도

rain *n.* pi 비; *v.* pi o-da 비오다

rainbow *n.* mu-ji-gae 무지개

raincoat *n.* u-jang 우장

rainy *adj.* pi manh-i-o-nŭn 비많이오는

raise *v.* (lift up) ir-ŭ-k'i-da 일으키다; (lift) ol-li-da 올리다; (rear) kil-lŭ-da 길르다

raisin *n.* kŏn p'o-do 건포도

rake *n.* kal-k'wi 갈퀴; *v.* kal-k'wi-jil ha-da 갈퀴질하다

ram *n.* sut-yang 숫양; *v.* pu-di-ch'i-da 부디치다

ramble *v.* kŏ-nil-da 거닐다

ramp *n.* sŏng-sa-myŏn 성사면

rampart *n.* sŏng-byŏk 성벽

random *adj.* maeng-mok-jŏk in 맹목적인

range *n.* (scope) pŏm-wi 범위; (mountain) san-maek 산맥; (rifle) sa-jang 사장; (distance) kŏ-ri 거리

rank *n.* (row) chul 줄; (grade) kye-kup 계급

ransack *v.* yak-t'al ha-da 약탈하다

ransom *n.* sok-joe-gŭm 속죄금; *v.* mom-kaps-ŭl chu-go bae-nae-da 몸값을주고빼내다

rap *v.* dang-dang tu-dŭ-ri-da 땅땅 두드리다

rape *v.* kang-gan ha-da 강간하다

rapid *adj.* ba-rŭn 빠른

rare *adj.* tŭ-mŭn 드믄

rascal *n.* ak-han-nom 악한놈

rash *adj.* mu-mo han 무모한; *n.* pal-jin 발진

rashly *adv.* mu-mo ha-ge 무모하게

rat *n.* chwi 쥐　　　「do 속도

rate *n.* pi-ryul 비률; (speed) sok-

rather *adv.* ch'a-ra-ri 차라리

ratification *n.* pi-jun 비준

ration *n.* pae-gŭp 배급

rational *adj.* i-sŏng-jŏk 이성적

rattle *v.* so-ri na-da 소리나다

ravage *v.* hwang-p'ye ha-ge ha-da 황폐하게하다

raven *n.* ga-ma-gwi 까마귀

ravine *n.* san-kol-ja-gi 산골짜기

raw *adj.* saeng…… 생……

ray *n.* kwang-sŏn 광선

razor *n.* myŏn-do k'al 면도칼

reach *v.* p'yŏ-da 펴다

read *v.* ilk-da 읽다

reader *n.* tok-bon 독본

readily *adv.* swip-sa-ri 쉽사리

reading *n.* ilk-gi 읽기

ready *adj.* chun-bi-ga doen 준비 가된

real *adj.* chin-jŏng han 진정한

reality *n.* hyŏn-sil-sŏng 현실성

realize *v.t.* sil-hyŏn ha-da 실현하다

really *adv.* sil-sang ch'am-ŭ-ro 실상참으로

reap *v.* kŏd-ŏ tŭ-ri-da 걷어드리다

reappear *v.* ta-si na-t'a-na-da 다시나타나다

rear *n.* twi 뒤; *v.t.* kil-lŭ-da 길르다

rearrange *v.* ta-si pa-ro chap-da 다시바로잡다

reason *n.* i-sŏng 이성; (cause) i-yu 이유

reasonable *adj.* hap-ni-jŏk-in 합리적인

reassure *v.* an-sim-si-k'i-da 안심시키다

rebel *n.* pan-yŏk-ja 반역자; *v.i.* pan-yŏk ha-da 반역하다

rebellion *n.* pan-yŏk 반역

rebuild *v.* che-gŏn ha-da 재건하다

rebuke *v.* gu-jit-da 꾸짖다

recall *v.* ki-ŏk ha-da 기억하다

recapture *v.* ta-si put-chap-da 다시붓잡다

recede *v.* mul-lŏ-sŏ-da 물러서다

receipt *n.* yŏng-su-jŭng 영수증

receive *v.t.* pat-da 받다

receiver *n.* su-hwa-gi 수화기

recent *adj.* yo-jŭm-ŭi 요즘의

recently *adv.* yo-jŭm-e 요즘에

reception *n.* hwan-yŏng 환영; (party) hwan-yŏng hoe 환영회

receptivity *n.* kam-su-sŏng 감수성

recess *n.* hyu-gye 휴계

recipe *n.* yo-ri-pŏp 요리법

reciprocal *adj.* ho-sang 호상

recitation *n.* nang-dok 낭독

recite *v.* nang-dok ha-da 낭독하다

reckless *adj.* mu-mo han 무모한

reckon *v.* kye-san ha-da 계산하다

reclaim v· kae-ch'ŏk ha-da 개척하
다

recognize v· (know) ar-a po-da 알
아보다; (admit) in-sik ha-da 인
식하다

recollect v· saeng-gak ha-da 생각
하다

recollection n· hoe-sang 회상

recommend v· ch'u-ch'ŏn ha-da 추
천하다

recommendation n· ch'u-ch'ŏn 추
천

reconcile v· hwa-hae si-k'i-da 화해
시키다

reconnaissnce n· chŏng-ch'al 정찰

reconsider v· chae-ko-ryŏ ha-da
재고력하다

reconstruct v· chae-gŭn ha-da 재
건하다

record n· ki-rok 기록; v· ki-rok
ha-da 기록하다

recover v· hoe-bok ha-da 회복하
다

recreation n· o-rak 오락

recruit n· sae pyŏng-jŏng 새병정;
v· po-ch'ong ha-da 보총하다

rectangle n· ku-hyŏng 구형

rectify v· ko-ch'i-da 고치다

recuperate v· hoe-bok-doe-da 회복
되다

red adj· pulk-ŭn 붉은

redeem v. to-ro ch'at-da 도로찾다

redemption n. (from sin) sok-choe
속죄

reduce v. kam-so ha-da 감소하다

reduction n. kam-so 감소

reed n. kal-dae 갈대

reef n. am-ch'o 암초

reel n. mul-le 물레; v. kam-ta
감다

reelect v. chae-sŏn ha-da 재선하
다

reestablish v. ta-si se-u-da 다시세
우다

reexamine v. chae kŭm-t'o ha-da
재금토하다

refer v. cho-hoe ha-da 조회하다

referee n. sim-p'an-gwan 심판관

reference n. ŏn-gŭp 언급

refine v. chŏ-je ha-da 저제하다

reflect v. pan-sa ha-da 반사하다

reform v. kae-hyŏk ha-da 개혁하
다

refrain v. sam-ka-da 삼가다

refresh v. sae-rop-ge he-da 새롭게
하다

refeshments n. ŭm-sik-mul 음식
물

refrigerate v. naeng-jang ha-da 냉
장하다

refrigerator n. naeng-jang-go 냉
장고

refuge *n.* p'i-nan-ch'ŏ 피난처

refugees *n.* pi-nan-mĭn 피난민

refusal *n.* kŏ-jŏl 거절

refuse *v.* kŏ-jŏl ha-da 거절하다

regain *v.* to-ro ch'at-da 도로찾
다

regard *v.* chu-si ha-da 주시하다;
n. chon-kyŏng 존경

regime *n.* chŏng-kwon 정권

regiment *n.* yŏn-dae 연대

region *n.* chi-bang 지방

register *v.* tŭng-gi ha-da 등기하
다

registrar *n.* (of school) kyo-mu-
jang 교무장

registration *n.* tŭng-nok 등록

regret *v.* yu-gam-ŭ-ro saeng-gak
ha-da 유감으로생각하다; *n.* yu-
gam 유감

regular *adj.* (usual) po-t'ong 보
통

regulate *v.* chŏng-je ha-ge ha-da
정제하게하다

rehabilitate *v.* pok-gu si-k'i-da
복구시키다

rehabilitation *n.* pok-gu 복구

rehearse *v.* yŏn-sŭp ha-da 연습하
다

reign *n.* sŏng-dae 성대; *v.* kul-
lim ha-da 군림하다

rein *n.* ko-pi 고삐

reindeer *n.* bul-sa-sŭm 뿔사슴

reject *v.* kŏ-jŏl ha-da 거절하다

rejection *n.* kŏ-jŏl 거절

rejoice *v.* ki-pŭ-ge ha-da 기쁘게하다

relate *v.* i-ya-gi ha-da 이야기하다

relation *n.* kwan-gye 관계

relative *n.* ch'in-ch'ŏk 친척; *adj.* pi-gyo-jŏk 비교적

relax *v.* nŭt-ch'u-da 늦추다

relay *v.* chŏn ha-da 전하다

release *v.* sŏk-bang ha-da 석방하다

relent *v.* nuk-ŏ-ji-da 눅어지다

relevant *adj.* chŏk-jŏl han 적절한

reliable *adj.* sïl-loe hal-su i-nŭn 신뢰할수있는

relief *n.* ku-je 구제

relieve *v.* ku-je ha-da 구제하다

religion *n.* chong-kyo 종교

relish *n.* ch'wi-mi 취미; *v.* chŭl-gi-da 즐기다

reluctant, to be, *v.* sïl-ta 싫다

rely *v.* ŭi-ji ha-da 의지하다

remain *v.* mŏ-mŭ-rŭ-da 머므르다; (be left over) nam-ta 남다

remainder *n.* na-mŏ-ji 나머지

remains *n.* yu-gol 유골

remark *v.* mal ha-da 말하다; *n.* mal-ssŭm 말씀

remarkable *adj.* du-ryŏt han 뚜렷한

remedy *n.* ku-hal pang-pŏp 구할 방법

remember *v.* ki-ŏk ha-da 기억하다

remembrance *n.* ki-ryŏm-p'um 기념품

remind *v.* saeng-gak ha-ge ha-da 생각하게하다

remit *v.* (send money) ton po-nae-da 돈보내다

remittance *n.* song-gŭm 송금

remnant *n.* na-mŏ-ji 나머지

remonstrate *v.* kan-ŏn ha-da 간언하다

remorse *n.* nwi-u-ch'ïm 뉘우침

remote *adj.* mŏn 먼

remove *v.* om-gi-da 옮기다

render *v.* che-ch'ul ha-da 제출하다

rendezvous *n.* chi-jŏng-doen chïp-hap-so 지정된집합소

renew *v.* sae-rop-ge ha-da 새롭게 하다

renounce *v.* pu-ïn ha-da 부인하다

renown *n.* myŏng-sŏng 명성

rent *n.* pil-li-nŭn sak 빌리는삯; *v.* (from) se-chu-go pil-li-da 세주고 빌려다; (to) se-pat-go pil-lyŏ chu-da 세받고빌려주다

reorganize *v.* ta-si cho-jik ha-da 다시조직하다

repair *v.* su-sŏn ha-da 수선하다

reparation *n.* pae-sang 배상

repay *v.* kap'-da 갚다

repeal *v.* p'ye-ji ha-da 폐지하다

repeat *v.* toe-p'ur-i ha-da 되풀이 하다

repel *v.* kyŏk-t'oe ha-da 격퇴하다

repent *v.* hu-hoe ha-da 후회하다

repetition *n.* toe-p'ur-i 되풀이

replace *v.* kal-da 갈다

replacement *n.* kyo-dae 교대

replenish *n.* po-ch'ung ha-da 보충 하다

reply *n.* tae-dap 대답; *v.* tae-dap ha-da 대답하다

report *n.* po-go 보고; *v.* po-go ha-da 보고하다

reporter *n.* ki-ja 기자

represent *n.* tae-p'yo ha-da 대표하 다

representative *n.* tae-p'yo 대표

reprieve *n.* chip-haeng-yu-ye 집행 유예

reprimand *v.* ching-gye ha-da 징계 하다

reproach *v.* gu-jit-da 꾸짖다

reproduce *v.* pok-sa ha-da 복사하 다

reprove *v.* pi-nan ha-da 비난하다

republic *n.* kong-hwa-guk 공화국

repudiate *v.* pu-in ha-da 부인하다

repulse *v.* mul-li ch'i-da 물리치다

reputation *n.* myŏng-sŏng 명성

request *n.* yo-gu 요구; *v.* yo-gu
ha-da 요구하다

require *n.* yo-gu ha-da 요구하다

rescue *v.* ku ha-da 구하다

research *n.* yŏn-gu 연구

resemble *v.* pi-sŭt ha-da 비슷하다

resent *v.* pu-hae ha-da 부해하다

reservation *n.* ye-yak 예약

reserve *v.* po-ryu ha-da 보류하다

residence *n.* kŏ-ju 거주

resign *v.* sa-jĭk ha-da 사직하다

resignation *n.* sa-jĭk 사직

resist *v.* chŏ-hang ha-da 저항하다

resistance *n.* chŏ-hang 저항

resolute *adj.* kyŏl-sĭm han 결심한

resolve *v.* kyŏl-sĭm ha-da 결심하
다; (settle) hae-gyŏl ha-da 해결
하다

resort *n.* po-yang-ji 보양지

resource *n.* chae-won 재원

respect *v.* chon-gyŏng ha-da 존경
하다; *n.* chon-gyŏng 존경

respectable *adj.* chŏm-jan-ŭn 점
잖은   「한

respectful *adj.* kong-son han 공손

respond *v.* ŭng ha-da 응하다

responsible *adj.* ch'aeg-im i-nŭn
책임 있는

responsibility *n.* ch'aeg-ĭm 책임

rest *v.* swi-da 쉬다; *n.* swi-gi 쉬
기; (remainder) na-mŏ-ji 나머지

restaurant *n.* yo-ri chǐp 요리집

restless *adj.* pur-an han 불안한

restoration *n.* hoe-bok 회복

restore *v.* (give back) tol-lyŏ chu-da 돌려주다; (repair) 회복하다

restrict *v.* che-han ha-da 제한하다

result *n.* kyŏl-gwa 결과

resume *v.* chae-gae ha-da 재개하다

resumption *n.* chae-gae 재개

resurrection *n.* pu-hwal 부활

retail *n.* so-mae 소매; *v.* so-mae ha-da 소매하다

retain *v.* po-ryu ha-da 보류하다

retaliate *v.* po-bok ha-da 보복하다

retard *v.* nǔ-ri-ge ha-da 느리게하다

retire *v.* (from office) t'wi-jǐk ha-da 퇴직하다

retract *v.* ch'wi-so ha-da 취소하다

retreat *n.* t'oe-gak 퇴각; *v.i.* t'oe-gak ha-da 퇴각하다

retrieve *v.* hoe-bok ha-da 회복하다

retroactive *adj.* so-gǔp ha-nǔn 소급하는

return *v.* (give back) pan-hwan ha-da 반환하다; (come back) tor-a o-da 돌아오다; (go back) to-ro ka-da 도로가다

reunion *n.* kan-ch'in-hoe 간친회

reunite *v.* chae-yŏn-hap ha-da 재연합하다

reveal *v.* na-t'a-nae-da 나타내다

revelation *n.* muk-si 묵시

revenge *n.* pok-su 복수

revenue *n.* su-ip 수입

reverence *n.* chon-gyŏng 존경

review *v.* (book) p'yŏng-non ha-da 평론하다; (lessons) pok-sŭp ha-da 복습하다; (troops) kŏm-yŏl ha-da 검열하다

revise *v.* kae-jŏng ha-da 개정하다

revive *v.* so-saeng ha-da 소생하다

revolt *v.* Pan-yŏk ha-da 반역하다

revolution *n.* (rebellion) pan-yŏk 반역

revolve *v.* tol-da 돌다

reward *n.* po-su 보수; *v.* po-su-rŭl chu-da 보수를주다

rheumatism *n.* ryu-mŏ-t'i-jŭ 류머 티즈

rib *n.* kal-pit-dae 갈빗대

rice *n.* ssal 쌀; (cooked) pap 밥; (cooked, polite form) chin-ji 진지; (shelled) ssal 쌀; (unshelled) pyŏ 벼; **r. field** non 논; **r. seed bed** mot cha-ri 못자리; **r. seed plant** mo 모; **r.-plant** *n.* pyŏ 벼

rich *adj.* ton-man-ŭn 돈많은

riches *n.* chae-san 재산

rick *n.* no-jŏk 노적

rickets *n.* ku-ru-pyŏng 구루병

rid *v.* ŏp-sae-pŏ-ri-da 없새버리다

riddle *n.* su-su-ke-ki 수수께끼

ride *v.* t'a-da 타다; *n.* t'a-gi 타기

ridge *n.* san-pong-o-ri 산봉오리

ridicule *n.* cho-rong 조롱

rifle *n.* so-ch'ong 소총

right *adj.* pa-rŭn 바른; *adv.* pa-rŭ-ge 바르게; *n.* (perogative) kwol-li 권리; **r.** side pa-rŭn p'yŏn 바른편

rightly *adv.* pa-rŭ-ge 바르게

right-wing *n.* u-ik 우익

rim *n.* ka 가

ring *n.* (circle) ko-ri 고리; (finger) Pan-ji 반지; *v.* ch'i-da 치다

rinse *v.* ka-si-da 가시다

riot *n.* p'ok-dong 폭동; *v.* p'ok-dong-ŭl ir-ŭ-k'i-da 폭동을일으키다

rip *v.* jit-da 찢다

ripe *adj.* ig-ŭn 익은

ripen *v.* ik-da 익다

ripple *n.* chan mul-kyŏl 잔물결

rise *v.* ol-la-ka-da 올라가다

risk *n.* wi-hom 위험; *v.t.* ……ŭl kŏl-go ha-da ……을걸고하다

rival *n.* kyŏng-jaeng-ja 경쟁자; *v.* kyŏng-jaeng ha-da 경쟁하다

river *n.* kang 강

rivulet *n.* si-nae 시내

road *n.* kil 길

roam *v.* pae-hoe ha-da 배회하다

roar *v.* pu-rŭ-jit-da 부르짖다

roast *n.* ku-ŭn ko-gi 구운고기;
v. kup-da 굽다

rob *v.* to-duk-jil ha-da 도둑질하다

robber *n.* kang-do 강도

robe *n.* ga-un 까운; *v.* ga-un-ŭl
ip-da 까운을입다

robin *n.* ro-bin-sae 로빈새

rock *n.* pa-wi 바위; *v.* hŭn-dŭl-
da 흔들다

rocket *n.* hwa-jŏn 화전

rocky *adj.* pa-wi man-un 바위많은

rod *n.* mak-dae-gi 막대기

rogue *n.* nom 놈

roll *v.i.* kul-da 굴다; *v.t.* kul-li-
da 굴리다

roller *n.* ro-la 로라

romantic *adj.* nang-man han 낭
만한

romp *v.* chang-nan ha-myŏ nol-da
장난하며놀다

roof *n.* chi-bung 지붕

room *n.* pang 방

roost *n.* hwae 홰

rooster *n.* su-tak 수귥

root *n.* bu-ri 뿌리

rope *n.* pat-chul 밧줄

rose *n.* chang-mi 장미; **R. of Shar-
on** (national flower of Korea)
mu-gung-hwa 무궁화

rot *v.* ssŏk-da 썩다

rotate *v.* tol-da 돌다

rotation *n.* yun-hwan 윤환;
(change in turn) kyo-dae 교대

rotten *adj.* ssŏg-ŭn 썩은

rough *adj.* kŏ-ch'in 거친

round *adj.* tung-gŭn 둥근; *prep.*
& *adv.* chu-wi-e 주위에

roundabout *adj.* tor-a-sŏ ka-nŭn
돌아서가는

rouse *v.* i-rŭ-k'i-da 이르키다

route kil 길

routine *n.* hang-sang ha-nŭn il 항
상하는일

row *n.* chul 줄; (disturbance) ya-
dan 야단; *v.* no chŏt-da 노젓다

royal *adj.* wang-ŭi 왕의

rub *v.* pi-bi-da 비비다

rubber *n.* ko-mu 고무

rubbish *n.* ssŭ-re-gi 쓰레기

rubble *n.* pu-sŭ-rŏ-gi tol 부스러기
돌

ruby *n.* hong ok 홍옥

rudder *n.* k'i 키

ruddy *adj.* bal-gan 빨간

rude *adj.* sang-sŭ-rŏ-un 상스러운

rudeness *n.* sil-ye 실예

rue *v.* nwi-u-ch'i-da 뉘우치다

rug *n.* yang-t'an-ja 양란자

ruin *n.* mol-lak 몰락; *v.* mol-lak
ha-da 몰락하다

rule *n.* chi-bae 지배; *v.* chi-bae ha-da 지배하다

ruler *n.* cha 자

rumor *n.* so-mun 소문

run *v.* dwi-ŏ ka-da 뛰어가다; **r. away** *v.* to-mang ka-da 도망가다; **r. for office** *v.* ip-hu-bo ha-da 입후보하다

rural *adj.* si-gol-ŭi 시골의

ruse *n.* mo-ryak 모략

rush *n.* tol-jin 돌진; *v.* tal-yŏ tŭl-da 달려들다

rust *n.* sang-nok 상녹; *v.* nok-sŭl-da 녹슬다

rustic *adj.* si-gol tŭ-gi-ŭi 시골뜨기의

rustle *v.* pa-sak pa-sak ŭl-li-da 바삭바삭을리다

rusty *adj.* nok-sŭl-ŭn 녹슬은

rut *n.* pa-k'wi cha-guk 바퀴자국

rye *n.* ssal po-ri 쌀보리

〔S〕

Sabbath *n.* an-sĭk-il 안식일

saber *n.* kun-do 군도

sable *n.* san-dal 산달

sabotage *n.* t'ae-ŏp 태업

sack *n.* cha-ru 자루

sacrament *n.* sŏng-sik 성식

sacred *adj.* sŏng-sŭ-rŏ-un 성스러운

sacrifice *n.* hŭi-saeng 희생

sad *adj.* sŭl-p'ŭn 슬픈

saddle *n.* an-jang 안장; *v.* an-jang-ŭl chi-u-da 안장을지우다

sadness *n.* sŭl-p'ŭm 슬픔

safe *adj.* an-jŏn han 안전한; *n.* kŭm-go 금고

safeguard *n.* po-ho 보호

safety *n.* an-jŏn 안전; **s. pin** an-jŏn P'in 안전핀

sage *n.* ch'ŏl-in 철인

sail *n.* tot 돛; *v.* hang-hae ha-da 항해하다

sailing *n.* ch'ul-bŏm 출범

sailor *n.* su-bu 수부; (navy) su-byŏng 수병

saint *n.* sŏng-ĭn 성인

sake of, for the, ...ŭl wi-ha-yŏ ......을위하여

salad *n.* ssael-la-dŭ 쎌타드

salary *n.* pong-gŭp 봉급

sale *n.* p'an-mae 판매

salesman, saleswoman *n.* chŏm-won 점원

saliva *n.* ch'ĭm 침

salmon *n.* yŏn-ŏ 연어

saloon *n.* sul chĭp 술집

salt *n.* so-gŭm 소금; *v.* so-gŭm ch'i-da 소금치다; **s. mine** *n.* am-yŏm-kul 암염굴

salty *adj.* jan 짠

salutation n. in-sa 인사

salute v. kyŏng-ye ha-da 경예하다

salvage v. ku-hae-nae-da 구해내다

salvation n. yŏng-hon ku-je 영혼 구제; **S. Army** ku-se-gun 구세군

salve n. ko-yak 고약

same adj. kat'-ŭn 같은

sampan n. ssam-p'an 쌈판

sample n. kyŏn-bon 견본

sanction n. chae-hŏ 재허; v. yun-hŏ ha-da 윤허하다

sand n. mo-rae 모래; **s. bar** n. sa-ju 사주; **s.-storm** sa-p'ung 사풍

sandwich n. ssaen-dŭ-wi-ch'wi 쌘드위취

sandy adj. mo-rae-ŭi 모래의

sane adj. on-gŏn-han 온전한

sanitary adj. wi-saeng-jŏk 위생적

sanitation n. wi-saeng 위생

sanity n. on-gŏn 온전

Santa Claus n. ssaen-t'ŏ k'ŭl-lo-sŭ hal-a-bŏ-ji 쌘터클로스할아버지

sap n. su-aek 수액

sarcastic adj. p'ung-ja-jŏk 풍자적

sardine n. chŏng-ŏ-ri 정어리

sash n. doe 뙤

Satan n. ma-gwi 마귀

satchel n. hak-saeng ka-bang 학생 가방

satellite n. wi-sŏng 위성

satin *n.* kong-dan 공단

satisfaction *n.* man-jok 만족

satisfactory *adj.* man-jok han 만족한

satisfy *v.* man-jok si-k'i-da 만족시키다

Saturday *n.* t'o-yo-il 토요일

sauce *n.* sso-o-ssŭ 쏘오쓰; **s.-pan** *n.* nam-bi 남비

saucer *n.* ch'a-chan pa-ch'ĭm 찻잔바침

saucy *adj.* yŏm-ch'i ŏp-nŭn 염치없는

sausage *n.* sso-sse-ji 쏘쎄지

savage *adj.* ya-man-ŭi 야만의; *n.* ya-man-in 야만인

save *v.* ku ha-da 구하다

savings *n.* chŏ-kŭm 저금; **s.-bank** *n.* chŏ-ch'uk ŭn-haeng 저축은행

saviour *n.* ku-jo-ja 구조자

saw *n.* t'op 톱; *v.* t'op-jĭl ha-da 톱질하다

sawmill *n.* che-jae-so 제재소

say *v.* mal ha-da 말하다

saying *n.* mal 말

scab *n.* hŏn-de-tak-ji 헌데딱지

scaffold *n.* pal-p'an 발판

scald *n.* ti-da 디다

scale *n.* (fish) pi-mul 비늘; (map) ch'ŏk-do 척도

scales *n*. chŏ-ul 저울

scalp mŏ-ri ka-juk 머리가죽

scan *v*. ŏl-lŭn hul-t'ŏ po-da 얼는 훑어보다

scanty *adj*. mo-ja-ra-nŭn 모자라는

scar *n*. hŭm 흠

scarce *adj*. tŭ-mun 드문

scarcely *adv*. kŏ-ŭi……ŏp-ge 거의 ……없게

scarcity *n*. pu-jok 부족

scare *v*. nol-la-ge ha-da 놀라게하다

scarecrow *n*. hŏ-su-a-bi 허수아비

scarf *n*. mok to-ri 목도리

scarlet *n*. chin-hong saek 진홍색

scatter *v*. hŭ-t'ŭ-rŏ-tŭ-ri-da 흐트러뜨리다

scavenger *n*. ch'ŏng-so-in 청소인

scene *n*. kwang-gyŏng 광경; (theatre) mu-dae 무대

scenery *n*. kyŏng-ji 경지

scent *n*. naem-sae 냄새

schedule *n*. si-gan-p'yo 시간표

scheme *n*. ke-hŭik 계획

scholar *n*. hak-ja 학자

school *n*. hak-kyo 학교; **s.fellow, s.mate** tong-ch'ang 동창; **s.house** kyo-sa 교사; **s.master** kyo-su 교수; **s.room** kyo-sil 교실

science *n*. kwa-hak 과학

scientific *adj*. kwa-hak-ŭi 과학의

scientist *n.* kwa-hak-ja 과학자

scissors *n.* ka-wi 가위

scold *v.* gu-jit-da 꾸짖다

scope *n.* pŏm-wi 범위

scorch *v.* gŭ-sŭl-da 끄슬다

score *n.* tŭk-jŏm 득점; *v.* tŭk-jŏm ha-da 득점하다

scorn *v.* myŏl-si ha-da 멸시하다

scorpion *n.* chŏn-gal 전갈

scoundrel *n.* ak-han 악한

scour *v.* tak-da 닦다

scout *n.* ch'ŏk-hu 척후

scowl *v.i.* ji-p'u-ri-da 찌푸리다

scramble *v.* ki-ŏ-o-rŭ-da 기어오르다

scrap *n.* cho-gak 조각

scrape *v.* kŭlk-da 긁다

scratch *n.* kŭlk-ki 긁기; *v.* kŭlk-da 긁다

scream *n.* a-u-sŏng 아우성; *v.* a-u-sŏng ch'i-da 아우성치다

screen *n.* pyŏng-p'ung 병풍

screw *n.* na-sa 나사; **s.driver** na-sa song gŏt 나사송곳

scribe *n.* tae-sŏ 대서

script *n.* (money) kun-p'yo 군표

scripture *n.* sŏng-kyŏng 성경

scrub *v.* sol-ŭl ssit-da 솔을씻다; **s. oak** *n.* kal na-mu 갈나무

scrupulous *adj.* tae-dan-hi dok-dok han 대단히똑똑한

sculptor *n.* cho-gak-sa 조각사

sculpture *n.* cho-gak-sul 조각술

scythe *n.* k'ŭn-nat 큰낫

sea *n.* pa-da 바다; s.**bathing** *n.* hae-su-yok 해수욕

seal *n.* (animal) mul-pŏm 물범; (mark) to-jang 도장; *v.* to-jang jik-da 도장찍다

seam *n.* ot-sol-gi 옷솔기

seaman *n.* su-bu 수부

seamstress *n.* ch'im-mo 침모

search *v.* ch'at-da 찾다

seashore *n.* hae-pyŏn 해변

seasickness *n.* pae mŏl-mi 배멀미

season *n.* si-jŏl 시절; *v.* (wood) mal-li-da 말리다; *v.* (flavor) yang-nyŏm ch'i-da 약념치다

seat *n.* cha-ri 자리; *v.* cha-ri-e ant-da 자리에앉다

seaweed *n.* hae-ch'o 해초

second *adj.* tul-chae-ŭi 둘째의; *n.* (time) ch'o 초

secondary *adj.* tul-chae-ŭi 둘째의

secrecy *n.* pi-mil 비밀

secret *n.* pi-mil 비밀; *adj.* pi-mil-ŭi 비밀의

secretariat *n.* pi-sŏ-gwa 비서과

secretary *n.* pi-sŏ-gwan 비서관; (government) chang-gwan 장관

sect *n.* kyo-p'a 교파

section *n.* ku-bun 구분

secular *adj.* sok-in-ŭi 속인의

secure *v.* hwak-sil ha-ge ha-da 확실하게하다; **be s.** an-jŏn ha-da 안전하다

security *n.* an-jŏn 안전; **S. Council (U.N.)** an-jŏn po-jang i-sa hoe 안전보장이사회

see *v.* po-da 보다

seed *n.* ssi 씨

seek *v.* ch'at-da 찾다

seem *v.* po-i-da 보이다

segregate *v.* pul-li ha-da 분리하다

seize *v.* chap-da 잡다

seizure *n.* ch'a-ap 차압

seldom *adj.* tŭ-mul-ge 드물게

select *v.* sŏn-t'aek ha-da 선택하다

self *n.* cha-gi 자기; **s.-control** kŭk-gi 극기; **s.-defense** cha-wi 자위; **s.-government** cha-ch'i 자치; **s.-help** cha-jo 자조; **s.-protection** ho-sĭn 호신; **s.-reliance** chŏ-rŭl mit-gi 저를믿기

selfish *adj.* i-gi-jŏk 이기적

sell *v.* p'al-da 팔다

semblance *n.* oe-yang 외양

semester *n.* hak-gi 학기

semicolon *n.* sse-mi-k'o-ul-lŭn 쎄미코울른

seminary *n.* sĭn-hak-kyo 신학교

senate *n.* sang-won 상원

senator *n.* sang-won-ŭi ŭi-won 상
원의의원

send *v.* po-nae-da 보내다

sender *n.* po-nae-nŭn sa-ram 보내
는사람

senior *n.* (chief) su-sŏk 수석;
(elder) chon-jang 존장

sensation *n.* kam-gak 감각

sense *n.* chŏng-sin 정신; (five
senses) o-gwan 오관; (meaning)
dŭt 뜻

sensible *adj.* chŏng-sin i-nŭn 정신
있는

sensitive *adj.* min-gam han 민감
한

sentence *n.* mun 문; (for crime)
hyŏng-ŭi sŏn-go 형의선고; *v.* sŏn-
go ha-da 선고하다

sentry *n.* p'a-su pyŏng 파수병

separate *v.* pul-li ha-da 분리하다;
adj. pul-li doen 분리된

separation *n.* pul-li 분리

September *n.* ku-wol 구월

septic *adj.* ssŏg-nŭn 썩는

sequence *n.* kye-yŏl 계렬

serenade *n.* so-ya-gok 소야곡

serene *adj.* ch'ŏng-myŏng han 청
명한

serf *n.* nong-no 농노

sergeant *n.* sang-sa 상사

serial *adj.* yŏn-sok-jŏk 연속적;
s. **number** (military) kun-pŏn-ho
군번호
sericulture *n.* yang-jam 양잠
series *n.* yŏn-sok 연속
serious *adj.* chung-dae han 중대한
seriously *adv.* ch'am 참
sermon *n.* sŏl-gyo 설교
serpent *n.* paem 뱀
servant *n.* ha-in 하인
serve *v.* sŏm-gi-da 섬기다
service *n.* kong-hŏn 공헌
serviceable *adj.* ssŭl man han 쓸
만한
set *v.* (put) no-ta 놓다; (sun) chi-
da 지다; (table) sang-po-da 상
보다
setting *n.* mu-dae chang-ch'i 무대
장치
settle *v.* hae-gyŏl ha-da 해결하다
settlement *n.* (Place) chŏng-ju 정
주
settler *n.* sik-min-ja 식민자
seven *n.* il-gop 일곱
seventeen *n.* yŏl-il-gop 열일곱
Seventh Day Adventist *n.* an-sik
kyo 안식교
seventy *n. & adj.* ir-hŭn 일흔
sever *v.* gŭn'-ta 끊다
several *adj.* myŏt 몇
severe *adj.* sim-han 심한

severely *adv.* sim ha-ge 심하게

sew *v.* pa-nu-jil ha-da 바누질하다

sewage *n.* ssŭ-re-gi 쓰레기

sewer *n.* su-ch'ae 수채

sewing *n.* pa-nu-jil 바누질

sex *n.* sŏng 성

shabby *adj.* hŏn 헌

shade *n.* kŭ-nŭl 그늘

shadow *n.* kŭ-rĭm-ja 그림자

shady *adj.* kŭ-nŭl-jin 그늘진

shaft *n.* cha-ru 자무

shaggy *adj.* t'ŏl man-ŭn 털많은

shake *v.* hŭn-dŭl-da 흔들다;
(hands) ak-su ha-da 악수하다

shall *auxil.* use the future tense of
the verb desired

shallow *adj.* yat'-ŭn 얕은

sham *n.* sok-im 속임

shame *n.* pu-kŭ-rŏ-um 부끄러움

shameful *adj.* su-ch'i-sŭ-rŏ-un 수
치스러운

shameless *adj.* yŏm-ch'i ŏp-nŭn
염치없는

shampoo *v.* mŏ-ri-rŭl kam-ta 머리
를감다

shape *n.* mo-yang 모양

share *n.* mok' 몫; *v.* pae-dang
ha-da 배당하다

shark *n.* sang-ŏ 상어

sharp *adj.* nal-k'a-ro-un 날카로운;
adv. nal-k'a-rop-ge 날카롭게

sharpen v. kal-da 갈다

sharpness n. nal-k'a-ro-um 날카로움

shatter v. pu-su-da 부수다

shave v. myŏn-do ha-da 면도하다

shawl n. syol 숄

she pron. kŭ-yŏ-ja 그여자

sheaf n. han-tan 한단

shear v. gŭn-ta 끊다; n. ka-wi 가위

sheath n. k'al chip 칼집

shed v. (drop off) t'ŏl-da 떨다; (tears) hŭl-li-da 흘리다; n. hŏt-gan 헛간

sheen n. kwang-hwi 광휘

sheep n. yang 양

sheet n. hot' i-bul 홑이불; (specific modifier used with anything flat) chang 장

shelf n. sŏn pan 선반

shell n. gŏp-jil 껍질; (gun) p'o-t'an 포탄; s. fire p'o-sa-gyŏk 포사격

shelter n. p'i-nan 피난; v. p'i-nan ha-da 피난하다

shepherd n. mok-ja 목자

shield v. po-ho ha-da 보호하다

shimmer n. pŏn-jŏk pŏn-jŏk ha-nŭn pit 번쩍번쩍하는빛; v. pŏn-jŏk pŏn-jŏk ha-da 번쩍번쩍하다

shin *n.* ap'-jŏng gaeng-i 앞정갱이
shine *v.* pit-na-da 빛나다; (polish) tak-da 닦다
ship *n.* pae 배; *v.* un-ban ha-da 운반하다; **sailing-s.** pŏm-sŏn 범선; **war-s.** *n.* kun-ham 군함
shipping *n.* sŏn-bak 선박
shipwreck *n.* nan-p'a 난파
shipyard *n.* cho-sŏn-so 조선소
shirk *v.* p'i ha-da 피하다
shirt *n.* wa-i-sya-ssŭ 와이샤쓰
shiver dŏl-da 떨다
shoal *n.* yŏ-ul 여울
shock *n.* ch'ung-gyŏk 충격
shoe *n.* ku-du 구두; (Korean) sïn 신; *v.* p'yŏn-ja-rŭl pak-da 편자를박다; **s.brush** *n.* ku-du-sol 구두솔; **s.horn** ku-du chu-gŏk 구두주걱; **s.lace** ku-du gŭn 구두끈; **s.shine** ku-du tak-gi 구두닦기; **s.polish** ku-du yak 구두약 **s.maker** ku-du jaeng-i 구두쟁이
shoot *n.* sun 순; *v.* sso-da 쏘다
shooting *n.* sa gyŏk 사격
shop *n.* chŏn pang 전방 「상인
shopkeeper *n.* so-mae sang-in 소매
shopman *n.* chŏm-won 점원
shore *n.* mul ga 물가
short *adj.* jalb-ŭn 짧은
shortage *n.* pu-jok 부족

shorten v. jalp-ge ha-da 짧게하다
shorthand n. sok-ki-sul 속기술
shorts n. un-dong yong cham-baeng-i 운동용잠뱅이 「의
short-sighted adj. kŭn-si-ŭi 근시
shot n. p'o-dan 포탄
shoulder n. ŏ-kae 어깨
shout n. ko-ham 고함; v. oe-ch'i-da 외치다
shove v. mil-da 밀다
shovel n. sap 삽
show v. po-i-da 보이다; n. ku-gyŏng kŏ-ri 구경거리
shower n. so-nak-bi 소낙비; (bath) sya-wo 샤워
shrapnel n. yu-san-t'an 유산탄
shred n. cho-gak 조각; v. chal-ge jit-da 잘게쩟다
shriek v. pu-rŭ-jit-da 부르짖다
shrimp n. sae-u 새우
shrine n. myo 묘
shrink v. chul-da 줄다
shroud n. su-ŭi 수의; v. tŏp'-da 덮다
shrub n. tŏn-bul 던불
shudder v.dŏl-da 떨다
shuffle v. pal-ŭl gŭl-go ka-da 발을끌고가다; (cards) sŏk-da 셔다
shun v. p'i ha-da 피하다
shut v. tat-da 닫다
shutter n. kŏt ch'ang 겉창

shuttle *n.* puk 북

shy *adj.* su-jip-ŭn 수집은

sick *adj.* pyŏng tŭn 병든

sickle *n.* nat 낫

sickness *n.* pyŏng 병

side *n.* yŏp' 옆

sideboard *n.* ch'an chang 찬장

sidewalk po-do 보도

sideways *adv.* yŏp'-ŭ-ro 옆으로

siege *n.* p'o-wi 포위

sigh *n.* han-sum 한숨; *v.* han-sum swi-da 한숨쉬다

sight *n.* si-ryŏk 시력; *v.* po-i-da 보이다

sign *n.* (symbol) pu-ho 부호; *v.* sŏ-myŏng ha-da 서명하다

signal *n.* sin-ho 신호; *v.* sin-ho ha-da 신호하다; **s.fire** *n.* Pong-hwa 봉화

signature *n.* sŏ-myŏng 서명

signboard *n.* kan-P'an 간판

significant *adj.* chung-yo han 중요한

silence *v.* ch'im-muk 침묵

silent *adj.* ko-yo han 고요한

silently *adj.* cho-yong-hi 조용히

silk *n.* pi-dan 비단; (Korean) myŏng-ju 명주

silkworm *n.* nu-e 누에

sill *n.* mun chi-bang 문지방

silly *adj.* ŏ-ri-sŏk-ŭn 어리석은

silver *n.* ŭn 은

similar *adj.* kat-ŭn 같은

simple *adj.* tan-sun han 단순한

simplicity *n.* tan-sun 단순

simplify *v.* kan-dan ha-ge ha-da 간단하게하다

simply *adv.* tan-sun-hi 단순히

sin *n.* choe 죄

since *conj.* (because) dae-mun-e 때문에; (time) ……i hu ……이후; *prep.* ……i hu ……이후

sincere *adj.* chin-sil han 진실한

sincerely *adv.* chin-sil ha-ge 진실 하게

sing *v.* no-rae ha-da 노래하다

singer *n.* sŏng-ak-ga 성악가

singing *n.* ch'ang-ga 창가

single *adj.* han 한

singular *adj.* koe-sang han 괴상한; *n.* tan-su 단수

sink *n.* su-ch'ae 수채; *v.* ba-ji-da 빠지다

sip *v.* bal-da 빨다

sir *n.* (Korean polite title) sŏn-saeng 선생

siren *n.* ssa-i-ren 싸이렌

sister *n.* (boy's older sister)nu-nim 누님; (boy's younger sister) nwi tong-saeng 뉘동생; (girl's young-er sister) tong-saeng 동생; (girl's older sister) hyŏng-nim 형님

sister-in-law, of a man *n.* (older brother's wife) hyŏng-su 형수; (younger brother's wife) kye-su 계수; (wife's older sister) ch'ŏ-hyŏng 처형; (wife's younger sister) ch'ŏ-je 처제; **of a woman** (older brother's wife) ol-k'e 올케; (younger brother's wife) a-u-nim 아우님; (husband's sister) si-nu 시누

sisters *n.* cha-mae 자매

sit *v.* ant-da 앉다

situation *n.* sa-jŏng 사정

six *n. & adj.* yŏ-sŏt 여섯 「섯

sixteen *n. & adj.* yŏl-yŏ-sŏt 열여

sixty *n. & adj.* ye-sun 예순

size *n.* k'ŭ-gi 크기

skate *n.* sŭ-k'et' 스켙; *v.* sŭ-k'et' ha-da 스켙하다

skeleton *n.* hae-gol 해골

sketch *n.* yak-do 약도

ski *n.* ssŭ-k'i 쓰카; *v.* ssŭ-k'i t'a-da 쓰키타다

skilful *adj.* son chae-ju i-nŭn 손 재주있는

skill *n.* son chae-ju 손재주

skin *n.* gŏp-jil 껍질; (animal) ka-juk 가죽; (human) p'i-bu 피부

skip *v.* dwi da 뛰다

skirmish *v.* cha-gŭn ch'ung-t'ol-ŭl ha-da 자근충돌을하다

skirt *n.* chi-ma 치마

skull *n.* tu-gol 두골

sky *n.* ha-nŭl 하늘; **s.lark** chong-dal sae 종달새; **s.scraper** ma-ch'ŏn-nu 마천두

slab *n.* p'an-sŏk 판석

slacken *v.* nŭt-ch'u-da 늦추다

slam *v.* gwang tat-da 광닫다

slander *n.* pi-nan 비난

slang *n.* sang-mal 상말

slap *n.* ch'al sak tu-dŭl-gim 찰삭 두들김; *v.* ch'al sak ch'i-da 찰 삭치다

slate *n.* sŏk p'an 석판

slaughter *n.* sal-yuk 살육

slave *n.* no-ye 노예

slavery *n.* no-ye che-do 노예제도

slay *v.* chuk-i-da 죽이다

sled *n.* ssŏl-mae 썰매

sleep *n.* cham 잠; *v.* cha-da 자다

sleeping-car *n.* ch'ĭm-dae ch'a 침대차

sleepy *adj.* chol-lĭn 졸린

sleet *n.* chin-nun ga-bi 진눈까비

sleeve *n.* so-mae 소매

sleigh *n.* ssŏl-mae 썰매; *v.* ssŏl-mae-rŭl t'a-da 썰매를타다

slender *adj.* ka-nyal-p'ŭn 가냘픈

slice *n.* ŏlb-ŭn jok 엽은쪽

slide *v.* mi-kŭ-rŏ-ji-da 미끄러지다

slight *adj.* ka-nyal-p'ŭn 가냘픈;
v. myŏl-si ha-da 멸시하다

slightly *adv.* cho-kŭm 조금

slime *n.* chin hŭk 진흙

sling *n.* di (팔다리매는) 띠; **s.shot**
tol-p'al-mae 돌팔매

slink *v.* ka-man-i tar-a-na-da 가
만이달아나다

slip *v.* mi-kŭ-rŏ-ji-da 미끄러지다;
n. (mistake) sil-su 실수

slipper *n.* ssŭl-li-p'ŏ 쓸리퍼

slippery *adj.* mi-kŭ-rŏ-un 미끄러운

slope *n.* kyŏng-sa 경사

sloth *n.* ke-ŭ-rŭm 게으름

slow *adj.* tŏn-din 더딘; *v.* sok-
yŏk-ŭl nŭt-ch'u-da 속력을늦추다

slowly *adv.* ch'an-ch'an-hi 찬찬히

sluggard *n.* ke-ŭ-rŭn-ja 게으른자

slumber *n.* cham 잠

sly *adj.* kyo-hwal han 교활한

smack *n.* ch'al-sak dae-ri-da 찰삭
때리다

small *adj.* chak-ŭn 작은

smallpox *n.* ma-ma 마마

smart *adj.* myŏng-min han 명민한

smash *v.* pu-su-da 부수다

smear *v.* pa-rŭ-da 바르다

smell *n.* naem sae 냄새; *v.* naem-
sae mat'-da 냄새맡다

smile *n.* mi-so 미소; *v.* mi-so ha-
da 미소하다

smiling *adj.* mi-so ha-nŭn 미소하
는

smith *n.* (blacksmith) tae-jang-
jaeng-i 대장쟁이

smoke *n.* yŏn-gi 연기; *v.* yŏn-gi
nae-da 연기내다; (cigarette)
tam-bae p'i-u-da 담배피우다

smoker *n.* tam-bae p'i-nŭn ɛa-ram
담배피는사람

smooth *adj.* p'yŏn p'yŏn han 편편
한; *v.* p'yŏng p'yŏng ha-ge ha-da
평평하게하다

smother *v.* sum-ŭl mak-da 숨을막
다

smuggle *v.* mil su-ip ha-da 밀수입
하다

snail *n.* tal-p'aeng-i 달팽이

snake *n.* paem 뱀

snap *v.* (break) t'ak gŏk-da 탁꺾
다; (dog) tal-lyŏ tŭl-da (개가) 달
려들다; *n.* sŭ-naep' tan-ch'u 스
냅단추

snare *n.* tŏt' 덫

snarl *v.* ŭ-rŭ-rŏng kŏ-ri-da 으르렁
거리다

snatch *v.* cha-ch'yŏ bae-at-da 자
쳐빼앗다

sneak *v.* ka-man-hi ta-ni-da 가만
히다니다

sneer *n.* myŏl-si 멸시; *v.* myŏl-si
ha-da 멸시하다

sneeze *n.* chae-jae 재재; *v.* chae-jae ha-da 재재하다

sniff *v.* kot-kim tŭr-i-swi-da 콧김들이쉬다

snip *n.* jo-gak 쪼각; *v.* cha-rŭ-da 자르다

snore *n.* k'o-kol-gi 코골기; *v.* k'o-kol-da 코골다

snout *n.* k'o 코

snow *n.* nun 눈; *v.* nun o-da 눈오다; **s·ball** *n.* nun mung-ch'i 눈뭉치; **s·drift** nun po-ra 눈보라; **s·fall** na-rin-nun 나린눈; **s·flakes** nun-song-i 눈송이; **s·man** nun sa-ram 눈사람; **s·shoe** nun sin 눈신; **s·storm** nun po-ra 눈보라

snowy *adj.* nun man-ŭn 눈많은

snug *adj.* p'o-gŭn p'o-gŭn han 포근포근한

so *adv.* kŭ-rŏ-ke 그렇게; **if s.** *conj.* kŭ-rŏ-myŏn 그러면; **s·called** *adj.* so-wi 소위

soak *v.* tam-gŭ-da 담그다

soap *n.* pi-nu 비누

soar *v.* sot-da 솟다

sob *n.* nŭ-kyŏ ul-gi 느껴울기; *v.* nŭ-kyŏ ul-da 느껴울다

sober *adj.* on-gŏn han 온건한; (not drunk) sul an mŏk-nŭn 술안먹는

sociable *adj·* sa-gyo-jŏk 사교적

social *adj·* sa-hoe-ŭi 사회의

society *n·* sa-hoe 사회

sock *n·* yang-mal 양말

socket *n·* sso-k'e-t'ŭ 쏘케트

sod *n·* chan-di 잔디

soda *n·* chae-mul 잿물; **s· water** so-da 소다; **s· pop** sa-i-da 사이다

sofa *n·* kin il-lak-ŭi-ja 기인락의자

soft *adj·* pu-dŭ-rŏ-un 부드러운

soften *v· t·* pu-dŭ-rŏp-ge ha-da 부드럽게하다

softly *adj·* pu-dŭ-rŏp-ge 부드럽게

soil *n·* hŭk 흙; *v·* tŏ-rŏp-da 더럽다

soldier *n·* yuk-gun kun-ĭn 육군군인

sole *n·* (shoe) ku-du pa-dak 구두바닥; (fish) sŏ-dae 서대

solemn *adj·* ŏm-suk han 엄숙한

solicitor *n·* pyŏn-ho-sa 변호사

solid *adj·* ko-ch'e-ŭi 고체의

solidify *v·* kut'-ge ha-da 굳게하다

solitary *adj·* oe-ro-un 외로운

solitude *n·* ko-dok 고독

solstice *n·* (winter) tong-ji 동지; (summer) ha-ji 하지

solution *n·* hae-gyŏl 해결

solve *v·t·* hae-gyŏl ha-da 해결하다

somber *adj·* ch'im-ch'im han 침침한

some *adj.* (a little) cho-kŭm sik
조금식; (*pron.*) ŏl-ma 얼마

somebody *n.* & *pron.* nu-ga 누가

somehow *adv.* kŭ-rŏk chŏ-rŏk 그
럭저럭

somersault *n.* chae-ju nŏm-gi 재
주넘기

something *pron.* mu-ŏt 무엇

sometime *adv.* ŏt-dŏn-dae 엇던때

sometimes *adv.* dae-dae-ro 때때로

somewhat *adv.* ŏl-ma-gan 얼마간

somewhere *adv.* ŏ-de-in-ji 어데인
지

son *n.* a-dŭl 아들

song *n.* no-rae 노래

son-in-law *n.* sa-wi 사위

soon *adv.* kot 곧

soot *n.* yŏn-mae 연매   「시키다

soothe *v.* chin-jŏng si-k'i-da 진정

soothsayer *n.* chŏm-jaeng-i 점쟁이

sorcerer *n.* pak-su 박수

sorceress *n.* mu-dang 무당

sore *adj.* a-p'ŭn 아픈

sorrow *n.* sŭl-p'ŭm 슬픔

sorry *adj.* sŏp-sŏp-han 섭섭한;
I am s. (my fault) mi-an-ham-
ni-da 미안합니다; I am s. (not
my fault) an-does-im-ni-da 안
됐입니다

sort *n.* chong-yu 종류; *v.* pul-yu-
ha-da 분류하다

soul *n.* yŏng-hon 영혼

sound *adj.* kŏn-jŏn han 전전한;
n. so-ri 소리; *v.* so-ri na-da 소
리나다

soup *n.* kuk 국

sour *adj.* sin 신

source *n.* kŭn-won 근원

south *n.* nam-jok 남쪽; *adj.*
nam⋯⋯ 남⋯⋯; **S. Pole** nam
gŭk 남극

southern *adj.* nam-jok-ŭi 남쪽의

sovereign *n.* chu-gwon-ja 주권자

sow *v.* ssi bu-ri-da 씨뿌리다; *n.*
am twae-ji 암돼지

soy-sauce *n.* kan-jang 간장

space *n.* sae 새; (celestial) kong-
gan 공간

spacious *adj.* nŏlb-ŭn 넓은

spade *n.* sap 삽

span *v.* kŏn-nŏ-not-da 전너놓다

spare *adj.* nam-nŭn 남는; *v.* (save)
yong-sŏ ha-da 용서하다; **s. part**
n. pu-sŏk p'um 부석품

spark *n.* pul got 불꽃

sparkle *v.* pŏn-chŏk kŏ-ri-da 번쩍
거리다

sparrow *n.* ch'am sae 참새

speak *v.* mal ha-da 말하다

speaker *n.* yŏn-sa 연사

spear *n.* ch'ang 창

special *adj.* t'ŭk-pyŏl-ŭi 득별의

specialize *v.* chŏn-mun-hwa ha-da
전문화하다

specially *adv.* t'ŭk-pyŏl-hi 특별히

specialty *n.* chŏn-mun 전문

species *n.* chong-yu 종류

specific *adj.* t'ŭk-su han 특수한

specify *v.* cha-se-hi ssŭ-da 자세
히쓰다

specimen *n.* kyŏn-bon 견본

speck *n.* a-rong 아롱

spectacle *n.* kwang-gyŏng 광경

spectacles *n.* an-gyŏng 안경

spectator *n.* ku-gyŏng-gun 구경군

spectroscope *n.* pun-gwang-gi 분
광기

speculate *v.* sa-saek ha-da 사색하
다

speculation *n.* sa-saek 사색

speech *n.* yŏn-sŏl 연설

speed *n.* sok-do 속도

spell *n.* chu-mun 주문; *v.* ch'ŏl-
ja ha-da 철자하다

spelling *n.* chŏl-ja pŏp 철자법

spend *v.* ssŭ-da 쓰다

sphere *n.* ku-hyŏng 구형

spice *n.* yang-yŏm 약념

spider *n.* kŏ-mi 거미

spike *n.* mot 못

spill *v.* ŏp'-ji-rŭ-da 엎지르다

spin *v.* pang-jŏk ha-da 방적하다

spinach *n.* si-gŭm-ch'i 시금치

spindle *n.* gu-ri 꾸리

spine *n.* ch'ŏk-ch'u 척추

spinning-wheel *n.* mul-le 물레

spinster *n.* no-ch'ŏ-nyŏ 노처녀

spire *n.* byo-jok t'ap 뾰족탑

spirit *n.* yŏng-hon 영혼

spiritual *adj.* yŏng-jŏk 영적

spit *v.* ch'im paet'-da 침뱉다

spite *n.* ak-ŭi 악의

spiteful *adj.* sim-sul-guch'-ŭn 심 술궂은

splash *v.* t'wi-gi-da 튀기다 「한

splendid *adj.* hul-lyung han 훌륭

splendor *n.* kwang-ch'ae 광채

splinter jok 쪽; *v.* jo·gae-da 쪼 개다

split *v.* ka-rŭ-da 가르다

spoil *n.* yak-t'al-p'um 약탈품; *v.* mang-ch'i-da 망치다

sponge *n.* hae-myŏn 해면

sponsor *n.* hu-won-ja 후원자

spoon *n.* su-ka-rak 숟가락

sport *n.* un-dong 운동

sportsman *n.* un-dong-ga 운동가

spot *n.* (place) chi-jŏm 지점; (dot) a-rung 아룽; *v.* (get dirty) tŏ-rŏ-wo-ji-da 더러워지다

spotless *adj.* gae-kŭt han 깨끗한

spout *v.* nae-p'um-da 내품다; *v.* chu-dung-i 주둥이

sprain *n.* bim 삠; *v.* bi-da 삐다

sprawl v. su-jok-ŭl bŏt-hi-da 수족을뻗히다

spray v. pun-mu ha-da 분무하다

spread v. nŏlb-hi-da 넓히다

sprightly adj. k'wae-hwal han 쾌활한

spring n. saem 샘; (season) pom 봄; (wire) sŭ-p'u-ring 스푸링; v. dwi-da 뛰다

sprinkle v. bu-ri-da 뿌리다

sprout v. na-da 나다

spruce n. pi-nul ka-mun-bi 비늘가문비

spur n. pak-ch'a 박차; v. kyŏng-nyŏ ha-da 격려하다

spurn v. mul-li-ch'i-da 물리치다

sputter v. ch'im-ŭl t'wi-ge ha-da 침을뛰게하다

spy n. t'am-jŏng 탐정; v. chŏng-t'am ha-da 정탐하다 「경

spyglass n. mang-won-gyŏng 망원

squad n. pun-dae 분대

squadron n. (air force) pi-haeng chung-dae 비행중대; (navy) ham-dae 함대

square n. chŏng-bang-hyŏng 정방형

squash n. ho-bak 호박

squat v. gŭr-ŏ ant-da 끌어앉다

squeak v. jik-jik so-ri nae-da 찍찍소리내다

squeal *n.* a-u-sŏng 아우성; *v.* a-u-sŏng ch'i-da 아우성치다

squeeze *v.* ja-da 짜다

squirrel *n.* ta-ram-chwi 다람쥐

stab *v.* ji-rŭ-da 찌르다; *n.* ji-rŭ-gi 찌르기

stable *n.* ma-gu-gwan 마구관

stack *n.* ka-ri 가리

staff *n.* ch'am-mo 참모; **chief of s.** ch'ong ch'am-mo-jang 종참모장

stag *n.* sut-sa-sŭm 숫사슴

stage *n.* mu-dae 무대

stagger *v.* pi-t'ŭl kŏ-ri-da 비틀거리다

staid *adj.* ch'im-ch'ak han 침착한

stain *v.* tŏ-rŏp-hi-da 더렵히다

staircase *n.* ke-dan 게단

stairs *n.* kye-dan 계단

stake *n.* mal-tuk 말뚝 「타진

stale *adj.* mas-i tal-la-jin 맛이달

stalk *n.* chul-gi 줄기; *v.* pŏ-t'wi-go kŏt-da 버튀고걷다

stall *n.* ma-gut-kan 마굿간

stalwart *adj.* ŏk-sen 억센

stamen *n.* su-sul 수술 「다

stammer *v.* mal tŏ-dŭm-da 말더듬

stamp *n.* (postage) u-p'yo 우표; (seal) to-jang 도장; *v.* (impress) jïk-da 찍다, *v.* (feet) pal-ŭl kul-li-da 발을굴리다; **revenue s.** in-ji 인지

stand *n.* (position) ip-jang 입장; (support) tae 대; *v.* sŏ-da 서다

standard *n.* p'yo-jun 표준; (flag) ki 기

standing *n.* chi-wi 지위

star *n.* pyŏl 별

starboard *n.* pa-rŭn-p'yŏn 바른편

starch *n.* chŏn-bun 전분; (clothes) p'ul 풀

stare *v.* no-ryŏ po-da 노려보다

starfish *n.* sŏng-ŏ 성어

starry *adj.* pyŏl man-ŭn 별많은

start *n.* si-jak 시작; *v.* si-jak ha-da 시작하다

starting-point *n.* ch'ul-bal-jŏm 출발점

startle *v.* gam-jak nol-la-ge ha-da 갑짝놀라게하다

starvation *n.* chu-rĭm 주림

starve *v.* chu-ri-da 주리다; **s. to death** *v.* kulm-ŏ chuk-da 굶어죽다

state *n.* chu 주; (condition) sang-t'ae 상태; *v.* ŏn-myŏng ha-da 언명하다

statement *n.* chin-sul 진술 「가

statesman *n.* chŏng-ch'i-ga 정치

station *n.* chŏng-gŏ-jang 정거장; *v.t.* chu-dun ha-da 주둔하다

stationary *adj.* ka-man-hi i-nŭn 가만히 있는

stationery *n.* mun-bang-gu 문방구

statue *n.* sang 상

stature *n.* sin-jang 신장

statute *n.* pŏm-yŏng 법령

stay *v.* mŏ-mul-da 머물다

steadfast *adj.* gut-gut han 꿋꿋한

steadily *adv.* han-gyŏl kach-i 한 결같이

steady *adj.* kut-ge pak-hin 굳게박 힌

steak *n.* sŭ-t'e-ik' 스테잌

steal *v.* hum-ch'i-da 훔치다

steam *n.* chŭng-gi 증기; *v.* ji-da 찌다; **s. engine** *n.* chŭng-gi ki-gwan 증기기관; **s. ship** *n.* ki-sŏn 기선

steel *n.* kang-ch'ŏl 강철

steep *adj.* ka-p'a-rŭn 가파른; **to be s.** *v.* ka-p'a-rŭ-da 가파르다

steeple *n.* byo-jok-t'ap 뾰족탑

steer *v.* cho-jong ha-da 조종하다

stem *n.* chul-gi 줄기

stenographer *n.* sok-ki-ja 속기자

stenography *n.* sok-ki-sul 속기술

step *v.* palp-da 밟다; *n.* han kŏr-ŭm 한걸음

stepbrothers *n.* i-bu hyŏng-je 이부 형제

stepchild *n.* i-but cha-sik 이붓자 식

stepfather *n.* kye-bu 계부

stepmother *n.* kye-mo 계모

sterilize *v.* sal-gyun ha-da 살균하다

stern *adj.* ŏm-gyŏk han 엄격한; *n.* sŏn-mi 선미

stick *n.* chi-p'ang-i 지팡이; *v.* (to) put'-da 붙다; *v.* (into) ji-rŭ-da 찌르다; *v.* (catch) kŏl-li-da 걸리다

sticky *adj.* gŭn-jŏk gŭn-jŏk han 끈적끈적한

stiff *adj.* bŏt-bŏt han 뻣뻣한

stifle *v.* chil-sĭk si-k'i-da 질식시키다

still *adj.* ko-yo han 고요한; *adv.* (time) a-jik 아직

stimulant *n.* hŭng-bun-je 흥분제

stimulate *v.* cha-gŭk ha-da 자극하다

sting *n.* sal 살; *v.* sso-da 쏘다

stingy *adj.* in-saek han 인색한

stint *v.* che-han ha-da 제한하다

stipulate *v.* kyu-jŏng ha-da 규정하다

stir *v.* hwi-jŏt-da 휘젓다

stirrup *n.* tŭng-ja 등자

stitch *n.* han pa-nŭl 한바늘

stock *n.* ka-ch'uk 가축; (family) hyŏl-t'ong 혈통

stocking *n.* yang-mal 양말; (Korean) pŏ-sŏn 버선

stomach *n.* pae 배; **to have a s.
ache** *v.* pae-ga a-p'ǔ-da 배가아
프다

stone *n.* tol 돌; **s.mason** sŏk-su
석수; **s.work** sŏk-jo-mul 석조
물

stony *adj.* tol-man-ǔn 돌많은

stool *n.* kŏl-sang 걸상

stoop *v.* kup-hǔ-ri-da 굽흐리다

stop *n.* chung-ji 중지; *v.* mŏm-
ch'u-da 멈추다

storage battery *n.* ch'uk-jŏn-gi 축
전기

store *n.* ka-ge 가게; *v.* chŏ-ch'uk
ha-da 저축하다

storehouse *n.* ch'ang-go 창고

stork *n.* hwang-sae 황새

storm *n.* p'ok-p'ung-u 폭풍우; *v.*
p'ok-p'ung-u-ga i-rŏ-na-da 폭풍
우가이러나다 「우의

stormy *adj.* p'ok-p'ung-u-ǔi 폭풍

story *n.* i-ya-gi 이야기

stout *adj.* dung-dung han 뚱뚱한

stove *n.* nal-lo 난로; **s.pipe** yŏn-
t'ong 연통

stowaway *n.* mil-hang-ja 밀항자

straight *adj.* gok-pa-rǔn 꼭바른

strain *v.* (filter) kŏ-rǔ-da 거르다;
(body) bi-da 삐다

strainer *n.* ch'e 체

strait *n.* hae-hyŏp 해협

strange *adj.* i-sang-han 이상한

stranger *n.* mo-rŭ-nŭn sa-ram 모르는사람

strangle *v.* mok-mae-ŏ chuk-i-da 목매어죽이다

strap *n.* ka-juk-gŭn 가죽끈; *v.* ka-juk-gŭn-ŭ-ro mae-da 가죽끈으로매다

stratagem *n.* sul-ch'aek 술책

strategy *n.* chŏl-lyak 전략

straw *n.* chip 집

strawberry *n.* dal-gi 딸기

stray *v.* kil-ŭl chal-mot tŭl-da 길을잘못들다

streak *n.* chul-ja-uk 줄자욱

stream *n.* nae-mul 냇물

street *n.* kŏ-ri 거리; **s. car** *n.* chŏn-ch'a 전차

strength *n.* him 힘

strengthen *v.* se-ge ha-da 세게하다

strenuous *adj.* pun-t'u-jŏk 분투적

stretch *v.* (spread) p'yŏ-da 펴다; (elastic) nŭl-da 늘다

strict *adj.* ŏm-gyŏk-han 엄격한

stride *v.* sŏng-k'ŭm sŏng-k'ŭm kŏt-da 성큼성큼걷다

strife *n.* ssa-um 싸움

strike *v.* dae-ri-da 때리다; **to go on s.** tong-maeng p'a-ŏp ha-da 동맹파업하다; *n.* (industry) tong-maeng p'a-ŏp 동맹파업

string *n.* gŭn 끈

strip *v.* pe-ki-da 베끼다; *n.* kil-juk han cho-gak 길죽한조각

stripe *n.* chul 줄

strive *v.* him-ssŭ-da 힘쓰다

stroke *n.* (illness) pal pyŏng 발병; *v.* ssŭ-da tŭm-da 쓰다듬다

stroll *n.* san-po 산보; *v.* san-po ha-da 산보하다

strong *adj.* kut-sen 굳센

structure *n.* ku-jo 구조; (building) kŏn-mul 건물

struggle *n.* no-ryŏk 노력; *v.* him-ssŭ-da 힘쓰다

stub *n.* gŭ-t'ŭ-re-gi 끄트레기

student *n.* hak-saeng 학생

studio *n.* hwa-sĭl 화실

study *n.* kong-bu 공부; *v.* kong-bu ha-da 공부하다; *n.* (room) sŏ-jae 서재

stuff *n.* mul-gŏn 물건; *v.* ch'ae-u-da 채우다

stumble *v.* nŏm-ŏ-jĭl-bŏn ha-da 넘어질뻔하다

stump *n.* kŭ-ru 그루

stun *v.* chŏng-sĭn il-ke ha-da 정신잃게하다

stupid *adj.* ŏ-ri-sŏg-ŭn 어리석은

sturdy *adj.* t'ŭn-t'ŭn han 튼튼한

stutter *v.* mal-tŏ-dŭm-da 말더듬다

sty *n.* twae-ji-u-ri 돼지우리; (eye) nun ta-rae-ki 눈다랫기

style *n.* yu-haeng 유행

subdue *v.* chŏng-pok ha-da 정복하다

subject *n.* (theme) che-mok 제목

subjugate *v.* chŏng-pok ha-da 정복하다

subjunctive *n.* ka-jŏng pŏp 가정법

submarine *adj.* pa-da-mit-ŭi 바다밑의; *n.* cham-su-ham 잠수함

submerge *v.* mul-e cham-gŭ-da 물에잠그다

submission *n.* pok-jong 복종

submit *v.* (present) che-ch'ul ha-da 제출하다; (surrender) kul-bok ha-da 굴복하다

subscribe *v.* ye-yak ha-da 예약하다; (contribute) ki-bu ha-da 기부하다

subscription *n.* ye-yak 예약

subside *v.* ka-ra ant-da 가라앉다

subsistence *n.* saeng-hwal 생활

substance *n.* sil-ch'e 실체

substitute *n.* tae-ri 대리; *v.* tae-yong ha-da 대용하다

substitution *n.* tae-yong 대용

subtract *v.* kam ha-da 감하다

subtraction *n.* kam pŏp 감법

suburb *n.* kyo-ŭi 교의

subversive *adj.* p'a-goe-jok 파괴적

succeed *v.* sŏng-gong ha-da 성공
하다; (follow) hu-im ha-da 후
임하다

success *n.* sŏng-gong 성공 「공한

successful *adj.* sŏng-gong han 성

succession *n.* (inheritance) sang-
sok 상속; (continuation) yŏn-sok
연속

successor *n.* hu-gye-ja 후계자

such *adj.* kŭ-rŏ-han 그러한

suck *v.* bal-da 빨다

sudden *adj.* ch'ang-jul-ŭi 창졸의

suddenly *adv.* kap-ja-gi 잡자기

sue *v.* so-song ha-da 소송하다

suet *n.* so ki-rŭm 소기름

suffer *v.* koe-ro-wo ha-da 피로워
하다; (undergo) tang ha-da 당하
다

suffering *n.* ko-saeng 고생

sufficient *adj.* ch'ung-bun han 충
분한

suffix *n.* chŏp-mi-ŏ 접미어

sugar *n.* sŏl-t'ang 설탕; s. **cane**
sŏl-t'ang su-su 설탕수수; **cube**
s. kak sa-t'ang 각사탕

suggest *v.* che-an ha-da 제안하다

suggestion *n.* che-an 제안

suicide *n.* cha-sal 자살

suit *n.* (law) so-song 소송; (of
clothes) yang-bok 양복; *v.* mat-
da 맞다

suitable *adj.* chŏk-dang han 적당한

suitor *n.* ku-hon-ja 구혼자

sulk *v.* sĭm-sul nae-da 심술내다

sulky *adj.* sĭm-sul kut-ŭn 심술궂은

sullen *adj.* sĭm-sul naen 심술낸

sulphur *n.* yu-hwang 유황

sultan *n.* im-gŭm 임금

sultry *adj.* mu-dŏ-un 무더운

sum *n.* hap-gye 합계

summer *n.* yŏ-rŭm 여름

summit *n.* gok-tae-gi 꼭대기

summon *v.* pul-lŏ nae-da 불러내다; (legal) so-hwan ha-da 소환하다

sun *n.* hae 해; *v.* hae-pyŏt' jo-i-da 햇볕쪼이다; **s. beam** *n.* haes-sal 햇살; **s. burn** pyŏt-e t'a-da 볕에타다; **s. dial** hae-si-gye 해시계; **s. flower** hae pa-rae-gi 해바래기; **s. light** hae-pyŏt 해ㄷ; **s. shade** yang-san 양산; **s. shine** il-gwang 일광; **s. spot** t'ae yang-ŭi hŭk-jŏm 태양의흑점; **s. stroke** il-sa pyŏng 일사병

Sunday *n.* il-yo-il 일요일 「는

sunny *adj.* hae-pyŏt i-nŭn 해변있

superintendent *n.* kam-dok-ja 감독자

superior *adj.* tŏ-na-ŭn 더나온; *n.* ut sa-ram 웃사람

superlative *adj.* ch'oe-go-ŭi 최고
의

superstition *n.* mi-sĭn 미신

supervise *v.* kam-dok ha-da 감독
하다

supper *n.* chŏ-nyŏk pap 저녁밥

supply *n.* (stock) chae-go p'um 재
고품; *v.* po-gŭp ha-da 보급하다

support *n.* chi-ji 지지; *v.* chi-ji
ha-da 지지하다

supporter *n.* chi-ji-ja 지지자

suppose *v.* (think) saeng-gak ha-
da 생각하다; (assume) ka-jŏng
ha-da 가정하다

suppress *v.* nu-rŭ-da 누르다

supreme *adj.* ch'oe-go-ŭi 최고의

sure *adj.* hwak-sĭl han 확실한

surely *adv.* hwak-sĭl-hi 확실히;
exclam. a-mu-ryŏm 아무렴

surf *n.* mil-lyŏ-o-nŭn p'a-do 밀려
오는파도

surface *n.* p'yo-myŏn 표면

surgeon *n.* oe-gwa ŭi-sa 외과의사

surname *n.* sŏng 성

surplus *n.* ing-yŏ 잉여

surprise *n.* nol-lam 놀람; *v.* nol-
la-ge ha-da 놀라게하다

surrender *n.* hang-bok 항복; *v.*
hang-bok ha-da 항복하다

surround *v.* tul-lŏ ssa-da 둘러싸다

surroundings *n.* chu-wi 주위

survive v. sar-a-nam-da 살아남다

suspect n. hyŏm-ŭi-ja 혐의자; v. ŭi-sĭm ha-da 의심하다

suspend v. (hang) tar-a mae-da 달아매다; (from school) chŏng-hak sik-hi-da 정학식히다

suspenders n. mel-pang 멜빵

suspense n. pur-an 불안

suspicion n. ŭi-sim 의심

sustain v. (stand) kyŏn-di-da 견디다; (support) pach-yŏ chu-da 밭여주다

swallow n. che-bi 제비; v. sam-k'i-da 삼키다

swamp n. nŭp' 늪

swan n. paek-jo 백조

swarm n. de 떼; v. mo-yŏ tŭl-da 모여들다

sway v. hŭn-dŭl-li-da 흔들리다

swear v. (promise) maeng-sŏ ha-da 맹서하다; (curse) chŏ-ju ha-da 저주하다

sweat n. dam 땀

sweater n. sŭ-we-t'ŏ 스웨터

sweep v. ssŭl-da 쓸다; n. (oar) no 노

sweet adj. tan 단

sweetly adv. myo-ha-ge 묘하게

swell v. pu-p'ul-da 부풀다

swelling n. pu-ŭn-gŏt 부은것

swift adj. ba-rŭn 빠른

swiftly *adv·* ba-rŭ-ge 빠르게

swim *v·* he-ŏm ch'i-da 헤엄치다

swing *n·* kŭ-ne 그네; *v·* hŭn-dŭl-da 흔들다; *v·* (on swing) kŭ-ne dwi-da 그네뛰다

switch *n·* ssŭ-wi-ch'i 쓰위치; **s.-board** *n·* pae-jŏn-p'an 배전판

swoop *v·* nae-ryŏ tŏp'-ch'i-da 내려 덮치다

sword *n·* k'al 칼

sycamore *n·* mi-guk tan-ch'u na-mu 미국단추나무

syllable *n·* ŭm-jŏl 음절

syllabus *n·* yo-mok 요목

symbol *n·* sang-jing 상징

symbolize *v·* sang-jing ha-da 상징 하다

sympathetic *adj·* tong-jŏng i-nŭn 동정있는

sympathize *v·* tong-jŏng ha-da 동 정하다

sympathy *n·* tong-jŏng 동정

synagogue *n·* yu-d'ae-kyo-ŭi hoe-dang 유태교의회당

syphilis *n·* mae-dok 매독

system *n·* cho-jik 조직   「적

systematic *adj·* ke-t'ong-jŏk 계통

〔 T 〕

table *n·* sang 상; **t·cloth** sang-po 상보

tablet *n.* p'ae 패; (medicine) hwan-yak 환약

tadpole *n.* ol-ch'aeng-i 올챙이

tail *n.* go-ri 꼬리

tailor *n.* yang-bok-sang 양복상

take *v.* ka-ji-da 가지다

tale *n.* i-ya-gi 이야기

talent *n.* chae-gan 재간

talk *n.* mal-sŭm 말슴; *v.* mal ha-da 말하다

tall *adj.* k'i-ga-kŭn 키가큰

tallow *n.* chi-bang 지방

talon *n.* pal-t'op 발톱

tame *adj.* kil-dŭr-ŭn 길들은; *v.* kil-tŭr-i-da 길들이다

tan *n.* (color) hwang-gal-saek 황갈색; *v.* (leather) i-gi-da 이기다; *v.* (body) hae-pyŏt-e t'ae-u-da 햇볕에태우다

tangle *v.* ŏng-k'i-da 엉키다

tank *n.* t'aeng-k'ŭ 탱크; (army) chang-gap chŏn-ch'a 장갑전차

tap *v.* ka-byŏp-ge du-dŭ-ri-da 가볍게두드리다; *n.* (water) t'ong-ŭi chu-dung-i 통의주둥이

tape measure *n.* chul-ja 줄자

tar *n.* t'a-a-rŭ 타아르

tardy *adj.* nŭ-rĭn 느린

target *n.* p'yo-jŏk 표적

task *n.* il 일

tassel *n.* sul 술
taste *n.* mat 맛; *v.* mat po-da 맛
보다
tax *n.* se 세; *v.* kwa-se ha-da 과
세하다
taxi *n.* t'aek-ssi 택씨
tea *n.* ch'a 차
teach *v.* ka-rŭ-ch'i-da 가르치다
teacher *n.* sŏn-saeng 선생
teacup *n.* ch'at-chan 찻잔
tea-house *n.* ch'a chĭp 차집
teakettle *n.* (ch'a) chu-jŏn-ja (차)
주전자
team *n.* t'im 팀; (suffix) dan 단
teapot *n.* ch'a-chu-jŏn-ja 차주전자
tear *n.* (–drop) nun-mul 눈물;
n. (rip) jae-jĭn t'ŭm 째진틈;
v. jae-da 째다
tease *v.* sŏng ka si-ge kul-da 성가
시게굴다
technical *adj.* ki-sul-jŏk 기술적
tedious *adj.* chi-ri han 지리한
teeth *n.* i 이
teetotaler *n.* kŭm-ju-ga 금주가
telegram *n.* chŏn-bo 전보
telegraph *n.* chŏn-sin 전신; *v.*
chŏn-bo ch'i-da 전보치다
telephone *n.* chŏn-hwa 전화; *v.*
chŏn-hwa-rŭl kŏl-da 전화를걸다
telescope *n.* mang-won-gyŏng 망
원경

tell *v.* mal ha-da 말하다

temper *n.* pun 분; *v.* kang ha-ge ha-da 강하게하다

temperance *n.* chŏl-je 절제

temperate *adj.* chŏl-je i-nŭn 절제 있는

temperature *n.* on-do 온도

tempest *n.* tae-p'ok-p'ung 대폭풍

temple *n.* kwan-ja nol-i 관자놀이; (religious) sŏng-jŏn 성전; (Bud-dhist) chŏl 절

temporary *adj.* ĭm-si 임시

tempt *v.* yu-hŭk ha-da 유혹하다

temptation *n.* yu-hŭk 유혹

ten *n.* & *adj.* yŏl 열; **t. thousand** *n.* man 만

tenant *n.* so-jak-in 소작인 「키다

tend *v.* (look after) ch'i-k'i-da 지

tendency *n.* kyŏng-hyang 경향

tender *adj.* pu-dŭ-rŏ-un 부드러운; *n.* (boat) chong-sŏn 종선; (train) t'an-su ch'a 탄수차

tenderness *n.* pu-dŭ-rŏ-um 부드 러움

tennis *n.* t'e-ni-ssŭ 테니쓰

tense *adj.* kin-jang han 긴장한

tent *n.* ch'ŏn-mak 천막

term *n.* (school) hak-ki 학기; (pe-riod) ki-han 기한; (technical) sur-ŏ 술어; (condition) cho-kŏn 조건

terrace *n.* ch'uk-dae-ji 축대지
terrible *adj.* mu-sŏ-un 무서운
terrify *v.* mu-sŏp-ge ha-da 무섭게 하다
territory *n.* yŏng-t'o 영토
terror *n.* kong-p'o 공포
test *n.* si-hŏm 시험; *v.* si-hŏm ha-da 시험하다   「다
testify *v.* chŭng-ŏn ha-da 증언하
testimony *n.* chŭng-ŏn 증언
text *n.* kyo-sŏ 교서; (document) mun-gŏn 문건; **t. book** kyo-gwa-sŏ 교과서
than *conj.* po-da 보다
thank *v.* kam-sa ha-da 감사하다; **t. you** ko-map-sĭm-ni-da 고맙십니다
thankful *adj.* kam-sa han 감사한
thanks *n.* kam-sa 감사
thanksgiving *n.* kam-sa che 감사제
that *adj.* kŭ 그; *pron* kŭ-gŏt 그것
thatch *n.* i-yŏng 이영; *v.* i-yŏng-ŭ-ro it-da 이영으로잇다
thaw *v.* nok-da 녹다
the *art.* kŭ 그
theater *n.* kŭk-jang 극장
their *pron* kŭ-dŭl-ŭi 그들의
them *pron* kŭ-dŭl-ŭl 그들을
theme *n.* (composition) non-je 논제; (subject) chu-je 주제; (line) chu-sŏn-nyul 주선률

themselves *pron.* kŭ-dŭl cha-sĭn
그들자신

then *adv.* kŭ-dae 그때

theory *n.* i-ron 이론

there *adv.* cho-gi 조기

therefore *adv.* kŭ-rŏ-mŭ-ro 그러
므로

thermometer *n.* han-nan-gye 한난
계

they *pron.* kŭ-dŭl 그들

thick *adj.* tu-t'ŏ-ŭn 두터운; *adv.*
tu-kŏp-ge 두껍게

thicket *n.* tŏm-bul 덤불

thickness *n.* tu-t'ŏ-um 두터움

thief *n.* to-jŏk-nom 도적놈

thieve *v.* to-jŏk-jĭl ha-da 도적질하
다

thigh *n.* nŏp-jŏk ta-ri 넙적다리

thimble, *n.* kol-mu 골무

thin, to be, *v.* (solids) yalp-da 얇
다; (liquids) mulk-da 묽다

thing *n.* mul-gŏn 물건

think *v.* saeng-gak ha-da 생각하다

third *n. & adj.* che-sam 제삼; **t.**
class sam-dŭng 삼등

thirst *n.* mok-ma-rŭm 목마름

thirsty, to be, *v.* mok-ma-rŭ-da
목마르다

thirteen *n. & adj.* yŏl-set 열셋

thirty *n. & adj.* sŏr-hŭn 설흔

this *adj.* i 이; *pron.* i-gŏt 이것

thistle *n.* yŏng-gŏng-k'wi 영경퀴
thorn *n.* ka-si 가시
thorough *adj.* wan-jŏn han 완전한
thoroughfare *n.* t'ong-no 통로
thoroughly *adv.* wan-jŏn ha-ge
완전하게
though *adv.* yŏk-si 역시; *conj.*
(even if) pi-rok……ra-do 비록…
…라도
thought *n.* saeng-gak 생각
thoughtful *adj.* saeng-gak i-nŭn
생각있는
thoughtless *adj.* saeng-gak ŏp-nŭn
생각없는
thousand *n. & adj.* ch'ŏn 천; **ten
t.** man 만
thread *n.* sil 실; *v.* sil-ŭl gwe-da
실을꿰다
threadbare *adj.* hŏn 헌
threat *n.* wi-hyŏk 위혁 「다
threaten *v.* wi-hyŏk ha-da 위혁하
three *n. & adj.* set 셋
thresh *v.* kok-sik-ŭl du-dŭ-ri-da
곡식을두드리다
threshold *n.* mun-chi-bang 문지방
thrift *n.* chŏl-yak 절약
thrifty *adj.* chŏl-yak ha-nŭn 절약
하는
thrill *n.* chŏl-lyul 절률
thrive *v.* pŏn-ch'ang ha-da 번창하
다

throat *n.* mok 목

throne *n.* ok-chwa 옥좌

throng *n.* kun-jung 군중; *v.* mo-i-da 모이다

through *prep.* & *adv.* ······ŭl t'ong ha-yŏ ······을통하여

throughout *prep.* & *adv.* choe ta 최다

throw *v.* nae-tŏn-ji-da 내던지다

thrust *v.* mil-ch'i-da 밀치다

thumb *n.* ŏm-ji son-ka-rak 엄지손가락

thunder *n.* noe-sŏng 뇌성; *v.* noe-sŏng ha-da 뇌성하다; **t. bolt** pyŏ-rak 벼락; **t. storm** u-roe 우뢰

Thursday *n.* mok-yo-il 목요일

thus *adv.* i-wa kach-i 이와같이

thwart *v.* pang-hae ha-da 방해하다

tick *n.* chin-dŭ-gi 진드기; *v.* dok-dak-dok-dak ha-da 똑딱똑딱하다

ticket *n.* p'yo 표

tickle *v.* kan-ji-rŏp-ge ha-da 간지럽게하다

tide *n.* cho-su 조수; **ebb t.** ssŏl-mul 썰물; **flood t.** mil-mul 밀물

tidings *n.* so-sĭk 소식

tidy *adj.* chŏng-yŏn han 정연한

tie *v.* mae-da 매다; *n.* nek-t'a-i 넥타이

tiger *n.* ho-rang-i 호랑이; **t. lily**
na-ri 나리

tightly *adv.* tan-dan-hi 단단히

tile *n.* ki-wa 기와

till *prep.* ga-ji 까지; *v.* kal-da
갈다

timber *n.* su-mok 수목

time *n.* si-gan 시간; **what t.?**
mye-si 몇시

timely *adj.* dae-e chŏk-hap han 때
에적합한

times *n.* si-dae 시대; (arithmetic)
pae 배

timid *adj.* kŏp-i-nŭn 겁있는

tin *n.* chu-sŏk 주석

tint *n.* Pit-kal 빛갈; *v.* mul tŭr-
i-da 물들이다

tiny *adj.* cho-kŭ-ma han 조그마한

tip *n.* gŭt 끝; (money) t'ip' 팁;
v. (over) ŏp'-ŏ-dŭ-ri-da 엎어뜨
리다; (money) t'ip'-ŭl chu-da
팁을주다

tiptoe *n.* pal-gŭt 발끝; *v.* pal-
gŭt-ŭ-ro kŏt-da 발끝으로걷다

tire *n.* ta-i-ya 다이야; *v.* p'i-gon
ha-da 피곤하다

tiresome *adj.* chi-ru han 지루한

title *n.* che-mok 제목

to *prep.* (up to and including) ……
ga-ji ……까지; (place) ……e ge
……에게

toad *n.* tu-kŏ-bi 두꺼비

toadstool *n.* tok-i-nŭn pŏ-sŏt 독
있는버섯

toast *n.* t'o-o-sŭ-t'ŭ 로오스트

tobacco *n.* tam-bae 담배; **t. pouch**
tam-bae ssam-ji 담배쌈지

today *n.* o-nŭl 오늘

toe *n.* pal-ka-rak 발가락

together *adv.* ham-ke 함께

toil *n.* il 일; *v.* ae-ssŭ-da 애쓰
다

toilet *n.* (lavatory) pyŏn-so 변소;
t. paper twi-ji 뒤지

token *n.* p'yo-jŏk 표적

tolerable *adj.* ch'am-ŭl-su i-nŭn
참을수있는

toll *n.* t'ong-haeng-se 통행세

tomato *n.* il-yŏn-kam 일년감

tomb *n.* nŭng 능

tomorrow *n.* nae-il 내일; **day after t.** mo-re 모레; **three days
from now** kŭl-p'i 글피

ton *n.* ton 돈

tone *n.* so-ri 소리

tongs *n.* pul-jĭp-gae 불집개

tongue *n.* hyŏ 혀

tonic *n.* kang-jang-je 강장제

tonight *n. & adv.* o-nŭl-pam 오
늘밤

too *adv.* yŏk-si 역시

tool *n.* yŏn-jang 연장

tooth *n.* i 이; **t.ache** ch'i-t'ong 치룡; **t.brush** ch'i-sol 치줄; **t.-pick** i-ssu-si-gae 이쑤시개

top *n.* gok-dae-gi 꼭대기; (toy) p'aeng-i 팽이

topic *n.* hwa-je 화제

torch *n.* hwaet-pul 햇불

torment *n.* ko-t'ong 고룡; *v.* koe-rop-hi-da 괴롭히다

torpedo *n.* o-roe 오뢰; **t. boat** *n.* o-roe-jŏng 오뢰정

torrent *n.* kŭm-yu 급류

torrid *adj.* mop-ssi tŏ-un 몹씨더운

tortoise *n.* kŏ-buk 거북; **t. shell** *n.* kwi-gap 귀갑

torture *n.* ko-mun 고문; *v.* ko-mun ha-da 고문하다

toss *v.* tŏn-ji-da 던지다

total *adj.* & *n.* ch'ong-gye 총계; *v.* hap-gye ha-da 합계하다

totter *v.* pi-t'ŭl kŏ-ri-da 비틀거리다

touch *v.* (with hands) man-ji-da 만지다; (contact) chŏp-ch'ok ha-da 접촉하다

tough *adj.* chil-gin 질긴

tour *n.* man-yu 만유; *v.* man-yu ha-da 만유하다

tourist *n.* man-yu-ja 만유자

tournament *n.* si-hap 시합

tow *v.* gŭl-go ka-da 끌고가다

toward *prep.* ······jok-ŭ-ro ······쪽으
로

towel *n.* su-gŏn 수건

tower *n.* t'ap 탑

town *n.* to-si 도시

toy *n.* chang-nan-gam 장난감

trace *n.* hŭn-jŏk 흔적; *v.* ch'u-jŏk
ha-da 추적하다

track *n.* pal-ja-guk 발자국; (railway) ch'ŏl-do 철도; *v.* twi-rŭl
joch-da 뒤를쫓다

tract *n.* chi-dae 지대; (religious)
ch'ŏn-do-ji 천도지

trade *n.* ŏp 업; *v.* chang-sa ha-da
장사하다; (exchange) kyo-dae
ha-da 교대하다

trader *n.* sang-in 상인   「상인

tradesman *n.* so-mae sang-in 소매

tradition *n.* chŏn-t'ong 전통

traffic *n.* kyo-t'ong 교통

tragedy *n.* pi-gŭk 비극

trail *n.* san-kil 산길; *v.* twi da-ra
o-da 뒤따라오다

train *n.* ki-ch'a 기차; *v.* hul-lyŏn
ha-da 훈련하다

traitor *n.* pal-yŏk-ja 발역자

tramcar *n.* chŏn-ch'a 전차

tramp *n.* pu-rang-ja 부랑자;
(walk) to-bo-yŏ-haeng 도보여행;
v. to-bo-yŏ-haeng ha-da 도보여
행하다

trample v. chit-palp-da 짓밟다

transact v. ch'ŏ-ri ha-da 처리하다

transaction n. ch'ŏ-ri 처리

transcribe v. pe-ki-da 베끼다

transfer n. chŏn-im 전입; v. olm-gi-da 옮기다

transform v. pyŏn-hyŏng ha-da 변형하다

transformer n. pyŏn-ap-gi 변압기

translate v. pŏn-yŏk ha-da 번역하다

translation n. pŏn-yŏk 번역

transparent adj. t'u-myŏng han 투명한

transplant v. olm-gyŏ sĭm-gŭ-da 옮겨심그다

transport v. su-song ha-da 수송하다

transportation n. su-song 수송

trap n. tŏt 덫; v. tŏch-ŭ-ro chap-da 덫으로잡다

travel n. yŏ-haeng 여행; v. yŏ-haeng ha-da 여행하다

traveller n. yŏ-haeng-ga 여행가

traverse v. kŏn-nŏ ka-da 건너가다

tray n. chaeng-pan 쟁반

treacherous adj. ŭm-hyung han 음흉한

tread v. palp-da 밟다

treason n. pan-yŏk 반역

treasure n. po-mul 보물

treasury *n.* kuk-go 국고

treat *v.* ch'wi-gŭp ha-da 취급하다

treatment *n.* tae-u 대우; (medical) ch'i-ryo 치료

treaty *n.* cho-yak 조약

tree *n.* na-mu 나무

tremble *v.* dŏl-da 떨다

tremendous *adj.* koeng-jang han 굉장한

trench *n.* (army) ch'am-ho 참호

trespass *v.* ch'im-ip ha-da 침입하다

trial *n.* (law) kong-p'an 공판

triangle *n.* sam-gak-hyŏng 삼각형

tribe *n.* chong-jok 종족

tributary *n.* chi-ryu 지류

tribute *n.* cho-gong 조공

trick *n.* kye-ryak 계략; *v.* sok-i-da 속이다

trickle *v.* dok-dok dŏr-ŏ-ji-da 똑똑 떨어지다

trifle *n.* sa-so han il 사소한일; *v.* chang-nan ha-da 장난하다

trifling *adj.* mi-mi han 미미한

trigger *n.* pang-a soe 방아쇠

trim *adj.* mal-ssuk han 말쑥한

trip *n.* yŏ-haeng 여행; *v.* chal-mot ti-di-da 잘못디디다

triumph *n.* sŭng-ni 승리; *v.* sŭng-ni ha-da 승리하다

trivial *adj.* mi-mi han 미미한

trolley n· (street car) chŏn-ch'a
전차

troop n· kun-dae 군대

trophy n· chŏl-li p'um 전리품

tropical adj· yŏl-dae chi-bang-ŭi
열대지방의

tropics n· yŏl-dae chi-bang 열대지
방

trot n· sok-bo 속보, v· sok-bo-ro
tal-li-da 속보로달리다

trouble n· su-go 수고; v· (worry)
kŭn-sĭm ha-ge ha-da 근심하게하
다 「지

trousers n· yang-bok pa-ji 양복바

trowel n· hŭk-son 흙손

truck n· t'ŭ-rŏk 트럭

true adj· ch'am-doen 참된

truly adv chin-sil-lo 진실로

trumpet n· na-p'al 나팔

trunk n· t'ŭ-rang-k'ŭ 트랑크;
(tree) chul-gi 줄기

trust n· (belief) sin-yong 신용;
(responsibility) sin-t'ak 신탁; v·
sin-yong ha-da 신용하다

truth n· chil-li 진리

truthful adj· chŏng-jĭk han 정직
한

try v· ha-yŏ po-da 하여보다; (law)
sĭm-ni ha-da 심리하다

tub n· t'ong 통; **bath t·** mog-yok
t'ong 목욕통

tube *n.* kwan 관; **inner t.** t'yu-u-bŭ 튜우브

tuberculosis *n.* p'e-pyŏng 페병

tuck *n.* chu-rŭm 주름

Tuesday *n.* hwa-yo-il 화요일

tuft *n.* ta-bal 다발

tug *n.* (boat) gŭl-sŏn 끌선; *v.* gŭl-da 끌다

tulip *n.* t'yu-ŭl-li-p'ŭ 튜을리프

tumble *v.* nŏm-ŏ-ji-da 넘어지다

tumbler *n.* kok-ye-sa 곡예사

tumult *n.* so-dong 소동

tune *n.* kok-jo 곡조; *v.* kok-ŭl ma-ch'u-da 곡을마추다

tunic *n.* kun-bok chŏ-go-ri 군복저고리

tunnel *n.* t'ŏn-nel 턴넬; *v.* kul-ŭl p'a-da 굴을파다

turbulent *adj.* kŏ-ch'in 거친

turf *n.* chan-di 잔디

turkey *n.* ch'il-myŏn-jo 칠면조

turn *n.* hoe-jŏn 회전; *v.* tol-da 돌다

turnip *n.* mu-u 무우

turpentine *n.* t'e-re-pin-yu 테레빈유

turret *n.* (gun) p'o-t'ap 포탑

turtle *n.* cha-ra 자라

tusk *n.* ŏ-gŭm-ni 어금니

tutor *n.* ka-jŏng kyo-sa 가정교사

twelve *n. & adj.* yŏl-tul 열둘

twenty *n.* & *adj.* sŭ-mul 스물

twice *adv.* tu pae-ro 두배로

twig *n.* chag-ŭn ka-ji 작은가지

twilight *n.* hwang-hon 황혼

twine *n.* no-kŭn 노끈

twinkle *v.* pan-chak-pan-chak pit-na-da 반짝반짝빛나다

twins *n.* ssang-dong-i 쌍둥이

twist *v.* go-da 꼬다

two *n.* & *adj.* tul 둘

type *n.* (sort) chŏn-hyŏng 전형; (printing) hwal-ja 활자; (suffix) sik 식; *v.* t'a-i-p'ŭ-ra-i-t'a-ro ch'i-da 타이프라이타로치다

typewriter *n.* t'a-i-p'ŭ-ra-i-t'a 타이프라이타

typhoid *n.* chang-jil-pu-sa 장질부사

typhus *n.* t'i-p'ŭ-sŭ 티프스

tyranny *n.* hak-jŏng 학정

tyrant *n.* p'o-gun 포군

〔 U 〕

ugly *adj.* ch'u-ak han 추악한

ultimate *adj.* ch'oe-hu-ŭi 최후의

ultimatum *n.* ch'oe-hu t'ong-ch'ŏp 최후통첩

umbrella *n.* u-san 우산

umpire *n.* sim-p'an-gwan 십판관

unable *adj.* ha-ji mot ha-nŭn 하지 못하는

unaccountable *adj·* sŏl-myŏng hal su ŏp-nŭn 설명할수없는

unaware *adj·* a-ji mot ha-nŭn 아지못하는

uncertain *adj·* pul an-jŏng han 불안정한

unclean *adj·* tŏ-rŏ-un 더러운 .

unclear *adj·* pul-myŏng han 불명한

uncomfortable *adj·* kwi-jung chung han 귀중중한

uncommon *adj·* pi-bŏm han 비범한

unconscious *adj·* ŭi-sik ŏp-nŭn 의식없는

uncover *v·t·* tu-kŏng-ŭl pŏt-ki-da 두껑을벗기다; *v.* (disclose) tŭ-rŏ nae-noh-ta 드러내놓다

under *prep·* & *adv* a-rae-e 아래에

underclothes *n·* sok-ot 속옷

undergo *v·* pat-da 받다

underground *adj·* chi-ha-ŭi 지하의; *n·* (activity) chi-ha un-dong 지하운동

underneath *adv·* a-rae-ro 아래로; *prep·* a-rae-e 아래에

understand *v·* al-da 알다

understanding *n·* i-hae 이해 「하다

undertake *v·* ch'ak-su ha-da 착수

undertaker *n·* chang-ŭi-sa 장의사

underwear *n·* sok-ot 속옷

undo *v·* (unfasten) pŏt-ki-da 벗기다; (untie) p'ul-da 풀다

uneasy *adj·* pul-an han 불안한

unemployment *n·* sil-ŏp 실업

uneven *adj·* ko-rŭ-ji an-ni han 고르지아니한

unexpected *adj·* saeng-gak-ji an-ni han 생각지아니한

unexpectedly *adv·* pul-ŭi-e 불의에

unfair *adj·* pul kong-p'yŏng han 불공평한

unfavorable *adj·* pul-li han 불리한

unfit *adj·* chŏk-dang ha-ji an-ni han 적당하지아니한

unfold *v·* p'yŏ-noh-ta 펴놓다

unforeseen *adj·* ye-ch'ŭk mot han 예측못한

unfortunate *adj·* pul-haeng han 불행한

unfrequented *adj·* wang-nae-ga tŭ-mŭn 왕래가드믄

unfurl *v·* p'yŏ-da 펴다

unhappy *adj·* sŭl-p'ŭn 슬픈

uniform *adj·* han kyŏl kat-ŭn 한결같은; *n·* che-bok 제복

unilateral *adj·* il-bang-jŏk-ĭn 일방적인

unimportant *adj·* chung-yo ha-ji an-ni han 중요하지아니한

union *n·* yŏn-hap 연합

unique *adj·* yu-il han 유일한

unit *n·* tan-wi 단위

unite *v·* yŏn-hap ha-da 연합하다

United Nations *n.* kuk-je yŏn-hap 국제연합; U.N. yu-en 유엔

universal *adj.* po-p'yŏn-jŏk 보편적

universe *n.* u-ju 우주

university *n.* tae-hak-kyo 대학교

unjust *adj.* pul kong-p'yŏng han 불공평한

unkind *adj.* pul ch'in-jŏl han 불친절한

unknown *adj.* al-ji mot ha-nŭn 알지못하는

unless *conj.* a-ni-ra-myŏn 아니라면

unlike, to be, *v.* ta-rŭ-da 다르다

unload *v.* pu-ri-da 부리다

unlucky *adj.* pul-haeng han 불행한

unnecessary *adj.* pul p'ir-yo han 불필요한

unpack *v.* chim-ŭl gŭ-rŭ-da 짐을끄르다

unpleasant *adj.* pul yu-k'wae han 불유쾌한

unravel *v.* p'ul-da 풀다

unreasonable *adj.* mu-ri han 무리한

unroll *v.* p'yŏ noh-ta 펴놓다

unseen *adj.* po-i-ji an-ni ha-nŭn 보이지아니하는

unselfish *adj.* yok-sim ŏp-nŭn 욕심없는

unsuccessful *adj.* sŏng-gong ha-ji mot han 성공하지못한

untie *v.* gŭl-lŭ-da 끌르다

until *prep.* ······ga-ji ······까지

unusual *adj.* tŭ-mun 드문

unwise *adj.* ŏ-ri-sŏg-ŭn 어리석은

unworthy of *adj.* ······hal ka-ch'i ŏp-nŭn ······할가치없는

up *adv.* & *prep.* wi-e 위에

uphill *adj.* ol-la ka-nŭn 올라가는

uphold *v.* (support) ch'an-jo ha-da 찬조하다

upon *prep.* wi-e 위에

upper *adj.* wi-ŭi 위의

upright *adj.* kot-ŭn 곧은; (honest) chŏng-jik han 정직한

uprising *n.* p'ok-dong 폭동

uproar *n.* ya-dan 야단　「엎다

upset *v.* twi-chib-ŏ ŏp'-da 뒤집어

upside-down *adv.* twi-chib-ŏ-jyŏ-sŏ 뒤집어져서

upstairs *n.* wi-ch'ŭng 위층

upward *adj.* wi-ro hyang han 위로 향한

urge *v.* chae-ch'ok ha-da 재촉하다

urgent *adj.* kin-kŭp han 긴급한

use *n.* sa-yong 사용; *v.* sa-yong ha-da 사용하다

useful *adj.* yu-yong han 유용한

useless *adj.* ssŭl-de ŏp-nŭn 쓸데없는

usher *n.* al-lae-in 안내인
usual *adj.* po-t'ong-ŭi 보통의
usually *adv.* hang-sang 항상
utensil *n.* ki-gu 기구
utilize *v.* i-yong ha-da 이용하다
utmost *adj.* kŭk-dan 극단
utter *adj.* tae-dan han 대단한; *v.*
　par-ŏn ha-da 발언하다
utterance *n.* par-ŏn 발언
utterly *adv.* a-ju 아주

〔 V 〕

vacant *adj.* pin 빈
vacate *v.* dŏ-na-da 떠나다
vacation *n.* hyu-ga 휴가
vaccinate *v.* chong-du ha-da 종두
　하다
vagabond *n.* pu-rang-ja 부랑자
vague *adj.* mag-yŏn han 막연한
vain *adj.* hŏt-doen 헛된; (con-
　ceited) hŏ-yŏng-sim i-nŭn 허영
　심 있는
vainly *adv.* hŏt-toe-i 헛되이
valiant *adj.* ssik-ssik han 씩씩한
valley *n.* kol-cha-gi 골짜기
valor *n.* yong-gi 용기
valuable *adj.* kwi-jung han 귀중한;
　n. kwi-jung-p'um 귀중품
value *n.* ka-ch'i 가치; *v.* chon-
　jung ha-da 존중하다; (appraise)
　p'yŏng-ga ha-da 평가하다

vane *n.* pa-ram-gae-bi 바람개비
vanish *v.* sa-ra-ji-da 사라지다
vanity *n.* hŏ-yŏng 허영
vapor *n.* chŭng-gi 증기
variety *n.* pyŏn-hwa 변화
various *adj.* yŏ-rŏ-ga-ji 여러가지
vary *v.* tal-li ha-da 달리하다
vase *n.* hwa pyŏng 화병
vaseline *n.* wa-sel-lin 와센린
vast *adj.* k'ŏ-da-ran 커다란
vault *n.* chŏ-jang-sil 저장실; *v.*
　dwi-da 뛰다
veal *n.* song-a-ji ko-gi 송아지고기
vegetable *adj.* sik-mul-ŭi 식물의;
　n. ch'ae-so 채소
vegetation *n.* sik-mul 식물
vehicle *n.* ch'a 차
veil *v.* kam-ch'u-da 감추다
vein *n.* chŏng-maek 정맥
velvet *n.* u-dan 우단
venerate *v.* chon-gyŏng ha-da 존경
　하다
vengeance *n.* pok-su 복수
ventilate *v.* hwan-gi ha-da 환기하
　다
ventilation *n.* hwan-gi 환기
veranda *n.* toet-ma-ru 됫마루
verb *n.* tong-sa 동사
verbal *adj.* mal-lo-ŭi 말로의
verge *n.* ka-jang-ja-ri 가장자리
verse *n.* si 시

versed *adj*. chŏng-t'ong han 정통한

very *adj*. pa-ro 바로; *adv*. tae-dan hi 대단히

vessel *n*. kŭ-rŭt 그릇; (ship) pae 배

vest *n*. chok-gi 족기

vex *v*. sŏng na-ge ha-da 성나게하다

vexation *n*. pun ham 분함

via *prep*. kŏ-ch'ŏ-sŏ 거처서

vibrate *v*. chĭn-dong ha-da 진동하다

vibration *n*. chĭn-dong 진동

vice *n*. choe-ak 죄악; (tool) gŏk-soe 꺽쇠; **vice······** (prefix) pu······ ······ 부······

vicinity *n*. kŭn-ch'ŏ 근처

vicious *adj*. kan-ak han 잔악한

victim *n*. hŭi-saeng-ja 회생자

victor *n*. sŭng-ni-ja 승리자

victorious *adj*. sŭng-ni-ŭi 승리의

victory *n*. sŭng-ni 승리

vie *v*. kyŏng-jaeng ha-da 경쟁하다

view *n*. (scene) kyŏng-ch'i 경치; *v*. po-da 보다

vigor *n*. chŏng-yŏk 정력

vigorous *adj*. chŏng-yŏk wang-sŏng han 정력왕성한

vile *adj*. pi-ru han 비루한

villa *n*. pyŏl-jang 별장

village *n*. ma-ŭl 마을

villain *n.* mo-ssŭl-nom 모쓸놈

vine *n.* nŏng-gul 넝굴

vinegar *n.* ch'o 초

vineyard *n.* p'o-do-won 포도원

violate *v.* wi-ban ha-da 위반하다

violence *n.* p'ok-haeng 폭행

violent *adj.* maeng-yŏl han 맹렬한

violet *n.* o-rang-k'ae got 오랑캐꽃

violin *n.* pa-yol-lin 바올린

virgin *n.* ch'ŏ-nyŏ 처녀

virtue *n.* tŏk 덕

virtuous *adj.* tŏk i-nŭn 덕있는

visible *adj.* po-i-nŭn 보이는

vision *n.* si-gak 시각

visit *n.* pang-mun 방문; *v.* pang-mun ha-da 방문하다

visitor *n.* son-nĭm 손님

visor *n.* mo-ja ch'a-yang 모자차양

vital *adj.* chung-yo han 중요한

vivid *adj.* sŏn-myŏng han 선명한

vocabulary *n.* ŏ-hwi 어휘

vocal *adj.* mok-so-ri-ŭi 목소리의

vocation *n.* chig-ŏp 직업

vogue *n.* yu-haeng 유행

voice *n.* mok-so-ri 목소리

volcanic *adj.* hwa-san-ŭi 화산의

volcano *n.* hwa-san 화산

volume *n.* pu-p'i 부피; (book) kwon 권

volunteer *n.* chi-won-ja 지원자; *v.* cha-won ha-da 지원하다

vote *v.* t'u-p'yo ha-da 투표하다

vow *n.* maeng-sŏ 맹서; *v.* maeng-sŏ ha-da 맹서하다

vowel *n.* mo-ŭm 모음

voyage *n.* hang-hae 항해

vulgar *adj.* ya-bi han 야비한

vulgarity *n.* ya-bi 야비

〔 **W** 〕

waddle *v.* a-jang-a-jang kŏt-da 아장아장걷다

wade *v.* mul-sok-ŭl kŏr-ŏ-ka-da 물속을걸어가다

wag *v.* hŭn-dŭl-da 흔들다

wage *n.* p'um-sak 품삯

wagon *n.* chĭm-ma-ch'a 짐마차

wail *v.* t'ong-gok ha-da 통곡하다

waist *n.* hŏ-ri 허리; **w.coat** *n.* cho-ki 조끼

wait *v.* ki-da-ri-da 기다리다

waiter *n.* we-t'ŏ 웨터

waiting-room *n.* tae-hap-sil 대합실

waitress *n.* yŏ-gŭp 여급

walk *n.* san-po 산보; *v.* kŏr-ŏ ka-da 걸어가다

wall *n.* pyŏk 벽

wake *v.i.* gae-da 깨다; *v.t.* gae-u-da 깨우다

wallet *n.* chi-gap 지갑

walnut *n.* ho-do 호도

wander *v.* tor-ŏ ta-ni-da 돌어다니
다

want *n.* p'ir-yo 필요; *v.* won ha-
da 원하다; *v.* (need) p'ir-yo ha-
da 필요하다

war *n.* chŏn-jaeng 전쟁

warble *v.* no-rae ha-da 노래하다

warder *n.* kan-su 간수

wardrobe *n.* ŭi-jang 의장

ware *n.* mul-p'um 물품

warehouse *n.* ch'ang-go 창고

warm *adj.* da-dŭt han 따듯한;
v. da-dŭt ha-ge ha-da 따듯하게
하다

warmth da-dŭt ham 따듯함

warn *v.* kyŏng-gye ha-da 경계하다

warning *n.* kyŏng-gye 경계

warrant officer *n.* chun-wi 준위

warrior *n.* kun-ĭn 군인

warship *n.* kun-ham 군함

wash *n.* bal-lae 빨내; *v.* (clothes)
bal-lae ha-da 빨내하다; *v.* (self)
ssit-da 씻다

washing *n.* bal-lae 빨내

waste *v.* nang-bi ha-da 낭비하다;
n. nang-bi 낭비

watch *n.* si-gye 시계; (look out)
kam-si 감시; *v.* kam-si ha-da
감시하다; **w. maker** si-gye-sa
시계사; **w·man** chi-k'i-nŭn sa-
ram 지키는사람

water *n.* mul 물; *v.* mul chu-da
물주다;   **w.color** *n.* su-ch'ae
hwa-yong 수채화용; **w.fall** p'ok-
p'o 폭포;   **w.-jar** mul-tok 물
독; **w.melon** su-bak 수박; **w.-
mill** mul-pang-a 물방아; **w.proof**
adj. pang-su-ŭi 방수의

watering-pot *n.* sal-su-gi 살수기

watt *n.* wat-t'ŭ 왓트

wave *n.* mul-gyŏl 물결; *v.* p'a-dong
ha-da 파동하다

wax *n.* mil 밀

way *n.* kil 길

waylay *v.* mae-bok ha-da 매복하다

wayward *adj.* pyŏn-dŏk-sŭ-rŏ-un
변덕스러운

we *pron.* u-ri 우리

weak *adj.* yak han 약한   「하다

weaken *v.* yak-ha-ge ha-da 약하게

weakness *n.* yak-jŏm 약점

wealth *n.* chae-mul 재물

wealthy *adj.* pu-yu han 부유한;
w. person *n.* pu-ja 부자

weapon *n.* mu-gi 무기

wear *v.* hae-tŭ-ri-da 해뜨리다;
(clothes) ip-da 입다

weary, to be, *v.* kon ha-da 곤하다

weather *n.* il-gi 일기; **w.-beaten**
adj. p'ung-u-e si-dal-lin 풍우에
시달린; **w.cock** *n.* pa-ram kae-
bi 바람개비

weave *v.* ja-da 짜다

web *n.* kŏ-mi chip 거미집

wedding *n.* kyŏl-hon sik 결혼식

wedge *n.* sswae-gi 쐐기

Wednesday *n.* su-yo-il 수요일

weed *n.* chap-ch'o 잡초; *v.* p'ul-ŭl bop-da 풀을뽑다

week *n.* il-chu-il 일주일

weekly *adj.* & *adv.* mae-chu 매주; *n.* chu-gan 주간

weep *v.* ul-da 울다   「수양버들

weeping-willow *n.* su-yang pŏ-dŭl

weigh *v.* tal-da 달다; (anchor) tach-ŭl kam-da 닻을감다

weight *n.* mu-ge 무게

weir *n.* ŏ-sal 어살

welcome *n.* hwan-yŏng 환영; *v.* hwan-yŏng ha-da 환영하다

welfare *n.* hu-saeng 후생

well *n.* u-mul 우물; *adv.* chal 잘; **to be w.** *v.* p'yŏng-an ha-da 평안하다

west *n.* sŏ-chok 서쪽

western *adj.* sŏ-yang 서양 「da 적시다

wet *adj.* chŏj-ŭn 젖은; *v.* chŏk-si-

whale *n.* ko-rae 고래

wharf *n.* pu-du 부두   「ŏt 무엇

what *adj.* ŏ-tŏn 어떤; (*tron.*) mu-

whatever *adj.* ŏ-nŭ……i-ra-do 어느……이라도; (*tron.*) ŏ-nŭ-gŏs i-ra-do 어느것이라도

wheat *n*. mil 밀

wheel *n*. pa-k'wi 바퀴

wheeze *v*. hŏl-dŏk-hŏl-dŏk ha-da
헐떡헐떡하다

when *adv*. ŏn-je 언제

whence *adv*. ŏ-de-sŏ 어데서

whenever *adv*. ŏn-je-na 언제나

where *adv*. ŏ-di-sŏ 어디서

whereabouts *n*. so-jae 소재

wherever *adv*. ŏ-di-dŭn-ji 어디든지

whether *conj*. ……in-ji ……인지

which *adj*. ŏ-nŭ 어느; (*pron.*) ŏ-
nŭ-gŏt 어느것

whichever *adv*. ŏ-nŭ-gŏs-i-dŏn-ji
어느것이던지

while *n*. tong-an 동안; *conj*.……
ha-nŭn tong-an-e……하는동안에

whim *n*. pyŏn-dŏk 변덕

whine *v*. sŭl-p'i ul-myŏ mal ha-da
슬피울며말하다

whinny *v*. hing-hing ul-da 힝힝울다

whip *n*. ch'ae-chuk 채죽; *v*. ch'ae-
chuk-ŭ-ro dae-ri-da   채죽으로때
리다

whiskers *n*. ku-re-na-rut 구레나룻

whisper *n*. sok-sak-im 속삭임;
v. sok-sak-i-da 속삭이다

whistle *n*. ho-gak 호각; (sound)
hwi-p'a-ram 휘파람; *v*. (mouth)
hwi-p'a-ram pul-da 휘파람불다;
v. ki-jŏk pul-da 기적불다

white *adj.* hŭin 흰; *n.* paek-saek
백색

who *pron.* nu-ga 누가

whoever *pron.* nu-gu-na 누구나

whole *adj.* chŏn-ch'e-ŭi 전체의;
n. chŏn-ch'e 전체

wholesome *adj.* yu-ik han 유익한

wholly *adv.* chŏn-yŏn 전연

whom *pron.* nu-gu-rŭl 누구를

whooping-cough *n.* paek-il-hae 백
일해

why *adv.* wae 왜

wick *n.* tŭng-sĭm 등심

wicked *adj.* hyung-ak han 흉악한

wickedness *n.* choe-ak 죄악

wide *adj.* nŏlb-ŭn 넓은

widow *n.* kwa-bu 과부

width *n.* nŏlb-i 넓이

wife *n.* (own) a-nae 아내; (another's) pu-in 부인

wig *n.* ka-bal 가발

wild *adj.* ya-saeng-ŭi 야생이

wilderness *n.* hwang-mu-ji 황무지

wilful *adj.* ko-ŭi-ŭi 고의의

will *auxil.* (no special word; use
the future ending with the desired
verb) (ha) ket-da (하) 겠다;
n. ŭi-ji 의지; (document) yu-ŏn
-sŏ 유언서; *v.* (bequeath) yu-ŏn
ha-da 유언하다　　　　「하는

willing *adj.* cha-jin ha-nŭn 자진

willingly *adv*. cha-jin hae-sŏ 자진
해서

willow *n*. pŏ-dŭl na-mu 버들나무

wilt *v*. si-dŭl-da 시들다

win *v*. i-gi-da 이기다

wince *v*. ŭi-ch'uk ha-da 의축하다

wind *n*. pa-ram 바람; *v*. kam-da
감다

windmill *n*. p'ung-ch'a 풍차

window *n*. ch'ang 창

windpipe *n*. ki-gwan-ji 기관지

windy *adj*. pa-ram pu-nŭn 바람부
는

wine *n*. sul 술

wing *n*. nal-gae 날개

wink *n*. gam-bak kŏ-rĭm; 깜박거림
v. gam-bak kŏ-ri-da 깐박거리다

winter *n*. kyŏ-ul 겨울

wipe *v*. (off) ssis-ŏ nae-da 씻어내
다; *v*. (eyes) nun mul tak-da 눈
물닦다

wire *n*. ch'ŏl-sa 철사; *v*. ch'ŏl-sa-
ro kam-da 철사로감다   「전신

wireless *n*. mu-sŏn chŏn-sĭn 무선

wisdom *n*. chi-hye 지혜

wise *adj*. hyŏn-myŏng han 현명한

wish *n*. so-won 소원; *v*. pa-ra-da
바라다

wisteria *n*. tŭng-na-mu 등나무

wistful *adj*. pa-ra nŭn-dŭt han 바
라는듯한

wit *n.* ki-ji 기지
witch *n.* mu-dang 무당
with *prep.* ……wa kach-i …와같이
withdraw *v.* hu-t'oe ha-da 후퇴하다
wither *v.* si-tŭl-da 시들다
withhold *v.t.* po-ryu ha-da 보류하다
within *adv.* an-e 안에
without *prep.* & *adv.* ŏps-i 없이
withstand *v.t.* kyŏn-di-da 견디다
witness *n.* chŭng-gŏ 증거; (person) chŭng-ĭn 증인; *v.* ip-jŭng ha-da 입증하다
witty *adj.* sŭl-gi i-nŭn 슬기있는
wizard *n.* yo-sul jaeng-i 요술쟁이
woe *n.* sŭl-p'ŭm 슬픔
wolf *n.* i-ri 이리
woman *n.* yŏ-ja 여자
wonder *n.* ki-gwan 기관; *v.* koe-sang ha-ge saeng-gak ha-da 피상하게생각하다
wonderful *adj.* koe-sang han 피상한
wondrous *adj.* nol-la-ul man-han 놀나울만한
wood *n.* na-mu 나무
woods *n.* sam-nĭm 삼림
wood–cutter *n.* na-mu-kun 나뭇군
wooden *adj.* mok-che-ŭi 목제의
woodpecker *n.* dak-da-ku-ri 딱다구리
wool *n.* yang-t'ŏl 양털

woollen *adj*. yang-mo-ŭi 양모의

word *n*. mal 말; (news) so-sik 소식

work *v*. il 일; *v*. il ha-da 일하다

workman *n*. il kun 일꾼

workmanship *n*. som-ssi 솜씨

workshop *n*. kong-jang 공장

world *n*. (physical) se-gye 세계; (abstract) se-sang 세상

worldly *adj*. se-sok-jŏk 세속적

worm *n*. po-le 버레

worn-out *adj*. hae-jin 해진

worry *n*. kŏk-jŭng 걱정; *v*. kŏk-jŭng ha-da 걱정하다

worse *adj*. tŏ-na-pŭn 더나쁜

worship *n*. sung-bae 숭배; (Christian) ye-bae 예배; *v*. (Christian) ye-bae ha-da 예배하다; *v*. (others) sung-bae ha-da 숭배하다 ⌜쁜

worst *adj*. ka-jang na-pŭn 가장나

worsted *n*. t'ŏl sil 털실

worth *n*. ka-ch'i 가치; *adj*. ka-ch'i i-nŭn 가치있는

worthless *adj*. ka-ch'i ŏp-nŭn 가치없는

worthy *adj*. hap-dang han 합당한

wound *n*. pu-sang 부상; *v*. pu-sang ha-da 부상하다

woven *adj*. jan 짠

wrap *v*. ssa-da 싸다

wrath *n*. no 노

wreath *n*. hwa-hwan 화환

wreck *n.* p'a-son 파손; *v.* p'a-goe
ha-da 파괴하다

wren *n.* kul-tuk-sae 굴뚝새

wrench *n.* sŭ-pa-na 스빠나

wretch *n.* pul-sang han sa-ram 불
상한사람

wretched, to be, *v.* pul-sang ha-da
불상하다

wriggle *v.* gum-t'ŭl kŏ-ri-da 꿈틀
거리다

wring out *v.* ja-nae-da 짜내다

wrinkle *n.* chu-rŭm 주름; *v.* chu-
rŭm chap-da 주름잡다

wirst *n.* pal' mok 팔목; **w.-watch**
p'al mok si-gye 팔목시계

writ *n.* yŏng-jang 영장

write *v.* ssŭ-da 쓰다

writer *n.* chak-ga 작가

writings *n.* chĭp 집

wrong *adj.* (bad) na-pŭn 나쁜;
(mistaken) t'ŭl-lĭn 틀닌; *adv.* na-
pŭ-ge 나쁘게; *n.* pu-dang 부당;
v. hak-dae ha-da 학대하다

〔 **X** 〕

x-ray *n.* ek-ssŭ kwang-sŏn 엑쓰꽝
선

xylophone *n.* mok-kŭm 목금

〔 **Y** 〕

yacht *n.* yo-t'ŭ 요트

Yalu *n.* am-nok-gang 압녹강

yam *n.* ko-gu-ma 고구마

yard *n.* ma-dang 마당; (measure) ma 마

yardstick *n.* cha 자

yarn *n.* gon-sil 끄실; (story) i-ya-gi 이야기

yawn *n.* ha-p'um 하품; *v.* ha-p'um ha-da 하품하다

year *n.* hae 해; (in compounds) nyŏn 년; **last y**· chang nyŏn 작년; **next y**· nae nyŏn 내년; **this y**· kŭm nyŏn 금년

yearly *adj.* hae ma-da 해마다

yearn *v.* (thing) kŭ-ri-wŏ ha-da 그리워하다; (person) sa-mo ha-da 사모하다

yeast *n.* nu-ruk 누룩

yell *n.* ham-sŏng 함성; *v.* we-ch'i-da 웨치다

yellow *adj.* nu-rŭn 누른

yelp *v.* ul-da 울다

yes *adv.* ne 네

yesterday *n.* ŏ-je 어제;   **day before y**· kŭ-jŏ-ke 그저게; **three days ago** kŭ-kŭ-jŏ-ke 그그저게

yet *adv.* a-jik 아직; (*conj.*) kŭ-rae-do 그래도

yield *v.* na-ta 낳다; (surrender) kul-bok ha-da 굴복하다; *n.* su-hwak 수확

yoke *n.* mŏng-e 멍에; *v.* mŏng-e-rŭl me-u-da 멍에를메우다

yolk *n.* no-rŭn cha 노른자 「의

yonder *adj & adv.* chŏ-jok-ŭi 저쪽

you *pron.* tang-sĭn 당신

young *adj.* chŏl-mŭn 젊은

youngster *n.* so-nyŏn 소년

your *pron.* tang-sĭn-ŭi 당신의

yourself *pron.* tang-sĭn cha-sĭn 당신자신

youth *n.* ch'ŏng-nyŏn si-dae 청년시대

youthful *adj.* chŏl-mŭn 젊은

〔 Z 〕

zeal *n.* yŏl-sĭm 열심

zealous *adj.* yŏl-sĭm i-nŭn 열심있는

zealously *adv.* yŏl-sĭm it-ge 열심있게

zebra *n.* chul chĭn mal 줄진말

zero *n.* kong 공

zest *n.* hŭng-mi 흥미

zigzag *adj.* tŭl-suk nal-suk han 들숙날숙한; *v.* tŭl-suk nal-suk ha-da 들숙날숙하다

zinc *n.* ham-sŏk 함석

zodiac *n.* sip-i-gung 십이궁

zone *n.* chi-dae 지대

zoo *n.* tong-mul-wŏn 동물원

zoology *n.* tong-mul-hak 동물학